LET'S WRITE TOGETHER!

A Collection of Short Stories by Aspiring Young Authors

VOLUME II

PUBLISHED BY TRIMARK PRESS, INC., DEERFIELD BEACH, FLORIDA.

LIBRARY OF CONGRESS CATALOGING-IN-PUBLICATION DATA

LET'S WRITE TOGETHER! A COLLECTION OF SHORT STORIES BY ASPIRING YOUNG AUTHORS
VOLUME II
WATSON, ALEX AND ROBERT P. WATSON, EDITORS

P. CM.
ISBN: 978-0-9904211-4-6
LIBRARY OF CONGRESS CONTROL NUMBER: 2015938671
E15
10 9 8 7 6 5 4 3 2 1
FIRST EDITION
PRINTED AND BOUND IN THE UNITED STATES OF AMERICA

publishing the written word
trimarkpress

A PUBLICATION OF TRIMARK PRESS, INC.
368 SOUTH MILITARY TRAIL
DEERFIELD BEACH, FL 33442
800.889.0693
WWW.TRIMARKPRESS.COM

LET'S WRITE TOGETHER!

A Collection of Short Stories by Aspiring Young Authors

VOLUME II

Edited by
Alex Watson & Robert P. Watson

PUBLISHED BY TRIMARK PRESS, INC.
800.889.0693
WWW.TRIMARKPRESS.COM

TABLE OF CONTENTS

LOWER SCHOOL AUTHORS

LOWER SCHOOL AUTHORS
(CONTINUED)

MIDDLE SCHOOL AUTHORS

UPPER SCHOOL AUTHORS

UPPER SCHOOL AUTHORS
(CONTINUED)

PREFACE

The idea for this book started with the terrible tsunami that struck Japan in the year 2011. I have always found natural disasters to be fascinating, so I decided to research the causes and consequences of the 2011 tsunami and other tsunamis. I discovered that there have been many tsunamis throughout history. Two of them struck Hawaii in the years 1946 and 1960. Because I was born in Hawaii, I have always been interested in America's fiftieth state and decided I would write a book about a devastating tsunami that hits the islands and a group of kids that struggle to survive the monster wave. In part, I based my story and characters on the real events and people in Hawaii in 1946 and 1960.

The book, *Tsunami,* was published in 2012. I had such a fun time writing the book (I managed to get a vacation to Hawaii after telling my father I needed to do "research" for the book!) that I decided to try and encourage other kids to write. I was only eleven and twelve at the time I worked on the book and wanted to show other kids that it does not matter how old you are – you can write a book!

Therefore, I came up with an organization called Let's Write Together. Everyone from school teachers to librarians, from parents to politicians, tries to encourage kids to read. My thought was that we should also encourage them to write. Writing is fun and rewarding, and can be done alone, with friends, or with family members. My father worked with me on the book and I wanted people to experience what we experienced – that writing a story or book together is a lot of fun.

There are two ways LWT supports the efforts of kids that want to write. The first is that I created a website (www.letswritetogether.com) that includes a free writing guide to help kids and families write books. It is a step-by-step tool to help with questions about writing, editing, and the publishing process. The LWT website also has a blog and information for young authors. The second project is a writing contest. Lower school through upper school authors were invited to write and then submit short stories on any topic to LWT. Sure enough, students from throughout south Florida and several from around the country (who have families in south Florida) worked hard and submitted their writing. My father and I sent the stories to volunteers who helped us by reading and judging them. The winners were selected and the result of that contest is this book.

I wish to acknowledge and thank WPTV 5, the *Boca Raton Magazine,* the Palm Beach County Library System, the Broward County Library System, and the Literacy Coalition of Palm Beach County for announcing and promoting the writing contest. I also wish to thank the many former school teachers and librarians that volunteered to read the short stories and serve as judges for the contest. Thanks to Jessica Burke, Christelle Mehu, and Kevin Studer, who volunteered to serve as editorial assistants. They read and helped edit the stories. I also want to acknowledge my mother and entire family for being so supportive of my idea and this contest.

A special thanks to Barry Chesler and Veronica Rodriguez at TriMark Press for publishing this book. They not only supported the idea for a book of stories by kids, but they were interested in supporting the writing efforts of young, aspiring authors. Most importantly, I wish to recognize the students that contributed short stories. I hope this project helped build confidence in your writing and inspire you to continue to write.

I am proud to announce...

Let's Write Together: The book, volume 2!

—Alex Watson
  Boca Raton, Florida

FOREWORD

Kelley Dunn, Anchor
WPTV News Channel 5 (NBC)

I f you want to see what makes reading and writing fun and interesting, take a look at these stories written by students.

Through short stories like these we can use our imagination to put ourselves in the place of the characters, travel to all parts of the world, and face all types of challenges. The best part, we can do it all in an afternoon without leaving our homes.

Reading stories like the ones in this book gives us a chance to develop new interests while also developing our reading and writing skills. No matter where you go or what you do, you will always rely on your ability to read and write.

As these stories can open doors to your imagination, reading and writing can open opportunities and adventures in your life. When I was the age of the young authors featured in this book, I loved to read and write. That passion has served me well in my career as a journalist and news anchor. I still love stories and books.

Enjoy the work of these authors, enjoy the book, and always enjoy reading and writing. I congratulate all the winners of this writing contest on having the courage and commitment to write and for writing such wonderful stories.

INTRODUCTION

Douglas Crane, Director
Palm Beach County Library System

What do a big red dog, a pigeon, and a hungry caterpillar have in common? They are all star characters from popular books that children around the world adore. As a librarian, I know the importance of fostering a love of reading at an early age. I have presented story times to children ages three to five, an age range where children are beginning to learn the alphabet and recognize the familiar patterns of stories. The public library has always collected books that excite and inspire children to dream and discover. There are few things more heartwarming for a librarian than to see young boys and girls walking out of the library carrying stacks of books in their small hands.

One of my greatest joys has been introducing my daughter, Sierra, to books. Since she was very young, I would bring home books to read to her in the bathtub or at bedtime. She would race to meet me at the door and grab the book bag out of my hand to see what treasures were inside. Now Sierra, a six year old, is a very quick reader of chapter books, which we pick out every Sunday on our visit to the neighborhood library. She enjoys the adventures of Jack and Annie in their Magic Tree House, and Cam Jansen solving mysteries with her photographic memory, and Harold and Chester, the cat and dog that live in the house of Bunnicula, the vampire bunny.

Like me, Dr. Robert Watson shared his love of reading with his son, Alex. They have even taken the next step of writing stories for others to enjoy. Alex's first book was called *Tsunami,* and he shared it with families at several library programs. This success inspired the Watsons to share their love of reading and writing even further by creating the "Let's Write Together" contest. The first book, published last year, was a tremendous hit. All the children who contributed to the book gathered at our West Boca Branch to celebrate its release. I am very pleased that the Watsons have repeated the contest so that a new group of young writers can earn a chance to share their writing with the world.

A love of reading would be impossible without writers. Writing is an art and a skill that takes a lifetime to master. I congratulate all the young writers who took this brave step of submitting their stories for publication. As well, I encourage them all to keep going forward by practicing the art of writing every day. With perseverance and resolve, they may soon write the books that fill our physical and electronic libraries. Finally, thank you Dr. Watson and Alex for birthing this contest and sharing your love of reading and writing. Write on!

ABOUT THE EDITORS

Alex Watson is a high-school student in Boca Raton, Florida. He enjoys playing sports and music, traveling, and hanging out with his friends. He coauthored the books *Tsunami* and *The Crossing*, the first in the *Time Zone* series, and is the editor of *Let's Write Together*, the multivolume collection of short stories by kids based on the annual writing contest he created.

Robert P. Watson, Ph.D. is Professor of American Studies at Lynn University, a commentator for several news outlets, and an author who has published 40 books and hundreds of scholarly articles, chapters, and essays on topics in American history and politics.

ABOUT THE CONTRIBUTORS

Katie Berlatsky is a ninth-grade aspiring author and astrophysicist at Grandview Preparatory School who, despite being generally fabulous, hasn't had a very exciting life so far. This, as you can imagine, has led to a dearth of things to put in her bio.

I started expressing myself through drawing before I could write. Now I love writing! My name is **Elizabeth Berman** and I am seven years old and a first grader from Ben Gamla Charter School in Palm Beach County. I would like to be a scientist when I grow up.

Kayla Blake is in the ninth grade at Wellington High School.

Adriana Bockman-Pedersen has known that she loved to write since she was in the fourth grade. She wrote her first book at 10 and it was published in her school library. She recently finished writing her first fantasy novel, which will be self-published sometime this year. She loves to read and her favorite series include *Harry Potter* and *Lord of the Rings*. She is now 14 and in the eighth grade.

Olivia Buzzanca is a freshman who attends Wellington High School. She is on her school's varsity cheerleading team. She is also in Wellington's marketing program (DECA) and is a member of the Key Club and an Honor Roll student.

Brendan Darden is eight years old and is a third grader at Grandview Preparatory School. He enjoys making books and hopes to have his own bookstore someday. Some of his hobbies are fishing, writing books, and playing baseball.

Olivia Eames and **Tim Eames** are aspiring authors who both enjoy sports, food, and things that make them laugh. They live and play in Wellington.

David Fahim is an eight-year-old third grader who attends BRCH. He is passionate about soccer and has played competitively for Team Boca, winning the Jupiter Cup in 2014. He is also a member of the Boca Mantas Swim Team and has won numerous medals in relay, butterfly, and backstroke. This year, he was chosen to represent his school at the Spelling Bee and Math Olympics. **Myriam Fahim** holds two law degrees and practiced family law in Canada before pursuing a career in public education. In 2010, she was awarded the YBAM's Lawyer of the Year Award.

Myriam is currently studying to become a teacher. She enjoys writing, travelling, playing volleyball, and being Emily and David's mom.

Emily Fahim is a ten-year-old fifth grader who attends BRCS. She is passionate about ballet and has been cast twice in BBT's Nutcracker productions. She is a member of the Boca Mantas Swim Team and has won a silver medal in relay at the 2014 swimming championships. In 2015, she competed in the elementary and middle school geography bee and won second place. Emily enjoys reading, writing, and traveling. **Monica Farag** holds a Bachelor of Education degree. She taught third grade, fourth grade, and pre-school for a number of years, wrote and directed a school play, went on a mission trip to Tanzania, and created programs for at-risk high school girls. An adventurer at heart, Monica has cliff dived, white water rafted, mountain climbed, and just got married. She enjoys being Emily and David Fahim's aunt.

Sydney Lyn Gordesky lives with her mother, father, and two-year-old brother in Brooklyn, New York. She attends first grade in a public school and her interests are gymnastics, books, words, and asking questions. Most of all, her passion is cooking and baking, which she does regularly with her mom and dad. She also likes to visit her grandmother, **Ellen A. Gordesky,** who lives in Boynton Beach, Florida.

Jett Hollister is a freshman at Wellington High School where he runs on the varsity track and cross country teams.

Younger than he looks, **Pablo Jaramillo** was born in Santiago de Chile to Colombian parents in September of 2000. He is an eighth grader at Spanish River Christian School and at the height of six-foot-three, he is a passionate basketball player who also likes animals, and donkeys in particular. Pablo is friendly and easy to get along with.

Courtney Kleino is 15 years old and in ninth grade at Wellington High School. She enjoys being a varsity cheerleader and loves cats.

Willow Kristich is seven years old and is in the first grade at Conewago Elementary School. She dances six days a week at the Central Pennsylvania Youth Ballet, was awarded a scholarship for her dance, and has performed many roles in their productions. This year marked Willow's third annual Thanksgiving food drive and she has donated over 3,000 pounds of food and raised over $1,000 for the local food bank. Willow also loves horses, jumping rope, swimming, reading books, writing, playing with her two dogs, and spending time with her family and friends. **Wendy Kristich,** a former dancer and swimmer herself, is Willow's proud mother. They both like to visit their family members in South Florida!

Bailey Maher is 14 and is a freshman attending Wellington High School. Bailey enjoys drawing and writing.

Jamie Moubarak is a ninth grader at Wellington High School.

Benjamin Pierce Oppenheimer is in the third grade at Grandview Preparatory School in Boca Raton.

Kaitlyn Osmond is 15 years old and is in the ninth grade at Wellington High School. One of her hobbies is playing soccer.

Jakub Pawlowski is 13 years old and is in the eighth grade at Christa McAuliffe Middle School.

Sam E. Perez is 14 years old and was born on Halloween. When she grows up, she wants to be an author or singer. She enjoys playing soccer, acting, and participating in sports. Sam would love to thank her best friends Sarah D. and Victoria G. Stone, and also acknowledge her family and eighth grade teachers at Grandview Preparatory School for believing in her!

Tommy Reid is 15 years old and is a freshman currently attending Wellington High School. His hobbies include hanging out with his friends and solving Rubik's Cubes.

Cadence Rochlen is currently a ninth grader attending Wellington Community High School. She is 15 and her hobbies include reading, writing, and practicing her flute.

Sean Scott is nine years old and in fourth grade at Newbridge Elementary School. He likes soccer, football, hockey, baseball, golf, track, dancing, and band. He was in student council in third grade and is in the school talent show for the third year in a row. He spoke at a March of Dimes 2015 kickoff event (March for Babies). Sean's short story is about his favorite subject – the presidents – and you can see two videos of him talking about them on YouTube. **Edward Scott** is Sean's dad.

Shayna Silverstein is nine years old and is a fourth grade student at Del Prado Elementary School. Her hobbies are gymnastics, writing, and day-dreaming. **Mallory Thomas** is 10 years old and is also in the fourth grade at Del Prado Elementary School. She likes to paint and write.

Rachel Stauffer is 14 years old and in the eighth grade at Martin GT Magnet Middle School in Raleigh, North Carolina. She enjoys writing (obviously), theater (both acting and behind-the-scenes), and dance (jazz, ballet, and pointe). She thoroughly enjoyed writing this story and did her best to make it as historically accurate as possible (the event in the story did happen, although the main character is entirely fictitious). This is her second time entering the *Let's Write Together* contest and she feels honored and overjoyed to be back this year!

Devereaux Stephens is 14 years old and currently attends Wellington High School as a freshman. He loves watching anime and wishes to start learning to code Javascript and maybe HTML. His brother, **Etienne Stephens,** is a huge influence in his life and really helped him come up with ideas for this story.

Victoria Gallastegui (a.k.a, Victoria Stone) lives in Boca Raton. She is 14 years old and is in eighth grade in Grandview Preparatory School. In her free time, she enjoys reading, writing, playing soccer, and singing. Victoria loves writing because it allows her to use her imagination and look at things from different perspectives.

Isabella Watson is a fifth grader at Saint Andrew's School, where she is a student ambassador, participates in the school musicals, and plays the trumpet in the concert band and drums in the pipe and drum band. She enjoys dancing, volleyball, and singing and wants to give a shout out to all her friends. **Claudia Watson** is a professor of languages and proud mother of Isabella and Alex!

Bobbi Zimmelman is a fourth grader at Citrus Cove Elementary School.

ABOUT THE PUBLISHER

TriMark Press, based in Deerfield Beach, Florida, is known as a pioneer in independent and participatory publishing, with over twenty-five years of book publishing expertise. Our clients include independent authors, journalists, photographers, financial institutions, financial firms, and non-profit and philanthropic organizations. Our publishing programs are designed to elevate the credibility and increase the exposure of our clients, accentuating their creativity and/or positioning them as experts in their field. For more information, call 800-889-0693 or 561-953-1777 or visit www.TriMarkPress.com.

LOWER SCHOOL AUTHORS

ALL ABOUT FRIENDS

Elizabeth Berman

My Friends

I have friends, including a best friend, and I would like to tell you all about them.

I have a friend. Isabella Kaplan is her name. I met Isabella on the first day of kindergarten. I was very shy and then I got used to my new school and that is when I started to have some friends like Isabella and some other friends like Lauren W. and Lauren G. They make school more fun every day.

My friend Isabella is kind, and that is how a friend should act. I help to clean up Isabella's playroom. She helps me with homework and other stuff. I also helped her when she lost her toy at the beach. We could not find it that day. I hope that one day we can find it. Isabella will be happy. Because she is my friend, that will make me happy.

Isabella is my best friend. Do you know why? It is because she is really kind. She likes sports, running, chess, and some classes. We have a lot in common. We have so much fun together and I like her a lot. Every day after school, we wait for each other and walk together to the parking lot. To show my love to her, I gave her a friendship necklace. She gave me a gift for the holiday. She knows I love Legos, so she gave me a Lego set.

Isabella and I like Legos because we can express our ideas through the Legos. When I build things with the Legos it makes me feel happy. You should try playing with Legos.

Isabella and I also like Monopoly. I like Monopoly because you can buy houses and utilities and it is like real life on the game board.

I also like horseback riding. When I went to Boston, my dad took me to a farm. I got to ride a horse named Peek-a-Boo. The cute horse was light brown and white and was very friendly. My dad took me back to the farm the day before we left Boston to see my new friend. Animals can be our friends, too. I was impressed by Peek-a-Book and would like to see her again. I would like to have a horse and really wish I could go to horseback riding lessons. If Isabella could join me, that would be great.

Since my school only has up to fifth grade, Isabella and I may be apart after fifth grade, but we will still call, text, email, chat, Skype, and other stuff, too. Do you want to know why we are going to do this? To make sure each other is okay! Best friends forever and forever, always.

A Poem and Song about Friends

I wrote a poem and song for my friends.

"Best Friend"

They are my best friends
And nobody is like them
Isabella has a kindness in her mind
She makes everything okay
Lauren G has a spark in her mind
She always makes it okay
Lauren W is playful as can be
I know it's always okay
They are my best friends and...
Nobody is like them

Advice on Having Friends

I would also like to give you advice on having friends.

Friends never put you down. They bring you up. If you want a friend, be nice. If you have a friend, make sure he or she is your type. What do you like? Find that out and search for the same type of person. You should not give up on friendship. Friends are nice.

Friends listen to you no matter what. Day and night, they listen to you. A friend will care about you. Friends do not interrupt you and you will not interrupt them. If you ask your friend, she or he will listen and do what you ask.

Friends keep you company. If they get hurt, you will always be there for them. If you have a friend, I bet she or he is your type. You will stay together in good times and bad times.

If you have a friend and she has another friend, she or he is still your friend. Their friend may become one of your friends and you all could be friends together.

When you are mad at your friends, do not be mad. Explain how you feel. Friends can make mistakes. We all make mistakes. Open your mind, forgive.

Don't be jealous of your friends. Jealousy is no way to go. Be supportive, be kind. When your friends accomplish something, say "Congratulations!" Here are some other things to say to your friends when they accomplish something: "Great job," "excellent," "awesome," and "you rock!" The most important words you should say to your friends are: "Hi" or "hello," "sorry" or "I forgive you," "you are so kind" or "you are nice," and "I like you" or "I love you."

If you have a friend, that is good. You want to know why? Because they are very fun and kind and nice. Your BFF will like you and I am positive you will like her or him. If you are going to move away from your BFF, take my advice: Call her or him every night.

I say that friends are the best ever! Friends rock!

ADVENTURES OF THE RESCUE RABBITS

Brendan Darden

O nce upon a time, there were two green alien rabbits in space. One of them was named Fatty and the other was Slim. They had become very rich in space after they figured out that in their home planet of Cookie, there was gold.

It all happened a few months back when the rabbits were part of a construction crew working on a new building. They were drilling a hole in the ground for a pipe and accidentally made it too deep. Fatty saw something shiny in the hole, so Slim lowered him into the hole. On his way down, the hole became deeper and narrower. Soon Fatty got stuck. Fatty pulled on the rope to let Slim know that he needed to be pulled up a little, but this did not work and he got stuck again and gave up. This time, Slim went in with a shovel to dig down to the narrow area. Slim made it wider and was able to get down inside the hole where he found a large chunk of gold. The rabbits told the construction manager about the gold. Since they had found it, they got to keep the gold. There was enough gold to help them retire forever.

With the money from the gold, the rabbits were able to buy the building that they had worked on after it was finished. They even helped their construction worker friends by buying them a forklift and some tools. They also shared some of the gold with their family and friends. Fatty and Slim placed the rest of their gold in a chest and put it in their attic for safe keeping.

***

One day, the rabbits were relaxing on their planet. It was a hot summer day and Slim was tanning near the pool. Fatty was playing on his pool slide. Suddenly, they heard a crash and that crash came from a spaceship. They were astonished to see a big aircraft on their planet. Fatty and Slim decided to explore the aircraft. They looked all around it and found a sign that read "NASA." Fatty thought it meant nose picking Alien Slimy Apple. Slim thought NASA stood for Nasty Aquarium Shrimp Appetizers. But they were both wrong. By the time they discovered it meant National Aeronautics and Space Administration, a door popped open. There was a man in a white suit. For some reason, the man wasn't scared of Fatty and Slim. The reason was because the man in the white suit was having déjà vu. He felt like he had seen the alien rabbits before in a rabbit mobile. He had a flashback to when he was six years old.

The astronaut remembered seeing these rabbits through a telescope long ago when he was a young boy camping with his dad. He wanted to become an astronaut someday, so his father had bought him a telescope for his birthday. They were watching the stars through the new telescope. The boy noticed something flash through the sky. He thought he saw rabbit ears, but he ignored it. However, he couldn't sleep that night because he kept on thinking about those rabbit ears.

The man snapped out of his flashback. The rabbits spoke to him, but their English was rusty. They had learned English from a mysterious book they had found at a construction site. The man asked the alien rabbits for help. He wanted to get back to Earth and explained that his aircraft had wrecked and was therefore not working.

Fatty and Slim thought for one moment and Fatty replied, "We can fly you back to Earth."

The man in the white suit said, "My name is Steve Everheart." He told them that if they flew him back, their identity would not be concealed. The rabbits didn't understand what Steve meant by their "identity not being concealed." Steve had to explain to them that on Earth, alien rabbits were enemies.

Slim interrupted, saying he had a plan. He thought they could direct Steve back to his planet while they hid in the back of their rabbit mobile. The rabbit mobile would be covered by a large piece of cloth. The rabbits would then fly back to planet Cookie after dropping Steve off. Steve couldn't believe that the vision he had long ago was true. They had a deal and soon the three of them were friends.

The rabbits would need three days to plan out the rescue mission. While Steve was on planet Cookie, he and Slim tried to fix the space shuttle. They patched a few pieces of scrap metal on the damaged areas. In the meantime, Fatty watched them as he ate a donut. During Steve's time on planet Cookie, he told the rabbits that there were other living things on Earth. Fatty and Slim were excited but nervous to hear this. They only knew about living things on their own planet.

The rabbits learned a lot in those three days from Steve. For example, Steve told the rabbits that fire burns wood, which is what he did when he went camping. Steve told them all about his camping trip when he was six-years old. He also told them that he had seen them through a telescope, but couldn't believe it at first. After meeting Fatty and Slim, he now believed what he had seen.

Finally, it was time for Steve to leave. Steve's space shuttle could not be fixed, so it was left behind. They used the rabbit mobile to take Steve back to Earth. Steve captained it to Earth, while the rabbits paid attention on how to get there and back. They made it to Earth and Steve was home. Steve gave the rabbits a special telephone that they could use to call him from their home planet to keep in touch.

Before returning home, the rabbits were astonished to see many strange things on planet Earth. They had never seen so many trees. Fatty and Slim thought they looked like giant pieces of broccoli. Also, nothing seemed to float on Earth like it did in space. However, they thought the cars on Earth were similar to their rabbit mobile. They saw some rabbits that didn't walk or talk, which they thought was weird. The rabbits on Earth all looked the same and were furry. Fatty and Slim didn't have fur like them.

The rabbits returned to planet Cookie after exploring Earth for a half hour.

***

A few years later, while Fatty and Slim were watching T.V., they heard a BOOM! It was a pirate ship that had crashed into a welcome sign outside of their home. Fatty and Slim went outside and found two pirate rabbits in the pirate ship. The pirates said that they would attack at dawn and take all of the rabbits' gold. These pirate rabbits had been watching Fatty and Slim for two months and planning when to attack them for their gold. What they heard made Fatty and Slim panick. So, they called Steve to tell him all about the pirates and that they needed his help. Steve went to planet Cookie with a new and improved space ship and brought along an attack fleet. They were ready. The battle began!

First, they prepared the attack fleet. They filled the ships up with fuel, gathered their weapons, and made their plan. Each one of them had their own spaceship and position. The plan was that Steve would try to take down the captain's pirate ship first. Fatty would try to get one of the smaller ships As predicted, at dawn the pirates came back. The pirates shot a few cannon balls toward Fatty who was chewing on a carrot. Fatty dodged them and shot lasers back, causing all the pirates to go bananas! There were lasers and cannon balls flying everywhere... BEEW! BEEW! BAM! BAM!

During the fight, Slim shot down one of the pirate ships. Meanwhile, Steve tried to take down the captain's pirate ship, but he was hit several times and his engine failed. His space ship started to go down, but he jumped out right before crashing and landed on Slim's spaceship. Steve was hanging onto one of the wings by one hand. Slim popped open the door and helped Steve inside the spaceship.

Steve took a grappling hook and tied it to Slim's ship. Then he threw it at the pirate ship and managed to hook it. They were now pulling the pirate ship round and round at high speeds. The rope snapped and the pirate ship went flying back to pirate world. One down! Now it was up to Steve, Slim, and Fatty to eliminate the captain's pirate ship.

Meanwhile, one of the pirates had to crash land back on Pirate World and survived. He passed on the word to other pirates about how he needed more of them to go and attack the rabbits on planet Cookie. All of the pirate rabbits on Pirate World prepared to go into battle.

During the battle, the captain shot three cannon balls at Steve and Slim. They quickly deflected them and the cannon balls were now headed back toward the captain's pirate ship. One of the cannon balls hit the bottom deck. The second one hit the front deck. The third round went through one of the sails. The ship slowly started to go down.

Unfortunately, more pirates arrived at that moment. Two of them headed toward Steve. Fatty remembered that fire burned wood, so he decided he would try to set the other pirate ships on fire, then there would only be the captain's ship left. Fatty used the radio to tell Slim to get some large matches and get ready to throw them at the two ships.

Fatty and Slim were able to throw the large matches at the pirate ships before they crashed into Steve. The fire burned the ships to ashes. All three of the friends then targeted the pirate captain's sail and shot more lasers. Finally, the captain's pirate ship collapsed.

They had won the battle and saved their home and gold!

***

The rabbits thanked Steve for helping them. Steve said, "I'm returning the favor from when you helped me."

Steve decided to stay on planet Cookie the next day. Steve taught the rabbits all about Earth and how things worked. Slim paid attention while Fatty got back to eating his donuts and relaxing. Slim found out from Steve how trees grow on Earth. Fatty thought it would be cool to have trees on their planet, so they used some of their money to plant trees and crops on planet Cookie. Steve taught the rabbits that the seeds needed sunlight, water, and air. Since there was no air in space, they put all of the seeds into a giant dome that had oxygen tanks in it. Fatty's favorite part about planting was that he could have fresh fruits and vegetables to eat.

Steve was glad that the rabbits had won the battle. He was happy that they would have plants too. Steve said good-bye to the rabbits and they thanked him for participating in the battle and helping them. Steve returned to Earth.

Slim thought it was fun watching everything sprout and grow on planet Cookie. The two rabbits were happy about their exciting, new adventure and shared it with their family and friends. Thanks to Steve and the lessons from Fatty and Slim, now all the rabbits on planet Cookie were happy and eating healthier. They would also never have to worry about rabbit pirates trying to attack them ever again. Fatty and Slim were heroes!

THE WINNING GOAL

David Fahim and Myriam Fahim

"Goooooaal! Number 10 scores the winning goal for the team, and folks, that means the team is one game away from the championships!" declared the announcer. Ethan Glen, the team captain and star player, ran down the sidelines, high-fiving his teammates.

"Way to go!" yelled John.

"Awesome!" said Sebastián, slapping Ethan on the back.

The Tigers' coach tousled Ethan's hair enthusiastically. "You're an animal, Glen! Keep it up! I want that trophy on our stand!"

"Yes, Coach. I'll do my best!"

"I know you will, Glen! You always come through!" Coach blew his whistle. "Tigers bring it in! Don't be the last one in!" The Tigers formed a circle around Coach Thomas.

"Chang! Next time, don't let your man slip from you! Muller, great job in goal! Isaac, good pressure on defense! Hands in everybody! Let's give our best cheer."

"Tigers, Tigers, we're the best; we will put you to the test;

we will beat you; we'll defeat you; to our victory we will treat you! Gooooo Tigers!"

The fans went wild. One blond skinny-looking kid wasn't cheering. He was sitting dejectedly on the bench. His team had won but he never even got to touch the ball once. The coach spotted him and headed his way.

"Beeswax! What's with the long face? You should be celebrating with the team! It's all about team effort! What's important is that you tried your best and I know you did."

"Coach, I was only out there for two minutes. In that time, I managed to hit Ethan in the cleats and trip Lee as he was trying to take the ball from the attacker. Then, I screened the goaltender which led to the Hawks' one and only goal. I suck!"

"Now, now, Beeswax. You just need more practice. Put in the hours and you'll be a champ just like Glen. But working as a team is what's important in this sport. One man can't win it all!"

"Yes, Coach."

"Now come and shake hands with the other team."

Buzz Beeswax slowly got up and lined up with the rest of his teammates. As he was shaking hands with the Hawks, one of them whispered, "Thanks for helping us out, Beeswax. You singlehandedly took out your whole team!"

The other Hawks' players snickered. Buzz hung his head in shame.

"Why can't I be more like Ethan Glen?" he thought to himself. He eyed Ethan enviously, as parents crowded around to congratulate him on his goal. Ethan was everything a star player should be. He was tall and athletic. Next to him, Buzz looked like a little shrimp. Ethan's blue eyes shone with confidence as he shook hands with parents and players.

Buzz turned away and sat on the field, slowly removing his socks and cleats. Maybe the coach was right. Maybe he did need more practice. One thing was certain: he really couldn't get any worse. He found his soccer bag and took out his flip-flops just as his mom and dad rounded the corner.

"You were amazing, Buzz! I am so proud of you," said Mrs. Beeswax.

"Gusto, son! That's what you have!" added Mr. Beeswax excitedly.

Buzz didn't like it when his parents praised his disastrous performances. He took a deep breath and counted to 10. Now was not the time to get into a fight with them. As he left the field, Buzz was so angry that he forgot to pick up his soccer ball. Later that day, some young kids found it and decided to keep it. Although he didn't know it yet, that was the reason Buzz's life was about to dramatically change.

***

"Bzzz! Bzzz! Look who's coming. It's Beeeeeeeswax!

"Hey, bee man! How many 'own goals' did you score yesterday?" one of the kids snickered.

"Now go back to your beehive." They all laughed.

"Not funny!" Buzz mumbled under his breath and walked away.

This was going to be a long day at school. He hurried to his locker and opened it. Something fell out. It was a picture of him "photoshopped" into a beehive! He heard the laughter behind him. Correction: This was going to be a VERY long day at school.

"Hey Buzz!" It was Kenny, Buzz's only friend. Kenny was the smartest kid in school and the number one gamer in the state. He knew everything there was to know about mystical dragons, howling goblins, and demon robots. Buzz's eyes fell on Kenny's red t-shirt which said, "CTRL your minions before they delete you!" Buzz wondered if Kenny was the one that would be "deleted" by the school bullies, later today.

"I got to level 37 last night and almost defeated the griffin. I think if I spin three times and hit him twice on the wings, I'll get him!" Kenny rubbed his hands excitedly at the thought.

"Maybe. But I have bigger problems than your griffin, Kenny. Check this out."

"Whoah! That's terrible!" said Kenny.

"Tell me about it!" complained Buzz, showing his friend the photoshopped image.

"I mean, these people don't even know how to use the software. They need a class on advanced imaging techniques. The beehive is totally unrealistic and your body is way too big for the image."

"Dude, you're missing the point here!"

"Oh! Sorry!" Kenny looked down at his hands, "So what are you going to do about it?"

"Same as usual: nothing. You know, I think that if I practice soccer and get really, really good at it, they might just leave me alone."

"Maybe," said Kenny, unconvinced.

"Tonight, we have a big practice and I'll turn over a new leaf. I'll practice so hard that I'll be even better than Glen!"

"You do that!" said Kenny, thinking his friend had completely lost his mind. "Well, we better get to class. The bell's about to ring."

Buzz couldn't wait to finish school. He pictured himself with a soccer ball scoring goal after goal. Deep inside, he knew that he would be the one who would lead his team to victory.

***

Buzz stood on the field staring at the goal. It was time to put his plan into action. He reached into his bag to pull out his soccer ball. Buzz frowned as he looked and looked. Finally, he dropped on all fours and emptied his whole bag. The ball wasn't there!

"Problem, Beeswax?"

"No, Coach! I just seemed to have misplaced my soccer ball."

Nathan Isaac, Patrick Muller, and Ethan Glen rolled their eyes. Coach Thomas sighed, "Just grab any ball. You're holding up practice!"

Buzz found one and stood by the cone. The whistle screeched. Buzz dribbled the ball with determination. He ran past Isaac and tried to do a step-over to avoid Chang. Instead, he tripped over the ball and fell flat on his face. The whistle screeched again.

"I didn't touch him, Coach! He fell by himself," said Chang defensively.

"I saw it. He tripped over the ball," agreed Isaac.

Buzz took his hand reluctantly, indicating that he was alright, and got up.

"Beeswax! Why don't you go practice step-overs over there? When you've done 20 good ones, come back and see me," decided Coach Thomas.

"O.K., Coach."

"The rest of you continue with this drill. I want to see good defense and even better offense. Remember, we have a big game this Saturday. Glen, you're up! Isaac and Chang in defensive positions again! Go!" yelled Coach.

Buzz spent the rest of practice doing step-overs. Although by the end of practice he was able to do 16 good ones, he still felt like a loser. Maybe he needed to try something else like focusing on his shot strength.

Saturday's game quickly arrived. Buzz put on his cleats and felt confident. With Kenny's help, he had practiced every night and knew that his leg muscles had grown stronger. Boy would Coach Thomas be surprised!

As he expected, he wasn't part of the starting lineup. He watched with interest as Ethan Glen scored two goals. The other team, the Giants, seemed to have giant feet. They were tough and quickly tied the game. Coach Thomas turned to him, "You're up, Beeswax! Go out there and get 'em!"

Buzz ran to the field and took the center back position. He was so nervous that he could hear his own breathing. He looked up into the stands and saw Kenny giving him a thumbs-up. He tried to focus his mind on the game. The referee had already put the ball back in play and one of the Giants had it. The guy, who looked like he was made of steel, headed right for Buzz. Buzz let out a war cry and ran out to meet him. The Giant was taken by surprise. He didn't expect Buzz to run right at him! That gained Buzz an advantage and allowed him to take the ball. The crowd cheered.

Another Giant tried to get it back from Buzz. But Buzz did a step-over and was surprised when it worked. Today was obviously his lucky day! He passed the ball to Chang and ran forward. Chang passed it to Isaac who passed it back to Buzz. Buzz could see Glen waiting by the goal, asking for the ball. He decided to take the shot himself. After all, he had practiced his shot strength! Buzz stepped back and kicked the ball as hard as he could. That's when everything went wrong.

Instead of sailing straight into the goal, the ball spun in the air and hit Ethan Glen square in the head. Ethan went down. The referee blew his whistle. All the players made a circle around Ethan who was lying unconscious on the ground. The referee moved them away to give him some air. Ethan's eyes fluttered open.

"Where am I?"

"You're on the soccer field. You got hit by the ball," answered the referee.

Coach Thomas arrived on the scene. "You okay, Glen?"

"I'm fine but my head hurts."

Coach quickly motioned to Ethan's parents to come on the field.

"I'm so, so sorry Ethan!" blurted Buzz. "I should've just passed!"

"No worries," said Ethan rubbing his head. "If I were in your shoes, I would have taken that shot too!"

"Is there anything I can do?" pleaded Buzz.

"Not really. Oh wait! There is something. I left my soccer ball under the bench."

"Don't worry! I'll get it, Ethan. I'll keep it with me until our next practice," promised Buzz.

"Yea, I'll be there," said Ethan weakly as his parents took him by the arms and lead him toward the parking lot.

"What are you all standing there gaping for!" said Coach Thomas. "The game isn't over.

Go out there and finish it for Glen!"

***

The whistle sounded and the game resumed. No one bothered passing the ball to Buzz anymore.

It was as if he were invisible. He kept calling for a pass but none of the Tigers listened. With five minutes left in the game, Gonzales managed to score, leading the Tigers to a 3-2 victory.

The Tigers clapped each other on the back. They were in the mood to celebrate. That is until they saw Coach Thomas' face... He was fuming!

"Beeswax was clear! Why didn't any of you pass to him?"

"He would've messed it up again, Coach!" piped up Gonzales.

"Oh, I see!" said Coach Thomas with a dangerous glint in his eye. "None of you soccer pros have ever, ever messed up!"

The boys shuffled their feet uneasily.

"We are a team! We are only as strong as our weakest player. I don't ever want to see such poor sportsmanship again. Are we clear?"

"Yes, Coach!" answered the boys.

"Practice on Monday. Don't be late!"

Miserable, Buzz made his way to the bench. This was possibly the worst day of his life. Ethan was hurt and his teammates hated him for accidentally hitting the star player. He scooped up Ethan's ball nonchalantly. The minute he touched the ball however, he felt a strange surge of power. Before he had time to process what was going on, Kenny came up to him.

"Hard luck."

"Yea, I guess," shrugged Buzz.

"Want to play Xbox360 at my place?"

"Sure. That would be great!" The invitation lifted Buzz's spirits.

"Excuse me," a deep voice piped in.

"Yes?" said the boys, surveying the man who had addressed them. He was tall and dressed in a strange black outfit with a hood covering his head.

"That ball is mine! My son left it here. Could you please give it to me?"

Buzz frowned and looked down at the ball he was holding. The weird power surging from it became stronger. "You must be mistaken, Mister. This is my friend Ethan's ball. See: It has his name right there."

"Yes, I can see that," said the man. "If you give it to me, I'll give you $1,000 dollars and you can buy your friend an even better ball."

Buzz shook his head decisively, "It's not mine to sell. Sorry!" The man shrugged and walked away.

"That's a lot of money you just turned down!" said Kenny.

"I don't know why, but that guy gave me the creeps!"

"Yea, well, hopefully Ethan won't kill you when he finds out you turned down that sweet deal!" teased Kenny.

From a distance, the man watched the two boys as they headed to Kenny's house. He was not alone. A group of men dressed in the same black clothing awaited his orders. He turned to face them and said simply, "Get it!"

***

A few days later, Buzz was back at soccer practice. Since the game, he had the feeling that someone was always watching him. He shook the feeling off and took out Ethan's ball. He had decided to use it since Ethan was on bed rest and couldn't attend practice for the time being.

It seemed to be a very good day for Buzz because he was able to easily and flawlessly execute every skill Coach called for. From scissor-kicks to rainbows, he had everything down.

Buzz's teammates looked at him with astonishment as he outwitted their best defense and scored one goal after another.

"Excellent job, Beeswax! I knew you had it in you!" said Coach Thomas. "Gather around and don't be last! Tomorrow, we have our final game. I know you're all upset that Ethan won't be playing. However, our team is not dependant on one man. You've all practiced and if you do your best we'll beat the Bear Claws. Get a goodnight's sleep and I'll see you tomorrow!"

Buzz smiled to himself. He had never played soccer so well. He felt unbeatable. He kicked the ball around relishing his triumph. When he looked up, it seemed that everyone had left the park. He realized that he had lost track of time and that his parents would be worried. He headed for his bike but was blocked by a figure clad in black. More black-outfitted men seemed to materialize out of nowhere. He was surrounded.

"Give us the ball!" said the closest one to him.

"Get away from me or I'll scream!" answered Buzz.

"Go ahead. We've secured this area. Now, hand it over," they warned.

"Never," said Buzz.

The next thing he knew, the black outfits tried to take the ball by force. Buzz felt superhuman strength surging through him. He kicked the figure closest to him, then leaped over the next man. He didn't know who was more shocked – him or the man! Buzz ran to his bike, got on, and peddled at full speed. This was no easy task with the ball in his grip. The men followed on foot, bellowing at him. He rounded the corner at high speed.

The closest house was Kenny's. Buzz got off his bike and frantically rang the doorbell. When Kenny opened, Buzz rushed inside, slammed the door behind him, and locked it. He took a moment to catch his breath.

"What's wrong?" asked Kenny.

"There are men in black chasing me! We've got to call the police!"

"Men in black?"

"Yes. Like the guy at the park! They're after Ethan's ball," explained Buzz.

"Dude, calm down! Look outside. There's nobody!"

Buzz went to the window and looked out. Kenny was right! The street was completely deserted. Kenny was looking at him weirdly.

"I didn't dream this up! They're real!" pleaded Buzz.

"Let's take a look outside and see if the big bad men in black are gone," answered Kenny, as if he were talking to a four year old. The minute they stepped outside, they knew it was a mistake. The black figures rushed down from Kenny's roof and grabbed them. They shot something on the floor which exploded and produced smoke. Then, they disappeared with their prisoners.

***

When the smoke hit the floor, everything went dark for Buzz and Kenny. They realized that the men had blindfolded them. After walking for what seemed like an eternity, the men took off the boys' blindfolds. Buzz and Kenny gasped. They seemed to be in some kind of underground lair. It was huge! At every turn, there was a choice between several passages. The men never hesitated, knowing exactly which passage they wanted to take.

For Buzz and Kenny, it was bad news! They realized that even if they managed to escape their captors, they would be hopelessly lost underground. The group finally arrived in a chamber with a huge dragon statue overlooking vaults filled with treasure.

"Welcome, honored guests!" boomed a voice. A man slowly emerged from the shadows.

It was the man from the park!

"Wait a second..." said Kenny. "I know who you are! You're ninjas! I don't know how I missed that before. I played "Attack of the Ninjas" like about nine thousand times. Cool!"

"Yes, we are Dragon Ninjas, sworn protectors of the great dragon treasure. I am Master Shenobi. We are sorry we had to take the ball by force, but it was imperative we retrieve our treasure."

"Oh, please!" said Buzz, unimpressed. "Ethan's ball isn't part of some treasure!"

"Not the ball. What's inside. Look!" With that, Master Shenobi did an ancient hand motion and struck the soccer ball. Suddenly, the whole cave shook. Buzz and Kenny tried to keep their balance throughout the earthquake. When it stopped, the ball split in two revealing a green diamond. The ninjas let out a cheer.

"Behold. The sacred dragon diamond!"

"What's it doing in Ethan's ball?" asked Buzz, completely taken aback.

"An interesting story, my friend. Please sit down and I'll explain." The two boys did as they were told. "It was first discovered by our brothers in Japan. What they didn't know was that the diamond possessed great power. It allowed anyone using it to achieve their full potential. Let me demonstrate."

Master Shenobi got up and gently placed the diamond in a glass casing. He took a few steps to the right and pointed to a tiny hole in the wall. From his outfit, he quickly removed three knives, took aim, and threw. Only one of the knives buried itself in the hole. The other two slightly missed. Master Shenobi then removed the green diamond from its casing. Holding it, he repeated the exercise. Buzz and Kenny gasped as they saw all three knives bury themselves in the hole.

"Now, you understand why this gem is so powerful?" Master Shenobi asked.

Buzz and Kenny nodded.

"So that's why I played soccer so well at our last practice!" exclaimed Buzz. "That's also how I got away from your ninjas!"

"Yes. It was the power of the gem," confirmed Master Shenobi. "The gem is as dangerous as it is powerful. It can never fall into the wrong hands! That's why we needed to move it from Japan to a safer place. One of our ninjas constructed this soccer ball to hide the gem until it could be shipped to us in America. Unfortunately, during shipment, the ball was misplaced. Someone mistakenly put it with a shipment of normal soccer balls. It was sold in a store. It took us a long time to track it down to your friend Ethan."

"Master Shenobi, I have a very important soccer game tomorrow," said Buzz. "Could I sort of borrow the stone?"

"That would be cheating!" interjected Kenny, shocked.

"Not really. The ball is just getting out my full soccer talents," insisted Buzz. "It's using something that's already inside of me..."

"True," answered Master Shenobi. "However, you must fulfill your potential on your own, young Buzz. That is the way of the Dragon Ninjas. Once you find a way to tap into your own special powers, you will be a great soccer player and do extraordinary things. Now, it is high time we returned you to the surface. Oh, before I forget – this belongs to your friend Ethan."

Master Shenobi put the ball back together and tossed it to Buzz. The boys bade farewell to the ninjas, who accompanied them back to the surface. Before they knew it, Buzz and Kenny were home. They were both scolded by their parents, who did not believe a word they said about ninjas and magical gems.

The next day, Buzz went to his Championship game. Coach Thomas put him in during the final minutes. The Tigers and the Bear Claws were tied 1-1. Isaac passed the ball to Gonzales. Buzz ran forward and was clear. Gonzales spotted him and made a beautiful pass. Only one defender stood in Buzz's way. It was now or never! Buzz did a step-over and "deked" the defender. He took the shot. It hit the post and went in.

"Gooooaaal! Number 5 scores the winning goal for the team. The Tigers win it all!

Everyone, stay put as our trophy ceremony will begin in 5 minutes!"

Buzz never heard that announcement. He was too busy celebrating with his teammates what it meant to be a real team.

THE SEAMSTRESS OF SLAVEN

Emily Fahim and Monica Farag

Slaven Palace, May 2, 1311 (Emera's Journal)

Dear Journal,

The Queen, with her high pitched and nasally voice, was hammering my mother all morning with demands about the dress that she wanted completed quicker than lightning. "It must be as blue as a peacock's tail," the Queen declared. "There must be no less than seven lustrous diamonds across the bodice, and make sure the seams do not show or my eyes will bulge out of my head and roll away to never be seen again."

To be fair, she may not have said the last bit exactly like that, but you get the gist. If it weren't for the fact that we needed the money she paid us for those magical dresses, I don't think we'd be able to put up with her incessant chatter.

Mum's task is to design and sew enchanted dresses that give the Queen wisdom to reign. In exchange, we receive money for food and rent. I can sew almost as well as Mum, but I don't have her powers. Mum says I shouldn't worry, that I am a like those flowers that bloom right before the first snowfall; however, it's hard to be the only one who hasn't figured it out yet.

Today, I was glad that Mum only needed my help with the hemming since it allowed me time to go play with Princess Meredith. She was one year older than I was and had the prettiest blond locks of hair going down to her waist. I told her all about the Queen's ramblings as she graciously accomplished several pirouettes in the air, showing off her own set of magical prowess. She suddenly stopped, turned around and said, "Maybe your magical talent is being able to handle my mother!"

"Ha-ha very funny, you'd be worried too had your dancing skills not emerged! You know what they do to people like me? They ship them across the sea and we never hear from them again."

"Well, Emera, we have two choices: demand that your talent be manifested at once, or start sewing a majestic traveling gown so you can impress those talentless people across the sea!"

I smiled at her because I knew Meredith was trying to make me feel better, but that thought was nagging me all day.

Seeing my expression full of anxiety, Meredith held my hands and said, "Come on, Em, we've tried everything! We've eaten the special diet recommended by the Endike Elves and we've even tried Crazy Cousin Calliope's special cream! There's one more option you know about but refuse to even consider. If you'd just try..."

"No Meredith! We've discussed this too many times before, it's too dangerous."

"Then you'll just have to believe that your talent will show up when it is ready to, just like it did for me," she said.

I really hope she's right. I wish I was just like everybody else! What if the magic never happens for me and I'm just little, ordinary, magic-less me?

Slaven Palace, May 3, 1311 (Princess Meredith's Diary)

Dearest Diary,

Today after Mother yelled at me about my posture, my handwriting, and my bad manners, she sent me to my apartments to write a letter about my dedication to my lessons. I must say I despise palace life. Let the servants do everything for you, live in a house as big as twelve mazes, go to boring balls, and most of all, I hate being proper. The only thing I like about the palace is my best friend Emera.

Let me tell you about Emera. She is smart, funny, kind, and understanding. Emera's mother is the palace seamstress and that's why they are always here. I know from my description of her that Mother sounds like a grumpy old witch, but when she rules the kingdom she is a wise, fair, and generous ruler. That is the effect of the dresses: they make her what she is not.

Poor Emera's mother fell sick with a high fever and no

one knows if she will make it. Emera is heartsick. I tried to cheer her up but she was miserable. Today, I will try again to make her feel better, but cheering up a person at their worst time is hard. Anyway, with all the talk about Emera's mum and the possibility that those precious gowns will not be made in time, Mother's temper is as hot as a dragon's fire. Now she is starting to take her anger out on me. I don't know if Emera's mother is going to get better or how I'll help Emera find her talent or how I will get Mum to calm down, but maybe I'll find a way.

Slaven Palace, May 4, 1311 (Princess Meredith's Diary)

Dearest Diary,

Emera's mother is dead. There is no way to take away the sadness from Emera's family. This morning, when I saw Emera, I burst into tears. During the funeral, I stood close to my mother knowing how horrid it would be to lose her, even with Mum's fiery temper. Afterward, my mother held a banquet in honor of our seamstress. Then she declared something that no one was expecting; she told everyone in the banquet hall that Emera was now the new seamstress and that she was expected to make Mother's blue and golden birthday gown.

At that moment, poor Emera fainted. When I heard she was awake and well, I rushed into the infirmary to see her. I saw her pacing by her bed saying, "What am I to do! Oh, what am I to do?" When I asked her what the problem was with sowing a simple dress, she coldly said, "Magical dresses, Meredith, magical dresses!"

When I realized what she meant, I almost fainted. I understood how much trouble my friend was in.

Slaven Palace, May 5, 1311 (Emera's Journal)

Dear Journal,

Today I was what they call a royal mess, a walking disaster. The Queen, apart from not giving me any time or consideration for my grief, has set me up in front of the whole kingdom for the worst kind of failure. If the dress that I am to make in one week's time does not provide her with the required wisdom, not only will my father and I lose our home, but no one will trust me again.

I know I must have looked like I had lost my wits today; I was pacing back and forth, muttering to myself, eyes darting from one side to the other like marbles, with hair that looked like birds could nest in it. To make matters worse, there actually was a sparrow that kept following me everywhere, giving my already vagabond look an even odder edge. Oh, how I miss my Mom! She would have known what to do. I cried so much when they announced her death. My dad held me in his arms, arms that seemed stronger than I had ever felt them to be. He kept whispering that we would be okay. If he only knew what my duties were, he'd be just as scared as I am! I couldn't tell him the truth; I didn't want him to worry. He had to go back to the farm to try to cultivate what little crops had grown this year, and I was to remain here under the Queen's order and care and figure out how to make ends meet.

The only person I have left here is Meredith. She promised me that she'll help me with my colossal, life-changing problem. Meredith fears that the only solution is to see the creature that everyone pretends doesn't exist, the one that parents use to frighten their children into obedience, the one who lives beyond the kingdom's boundaries, and the one I had refused to consider until circumstances became dire: Silverbeard Stone. I dread this option, but what choice do I have?

Slaven Palace, May 5, 1311 (Princess Meredith's Diary)

Dear Diary,

I kept thinking about my idea. Supposedly, my ideas are always good but this one seemed a little risky. Silverbeard Stone was the king of the dragon clan. That means he has the most wisdom. It sadly also means he has the most power. This dragon is hated by most humans because instead of shooting out only fire, Silverbeard also shoots out fire stones. However, there is a legend that, in the past, humans went to Silverbeard asking for his help and wisdom. In return for his wisdom, humans had to go on quests for different rare items Silverbeard wanted to collect. Emera agreed to go to Silverbeard's lair, but now I am just a tiny bit nervous myself. After all he is a dragon.

Well, on the bright side, my mother is going away to the kingdom of Drethelspend to attend her distant cousin's wedding. On the down side, she is taking me with her because I am the royal princess and so on and so forth. It's a good thing that we've spent all this time thinking about Silverbeard that I forgot to do my royal assignment! Mother will definitely ground me and leave me here. Hopefully then, Em and I will be able to set out for the Elves' Forest as soon as Mother leaves. I hope my plan will work!

Slaven Palace, May 6, 1311 (Princess Meredith's Diary)

Dear Diary,

It worked! At breakfast tomorrow morning, Mother will leave without me! When she saw I had skipped out of my lessons, Mother was furious. She said that, as a punishment, I would spend the week in my apartments and not go to Cousin Louisa's wedding. I was so happy! When I broke the news to Emera this morning, she rejoiced as well. Finally, she would be able to find out how to sew magical gowns and maybe, just maybe, Emera would find out her talent, too.

Emera and I are trying not to talk about dragons or anything of the sort because we are so nervous about encountering magical creatures on our way to Silverbeard. Instead, I'm talking about trolls, witches, or even another dragon! Regardless of those fears, Emera and I are going to leave at sunset tomorrow. We are making plans to go through the Elves' Forest, which should take about a day of following the trail. Next we should enter the Witch Kingdom. And last but not least, we shall arrive at the Dragon Desert where we will follow a trail leading to Silverbeard's lair.

I am scared about the Witch Kingdom, but it should be easy because they live underground and sleep during the day. The other thing I'm worried about is the elves, because the elves are very generous hosts and always use their charm to make you stay longer. And, if you don't, they will always remember and if you ever go into their forest again, they will curse you with a magic spell. I am really nervous about tomorrow. Hopefully we will live to see another day.

Elves' Forest, May 7, 1311 (Emera's Journal)

Dear Journal,

Meredith had this idea that if we dressed like trees, the elves wouldn't notice us passing through their home. It might have worked if the elves disliked those leafy giants, but as we began to cross the Elves' Forest, a small, pointy-eared, wide-eyed, and button-nosed creature jumped unto Meredith's head and began to look through her paper leaves for a place to sit.

"What do I do?" mouthed Meredith.

"Hmm, stay still and act like a tree?" I weakly suggested.

"Emera! He is tickling me! I can't hold still any longer!"

I was about to respond when I felt something heavy land

on my head. The elf on Meredith began to speak in some foreign melodious language to the creature on me. Meredith couldn't hold herself any longer and began to giggle. The creature on her head looked down and began to speak quicker and louder to his companion. He then chanted, "The Elves, the Elves, how wonderful are we; it is we ourselves that enchant the trees. You will have to stay, and keep us company; we will have our way; the Elves, the Elves."

Meredith looked at me with a smug smile. I was so sure she had the solution to our problem that I began to relax. That's when she said, "Um, that last verse doesn't rhyme!"

"We know it to be so; sadly it breaks the flow; but chant we must to warn you; what we say we always do," they replied.

"If we help you create a verse that rhymes, will you let us go?" I quickly asked, seeing how important rhyming was to their way of life.

"Let you go you say? If you help us today; not only will you go on your way; we will protect you night and day. For my wife had pestered me 'make it rhyme,' she says incessantly. I tried and tried to think of one; but sadly I came up with none!" the lead elf sang.

"What about 'Don't you worry'?" Meredith suggested. The two elves whispered to each other and considered the line to finish their rhyme. I looked at Meredith hopefully.

"That is not acceptable; your idea is not usable!" sang the elf on Meredith's head. "We want people in a hurry; to stop and to worry."

It did not seem fair that the success of our journey depended on this answer, but we had come this far. It took all the courage I had to suggest, "This is your destiny?"

The two elves jumped off our heads and began to dance. They took us by the hand and sang "A feast, a feast, must be had; for you have solved what drove us mad. Tell us where you wish to go; for now we must surely know."

I took a deep breath and said, "Well, first we need to go through the Witch Kingdom."

"We know the secret way; it will only take half a day."

Meredith quickly added, "Then to the Dragon Desert." The elves looked at each other and then at us. Their wide eyes and opened mouths said it all: they thought we were doomed.

Dragon Desert, May 8, 1311 (Emera's Journal)

Dear Journal,

I have done a lot of crazy things in life, such as eating from Daphny Doogle's experimental cooking creations, which wasn't the brightest of choices. However, the monstrous creature sleeping only a few feet away from us made eating that terrible tummy-ache-making mush seem like such an easy and sane task!

Silverbeard Stone had scales that were as bright as diamonds, sharp teeth that protruded from his mouth, and hot silver smoke that burst out from his nostrils with every breath. Meredith kept nudging me to say something, anything, to awaken this dragon that was to solve my problem. "What do I say?" I whispered to her, hoping to delay the inevitable.

"I don't know, 'Hello' maybe?"

"Doesn't it say somewhere to never wake a sleeping dragon?" I countered.

"No Emera, that's for bears. Never wake a sleeping bear."

I took a deep breath, and in a voice that didn't seem like mine, I saluted the sleeping creature. At first, I thought he hadn't heard me, but then, there arose this great rumbling sound. The ground beneath us began to shake and the dragon opened his large yellow eyes. He stuck out his tongue like a snake and began to lift himself from his slumber.

"Who dares disturb the great Silverbeard Stone?" he roared!

In the smallest voice I could muster I said, "Umm, Emera and Meredith, Your Excellency. May I add that I find your scales to be as beautiful as the sunrise?"

"Flattery will not work with me, only truth will set you free. Speak now as I am getting hungry for two girls about this high." He said this as he put his claws right next to my head. I seemed to have forgotten how to speak when his hot breath covered my face.

Thankfully, Meredith came to the rescue.

"Silverbeard, we know that you are a wise dragon that is feared and respected in many kingdoms. We also know that you help those in need if they fulfill a quest. We need your help and we are ready to do your bidding."

"My help, huh? What seems to be the problem… Princess?" He spit out the last word as though it was poison on his lips. I felt like I had to step up and do this myself. After all, this was my fault.

"Your Excellency, I have not yet found my power, and if I do not find it soon, I will lose all that is dear to me. You see, the Queen thinks I am a magical seamstress like my mother was; she expects me to make her a magical dress in a week's time. If I do not find my power, all will be lost. Will you help me?"

I looked into his yellow eyes, hoping the hunger in them would turn to kindness when he responded. "Yes, I will help you, but your quest will not be an easy one. You must steal a diamond from the Queen's tiara, and bring it back to me."

Meredith and I looked at each other, knowing full well the severity of the consequences of such an act. How will we accomplish such a feat? The Queen never parted from her crown. Silverbeard looked at us expectantly; that's when we nodded and sealed our fate.

Dragon Desert, May 8, 1311 (Princess Meredith's Diary)

Dear Diary,
We camped outside of Silverbeard's lair. Honestly, he isn't really that scary. He just tries to instill fear in those he encounters. I really could not sleep tonight. By now, the whole kingdom will be searching for us. Since I couldn't

sleep, I whispered to Emera, "Are you awake?"

She turned over and I saw she was wide awake. "Meredith, I've been thinking a lot about what the dragon said. And I think it would be wrong to steal your mother's jewels. Tomorrow we should go to the dragon and tell him we failed."

I was baffled that she wanted to abandon the quest for which we worked so hard and taken so many risks to accomplish. So I told her that when I was a child, I used to sneak out of Governess Bernadette's lessons, go into my mother's apartments, take her jewels, and play with them; so I'm sure I can sneak out of my lessons again and grab that jewel.

Emera just shook her head and smiled. "You know that I could never take anything from anyone, it's just not in my heart."

I knew this was her quest, so I gave in. "Fine, we will tell the dragon we failed and ask him for another quest."

Emera smiled and replied, "I think now we can go to sleep."

Dragon Desert, May 9, 1311 (Emera's Journal)

Dear Journal,

After I told Silverbeard about our failure to complete the quest, I held my breath, expecting to be fried like a marshmallow. Instead, he simply called all this nail-biting, hair-raising experience a test! Looking carefully at the situation, it seemed that we had passed since we were still breathing, but I could not be sure.

"A test? What do you mean a test? Are you playing with us?" Meredith said, adopting her tone of royal indignation.

Seeing Silverbeard begin to rise to his full height, I quickly elbowed Meredith and tried to salvage the damage. "Your Excellency, I am sure that Princess Meredith meant to thank you for using our plight as a means to entertain yourself. We could not be more grateful that you are not having us for dinner, oh mighty, scaly, sharp-toothed magnificence."

Silverbeard began to tremble, letting frightening sounds escape his opened mouth while pounding his foot on the ground. I began to slowly back away, thinking I'd rather face the Queen's wrath and starve than be chewed on like a drumstick.

Meredith placed both her hands on her hips and said, "Your Excellency, why are you laughing at us?"

"You will have to excuse me, girls, as it's been years since someone stood up to me. It feels quite refreshing. I had to test you, Emera, to see what your true power was. As I suspected, your inability to do no wrong shows that you have a wise and good heart. This gift is rare and it is worth more than all the kingdoms of this world! Follow it, use it for good, and next time you visit, please bring me a few carrots from your farm. I can smell them from here."

Too stunned to say anything of significance, all I was able to say was, "Carrots, Your Excellency?"

"Yes, I am a vegetarian of course, and a few good carrots dipped in the right dressing would certainly make my day." Silverbeard Stone, the great and feared dragon of the North, curled up into a ball and began to snore.

Slaven Palace, May 11, 1311 (Princess Meredith's Diary)

Dear Diary,

Things have been much better since we went to the dragon. The day we returned home, everyone was worried and angry. When Mother demanded an explanation for our disappearance I looked at Emera. She had the "I-don't-want-to-get-in-trouble-or-lie" type of look on her face. So, I took a deep breath and told mother that we went to ask a dragon for advice. Mother looked solemn the whole time I spoke. And when I finished, to my utter surprise, she burst out laughing.

I gave Em a puzzled gaze. She just shrugged. When Mum calmed down, she told me that I had quite an imagination and that she hardly believed me. She then told me to go to my room until I was able to tell the truth. So I stayed in my room until I thought it safe to emerge. Mother was so busy with her birthday preparations that she didn't seem to remember our discussion. It seemed like she wouldn't have noticed if Emera and I had escaped to the moon!

Color had returned to my mother's cheeks as she saw Emera making her birthday gown and me, the heir of her thrown, safe and sound. Emera, too, is looking better now that she knows her talent is in her heart. We came up with a game plan: Emera would sew "magic" dresses and teach Mother to take care of others in the kingdom. And last but not least, Mother was happy and agreed to give Emera's family money for rent, food, and clothing.

So far, everything is working finely. Emera is so kind, that all the animals in the kingdom follow her wherever she goes! She even gave Silverbeard a good reputation by writing a story about how he assisted her! Not to be a braggart, but Emera wrote about how I helped, too. She visits Silverbeard every day to keep him company because the poor dragon is lonely. Now Silverbeard helps the peasants from the village in Krin harvest the supply for the winter. Mom gave him the "Best Dragon of the Year" award (she made this up in his honor) because he helped the villagers of Krin.

Speaking of Mother, she has never been wiser and kinder than she is now. As you can see, there was only one true princess on the inside: Emera.

FUN IN FLORIDA

Sydney Lyn Gordesky and Ellen A. Gordesky

I went to visit my Nana and PopPop's house. They live in the Indian Spring community in Boynton Beach, which is in Florida.

I like to visit Florida. It was my cousin Makenzie's birthday, so I was very excited. The first thing we did that day was that we went to Ruthie and Richard's house. They are our cousins and they also live in the Indian Spring community. We were there for about 30 or 40 minutes.

Ruthie served us cheese and crackers for appetizers along with some drinks. Then we went to the restaurant for lunch... there was a lot of eating! We were sitting in the very back of the restaurant, so we kind of had a private area for our family. It was fun.

After we ate, we went back to my Nana and PopPop's house and had dessert. We also sang "Happy Birthday" to Makenzie. She was 18-years old. It was a lot of fun. After the party, we went outside and saw a neighbor. She was also named Ellen, like my Nana. Ellen was walking her dog. He was so cute and is very small. His name is Tiki.

Ellen invited us to go into her house to play with Tiki. Makenzie and I snuggled on the sofa with the dog. Tiki felt like a big pillow. We played so much with Tiki that he got very sleepy. We wore the dog out!

***

It was time to go home to Nana and PopPop's house. Makenzie and I had fun going on the patio where they live. We could look at the lake by their house. We took pictures of the lake. We then went into the garage and found a mat. There is a lot of space in the garage without any of the cars in there, so Makenzie and I started to do gymnastics.

Makenzie lives in northern New Jersey and we live in Brooklyn, which is in New York. We live pretty close to each other, so we do see Makenzie several times a year. But this time, Makenzie and her mother were visiting relatives in Boynton Beach, Florida and they also wanted to see us and spend time with us.

I am very glad that Makenzie likes to play with me even though she is 18-years old and I am only six. She is very kind to me and shows that she likes me. I appreciate that, because sometimes older children don't want to spend time with younger ones.

I am very lucky to have a loving cousin like Makenzie.

My cousin Makenzie is the best. I always think about her. Makenzie loves me and I love her.

I had a great time with Makenzie at my Nana and Pop-Pops's house.

After Makenzie left, we snacked on a lot of food. There was more food left from the party than you can imagine. After eating more, I said "good night" and went to my room to change into my PJs and went to bed. That was a really good day, I gave my Nana a hug and said "goodnight."

***

The next day, I wanted to see Makenzie and play with her some more. I said, "Where is Makenzie, where is Makenzie?" And Nana and PopPop said Makenzie went home to her house in Florida.

I said, "It's okay. I will still miss her."

And Nana said, "Oh sweetheart, I'm glad. That is so nice. Would you like some breakfast?"

I said, "Yes, I would like some breakfast."

Nana got the cereal and asked if anything was wrong. I said that I kind of missed Makenzie. I kind of gave a little frown to her.

And Nana said, "Alright, how would you like to visit the puppy's house later?"

That made me very happy and I said, "Woo Hoo!"

After breakfast, as Nana said, we went to the other Ellen's house and snuggled with the puppy named Tiki. I said that I could remember playing with Makenzie on this couch. We all laughed, even the puppy gave a little laugh. I think we all missed Makenzie.

We had some milk and cookies. The puppy wanted some milk and cookies too. My new name for him was Cocoa, because I thought he looked like a cup of cocoa and he seemed to want treats and sweets.

We all sat at the table to eat – all the humans and the little puppy, too. After that we went home and I went to the patio. Then I checked outside and I saw Ellen walking the dog.

I yelled, "Nana, Nana, I see the other Ellen walking the dog. I'd like to walk the dog, too."

Nana said that she was coming and would walk the dog with me. We went outside and all walked the puppy together. It sure is fun to visit Florida. I love my Nana, my cousin Makenzie, and my new friend – Tiki-Cocoa!

FRIENDS HELPING FRIENDS

Willow Kristich and Wendy Kristich

Hi, my name is Willow. I just turned seven years old and this is the story of how one child can change the world.

It was a beautiful spring day on Rosebud Drive. When I woke up, my dad was calling me for breakfast. Mom made my favorite French toast with fresh strawberries on top. It looked yummy, but for some reason I did not want to eat my breakfast. I guess I was not hungry. Mom said that I needed to eat my food because there were children starving all over the world.

When I heard that, I that I froze in total shock. "What did you say, Mom?"

My mom repeated herself. I asked my mom and dad to explain this terrible news to me. Dad said that grandparents, mommies and daddies, brothers and sisters, and also friends are starving all over the world.

"I don't understand what you mean," I yelled in a very upset tone.

Then I learned that all types of people were starving in the world because they did not have enough food or any food to eat. Some of these people do not have nice clothes or houses either.

"Wow, I had no idea. This is very hard to believe since I always have lots of food to eat, clean clothes to wear, and a beautiful house to live in," I told my mom and dad. What they told me hit me like a horse thundering down the road. I started to cry and the tears would not stop.

"What can I do to help?" I asked.

Dad had a great idea. "Why don't we start a food drive?"

"Perfect," said Mom.

"How do I start a food drive since I am just a kid?" I thought to myself. I was only five years old then.

And that is the day it all began.

Getting to Work

Every day, my dad brought home a giant cardboard box from work. The boxes kept coming and coming. Soon they started to fill up the whole garage at home. Mom and I gathered up stickers, paints, crayons, and anything crafty to decorate my cardboard boxes. Dad also taped the bottoms of the boxes to make them sturdy.

I thought to myself, "This is going to be a lot of work for just one person." So I asked several of my little friends if they wanted to help with the food drive. They did not know what a food drive was, so I explained to them, "A food drive is when people help donate food to a food bank so the people that need help can get food for free."

My friends all said "yes." They wanted to help! We decided to make it a fun activity. We had a decorating party outside in my backyard and each friend had a cardboard box to decorate. We put a sign on each box that read, "Friends Food Drive." What a fun day that was, especially when we would take breaks and eat our snacks and drink lemonade.

Each of my friends took their box home to find a local business, school, store, or some other place to put their decorated box for people to donate food. I decided to make several boxes and put one of them at my ballet studio. One went to Daddy's work, one went to the gym where Pa Pa (my grandfather) works out, and another one went to my school. We also covered big coffee cans with a sign about the food drive and put those all around the community to collect money for the food drive.

The next day Mom took me to the grocery store and bought some non-perishable food items (non-perishable means food that would not go bad) to put in some of my boxes. At the store, I picked out lots of fruit and veggie cans since they are good for you to eat.

Lots of Food

About two weeks went by and I was wondering if anyone was donating food and money to my food drive. I asked Mom to drive me around to check it out.

When I went to Daddy's work and saw the boxes, I yelled, "I can't believe it. There is food in my box!" It was happening; people were starting to fill up my boxes with food. I was so excited.

My friend's boxes were filling up, too. We decided to give the food drive a few more weeks since it was almost Thanksgiving.

"Let's collect all the boxes and canisters and take them to the local food bank so people would have food to eat for Thanksgiving," I said to my friends.

They all smiled and said, "We agree!"

One of my neighbors had a store and they heard about my food drive. They asked me if I would like to set up a stand at the store to tell people about my food drive and to collect some donations. I said "Yes" with a huge smile on my face. I made a poster and brought some of my friends to the store to help set up our food drive stand.

When the doors opened I was a little nervous, but to my surprise it ended up being a lot of fun. We collected lots of food and money that day and met a lot of nice people. My mom and dad said they thought it was a huge success. I was very happy.

Thanksgiving Day

It was one week until Thanksgiving and I met with all my friends at the local food bank. We all came with big boxes full of food. The people running the food bank seemed surprised, but happy to see us. I think I know why they were surprised. They said that we were the youngest group to ever organize their own food drive. We brought so much food that they had to come out to our cars with dolly's (a dolly is a metal cart with two wheels and a handle to lift heavy boxes safely). One by one, the boxes were taken into the building and onto a giant scale.

The people from the food bank wanted to weigh all the food donations to get a total for the food collected. Okay, here it goes: 1,100 pounds of food and $635 dollars. When we heard how much there was, we all screamed with joy! The people from the food bank said our food drive would feed over 200 families for Thanksgiving. Wow!

They took lots of pictures and put us in the local newspaper. I liked my Thanksgiving dinner more than ever before.

I hope that this food drive will inspire other kids to get involved and help out. I loved helping to feed families, so I decided to do my food drive every year.

Now, besides collecting food every year, I also donate toys, books, and clothes to needy families in the area. It only takes one person to make a difference. Just think what would happen if everyone would have their own food drive! I bet there would be no hungry people in the world. Wouldn't that be great?

WILD

Benjamin Pierce Oppenheimer

<u>Note</u>: When a word is in italics, it means it is spoken in wolfish.

A boy named Charlie and his dog Sparko, a husky, were on a field trip in the Amazon rain forest. Suddenly, they heard a sound which turned into a treacherous howl. Ten gray images came zooming full speed ahead! Charlie was trembling. Sparko let out an ear piercing howl. Charlie jumped back and turned around. No one was there…

The only thing there was a backpack. In it were a pocketknife, bottle of honey, bow and arrows, string, journal, camera, seeds, flint, steel, and a portable tent. Charlie grabbed the backpack and ran. When he and Sparko stopped; they were hungry. Charlie decided to pitch his tent for the night. He went inside it and ate some honey and gave some to Sparko. It was cool out, so Charlie used Sparko as a cozy blanket. Charlie smiled and fell asleep.

The next morning Sparko licked Charlie to wake him up. He looked outside. Charlie was thirsty so he went exploring with Sparko. An hour later, they found a nice pond with a good source of rich soil and lots of trees with coconuts. Charlie decided to use the coconuts as tools and cups as well as for food. He was busy cracking coconuts all day. He also drank some water and then he went back to his tent.

It was evening, when suddenly they heard the same howl. Charlie's mouth dropped open and he ran as fast as he could. Sparko followed. They were surrounded by trees, which might offer some safety and a place to hide. But Charlie stopped dead in his tracks, Sparko could not climb. Fortunately, Charlie saw a bush. He called quietly to Sparko and led her behind the bush and then muzzled her. They didn't make a sound. It was a good thing because a pack of wolves ran by. But then one stopped. It noticed footprints and began following them, sniffing the ground.

Charlie's heart was pounding hard. The wolf froze. It saw the footprints lead into the bush. Neither Charlie nor the wolf moved for a second. Then Sparko farted. It was so loud it caused a redwood to fall over and catch fire. The stench was so bad you had to wear a gas mask.

Fortunately, the sound was so loud and the smell was so bad that the wolf was momentarily stunned. That gave Charlie and Sparko a chance. Charlie ran so fast that Sparko could hardly keep up. Then the wolf ran after them. But then Charlie tripped! He stumbled over the branch of a tree. The thin wolf found him. Charlie froze with fear. He thought he was a goner. But then the strangest thing happened: The wolf snuggled up next to him. It was friendly! The wolf even had a name – Jimmy.

The wolf called out to its pack and they came running. All of the wolves were curious. Charlie sighed in relief. The pack took Sparko and Charlie and began to run. In a few minutes, they arrived at a strange bush and the wolves stopped and began to howl. Like magic, the bush lifted and a hole appeared behind it.

***

The wolves took Charlie and Sparko to a hidden room and there sat a big alpha wolf. He was curious about the newcomers. *"Bow wow wow!"* said the alpha wolf.

The wolves took Charlie to a special room. It was filled with pipes connecting to the center of the mysterious room. A wolf dropped him in the center of the room. A red ruby-like liquid oozed through the pipes nearby. Charlie felt very dizzy. He felt like he was falling into a trance and his body was warping into a new shape. He could hear voices chanting; he was shrinking. He felt his nose expand and his ears grow. Four beacons lit up the room, swirling with color. Then it all stopped.

Charlie felt different. He looked down at his feet and saw two paws. He realized what had happened. He was a wolf!

Then he heard the wolves speak to each other in curiosity.

"What is he?"

"Smells clean," said one.

"And tasty," agreed another.

"Noooo — must not eat him!"

"Is he one of us?" asked one of the wolves.

"Smells too clean to be one of us."

Then Sparko spoke: *"What have you done to master?"*

"We have transformed him into one of us," said one of the wolves.

"Can master speak?" Sparko asked.

"Yes," the wolves agreed.

Charlie tried to speak: *"CCCCan I tow halm?"* He tried again: *"Can I go home?"*

The Alpha wolf said, *"Yes, but come back."*

So Charlie and Sparko left the wolves' secret place. Oddly, Charlie did not need directions on where to go. He could smell every spot where he had stepped. He was also so fast that he was back at the pond in a minute.

Charlie and Sparko were hungry. Charlie tore some honey out of his backpack and ate it. He gave some to Sparko. His knew his honey would only last two more days, so he yanked out some seeds. He read the label and smiled. It was his favorite fruit – starfruit. It grows very quickly, so Charlie planted it in the rich soil near the pond.

That night Charlie and Sparko went into the tent to sleep. Inside, they found the alpha wolf waiting for them. He had a letter. Charlie opened it. It was from one of the smaller wolves that looked sick. It read, *"This is from Jimmy. I am the wolf who snuggled up next to you. I am in trouble and I need your help. To find me, go past the strange bush, and you will find a waterfall."*

***

That night, Charlie was too tired to go to Jimmy's cave. He decided to go there first thing in the morning. When he woke up, he found Sparko digging a hole. Charlie told her that he had to go to Jimmy's cave.

"Do you want to come?" he asked.

Sparko said, *"Okay, but I am hungry. Can I eat?"* Charlie gave her some honey, and they both ran to Jimmy's cave. When they found the waterfall, they saw a cave behind it. They went inside and felt that it was cool. Inside was a big pond and there were some crystals spread around the cave.

Jimmy came out from nowhere. He asked, *"Can you bring me some food?"*

Charlie said, *"I don't have any food left. But I will give you some seeds for you to grow food."*

Jimmy thanked him, and Charlie and Sparko decided to go back to his tent and have some lunch. When they got home, they ate the last bit of honey from the backpack. Suddenly, they heard footsteps – not wolf paw steps, but FOOT steps! With their hearts racing, they quietly ran to the strange bush to hide. They hid in it and the people walked right by Charlie without seeing him.

They were hunters! It was a big group of them. Charlie was scared. Even though wolves were fierce, they were not fierce enough to scare away a pack of hunters with guns.

Charlie saw that the hunters were headed straight toward Jimmy's cave. Charlie had to do something. With his heart beating so fast it was vibrating, Charlie tried to think of a plan. He saw an old tree trunk over by the water fall by Jimmy's cave. With a little force, it might fall over. So Charlie ran so fast that he was a moving blur. He reached the waterfall, jumped into the water, and swam over to the tree. Charlie pushed it until it fell. It crashed to the ground with a loud explosion. Water shot high into the air. This scared the hunters away!

Charlie sighed in relief when he swam back. He was relieved. Jimmy thanked him and Charlie walked back to his tent ready to tell Sparko about his day. Sparko was fascinated by the story.

That night, Charlie went to bed and was thinking about this and how much his family probably missed him. Charlie decided to tell the alpha wolf that he wanted to be transformed back into a human. Then he and Sparko fell asleep and dreamed wolf dreams.

The next morning Charlie woke up before Sparko. He quietly got up and looked outside. His starfruit seeds were growing! Charlie knew he would miss his little tent, the beautiful pond, and his wolf friends. Feeling gloomy, he walked to the strange bush and howled. It opened and he walked inside and saw that everyone was awake. He asked the alpha wolf his question: *"Can you turn me back into a human?"*

"Okay," said the alpha wolf.

The wolves took him to the room full of strange pipes that were leading to the center of the cave. Charlie sighed.

The chanting began: *"Oh gods of animals take him and make his soul human."*

Next, a green gem-like liquid filled the pipes, replacing the red-oozing liquid. When the liquid reached the center, Charlie felt dizzy. He felt like he was duplicating and losing consciousness. Then he felt his back legs getting taller and his arms grow another joint. Four beacons lit the room up, swirling. Then, it all stopped.

***

Charlie was relieved. He told the alpha wolf that he had to go home to his family.

The wolf said, *"No. Not yet. We have gift."*

Charlie was surprised for two reason: First, he could still understand the wolves talk even though he was a human again; and second, he was surprised they would give him a gift.

The wolves led Charlie to a sparkling room deep in the large cave. In it was a little basket. It was a nursery. The alpha wolf picked up a small little cub. It was white with blue eyes.

It was so small that they were able to place it in Charlie's lap. The cub snuggled and went to sleep. Charlie thanked the wolves and gently put the cub in his backpack, wrapping her in a small towel.

He went back to the tent and woke up Sparko, who was still sleeping. Charlie asked her to get up because they were going home. Charlie took down the tent. He did not show Sparko the baby cub, however. He simply told her, "We have to go home now."

They went back the way they had come. Charlie sighed. He remembered the spot where he first saw the wolves. He stayed on the tracks in the hiking path until he saw his house. It was 10:30 p.m. when he finally got home. He got into his bed and cuddled the baby cub.

The next morning, Charlie's mom woke him up and asked where he had been and what on earth he was doing with a baby wolf cub. Charlie had a lot of explaining to do!

STUCK ON MOUNT RUSHMORE

Sean Scott and Edward Scott

In the summer of 2013, the Peterson family from Dallas, Texas, went to Great Wolf Lodge in California. While at Great Wolf Lodge their son Tim won a video game called "Save the Presidents on Mount Rushmore." Tim was 14 years old, 6 feet 3 inches tall, and amazing at video games. He and his sister, Rachel, had also won 100,000 tickets in the arcade. Since Tim had won just about all of the tickets, his parents let him choose the prize. It was an easy decision for Tim, since he really loved history – especially the Presidents!

Tim's sister, Rachel, was 16 years old and awful at video games. She had won just three tickets, which was only enough to get candy and she hated candy. However, like Tim, Rachel really loved presidents. If you asked her a question about any president she would blurt out the name or year right away. When Tim told her he chose a video game about presidents for his prize, she was excited and couldn't wait to play it!

The Petersons had fun on vacation, but were glad to be home again. Tim was especially excited to be home because he was now able to play the game that he wanted so badly. He played the game for hours every day, but he was going back to school in a week so he wouldn't be able to play so much in the days ahead. When Tim went back to school and saw all of his friends, all he could talk about for the first week or two was his new game. His friends all thought that the game sounded cool, even though most of them weren't really into video games that had to do with history or presidents.

However, Tim's friend, Anthony Carlos, a.k.a. Ant, loved video games. He would play any game even if he didn't like the type of game. "Save the Presidents on Mount Rushmore" was a popular game and Ant really wanted to play it. He asked Tim if he could borrow the game for two days. Tim wasn't sure that he could trust Ant to return the game, since he wasn't good with returning things on time. Tim told Ant that he could not borrow the video game and was surprised to see him walk off without saying a word.

That night, Ant was on a mission to steal the new game from Tim. Ant woke up in the middle of the night and ran to Tim's house. Ant was really athletic so he was able to climb up into Tim's bedroom window on the second floor. Tim's window was opened slightly, so Ant crawled through and tiptoed around his room looking for the video game. He quickly spotted the game in the console attached to the TV, but the game would not come out of the console without keying in the password. However, Tim had left the TV on and Ant was able to play the game quietly. Ant changed his plan and, instead, decided to mess with the game. He would then escape out through the window before getting caught.

**

The next morning, Tim wanted to play his game before school but his parents told him that there wasn't enough time to play before school. Tim was so excited about the game that he almost forgot it was Friday and he still had to get ready for school. While sitting at the table eating breakfast, Tim's parents asked him if they could play his video game. They had heard Tim and Rachel talking about it being a very popular game and they were curious to see what it was like. Tim told them not to touch his game because he didn't want them to mess with his score.

After Tim's parents took him to school, however, they thought they could quickly check out his game before leaving for work in an hour. Tim's parents were "bad" listeners and ignored the fact that Tim told them not to play with his game. His parents started to play the game. Then Tim's mom said to Tim's dad, "Are you sure we should be doing this?"

Tim's dad responded, "What's the worst thing that could happen....we vanish into thin air?" Sure enough, when Tim's dad touched the controller, he suddenly vanished. Tim's mom was in shock when she saw this and she fell to the ground.

On her way to the ground she hit the controller and disappeared, too.

When Tim got to school he saw Ant in the hall. Ant asked Tim if his game was still working properly. Ant told Tim that some other friends who have the same game were having problems with it. The reason he told Tim was because he was afraid that Tim might find out that he was being sneaky and trying to ruin his game. Tim told Ant that he hadn't played the game in a day or so, but it worked fine the last time he played it.

When classes finished, Tim stayed at school for a Boy Scout meeting while his sister, Rachel, was helping tutor a seventh grader. At 5:00 p.m., Rachel and Tim left the school and walked home together. Their parents would usually get home a few minutes before them on Friday afternoons. When they walked into the house, they noticed that their parents are not there. Rachel told Tim not to worry and it is possible that mom and dad went to get pizza for dinner and would be back soon.

Tim went to his room to play his video game while Rachel went to get a drink in the kitchen. When he picked up the controller, he thought he heard his mom and dad's voices. He thought to himself, "That couldn't be possible since they were not home." He was about to press the start button on the controller when he heard his parents yelling at him saying, "DON'T PRESS THE START BUTTON." However, it was too late and he had already pressed the start button; he too vanished.

***

"Where did everyone go?" Tim wondered. After disappearing, Tim landed on George Washington and almost broke Washington's nose. But this wasn't the real Washington. When he got up from the ground, he saw that George Washington was his dad! Tim was wondering why everyone he saw was dressed like a president. He thought for a moment and remembered what Ant asked him about his game working properly. He vaguely remembered thinking that he heard someone walking in his room while his was sleeping the other night. This made him suspicious of what Ant might have been up to.

Out of nowhere, Ant was standing next to him looking like Theodore Roosevelt. Surprised, Tim asked, "Why are we here at Mount Rushmore?"

Ant told Tim that he had messed with his game the other night. Ant also explained that when he went to the bathroom during math class on Friday, he vanished out of nowhere and landed on Mount Rushmore. While Ant was explaining why everyone was stuck in the video game on Mount Rushmore, Tim saw his parents hiding behind a rock pretending they weren't there.

Tim asked Ant to stop what he was saying and wait while he ran over to his mom and dad. Tim yelled at them and said, "What is wrong with you? I told you not to play my game; and now look where we are – we're here on Mount Rushmore! Do you ever listen to anybody?"

Then his parent's started laughing. He asked what was so funny. They said in a weird voice, "You are about 5 feet 4 inches tall, 100 pounds, with brown hair and a scar on your nose and you are also holding a copy of the Constitution." To his surprise they were describing him as looking like James Madison our fourth president, who also happened to be our smallest president. The next thing he noticed was that his mom looked like Martha Washington.

Even more ridiculous was that somehow the rest of Ant's family was at Mount Rushmore too! Ant's brother Tony was there and looked like Abraham Lincoln. Ant's dad was James Monroe and his mom was James Monroe's wife, Elizabeth. Last but not least, Ant's cousin was Thomas Jefferson. How crazy was that?

***

Meanwhile, back in Texas, Rachel called out to Tim to see if he wanted to watch a documentary about the presidents on the History Channel. He did not answer. She walked around the house looking for Tim. She went into his room, only to find the TV on and the console with broken wires and the game manual shredded to pieces. Rachel immediately began trying to fix the wires. Once the wires were fixed, she started to play the game but realized that she needed a manual to help her play the game.

Back in the game, Tim and Ant's parents were talking about a plan for how to get back home. Tim offered a solution. Each of the presidents had special skills and Tim suggested that they combine them so that they could find a way out of the video game and return home. George Washington was a great general and fighter and Jefferson was really smart. So together they made a plan. Jefferson said that the game had eight levels. When you beat all the levels and someone isn't playing the game, the people who were on the quest will go to wherever the controller is.

So we have to beat all eight levels to get back to Texas. Washington said that they would have to split up into groups. Each group would try to beat four levels. Washington, Mrs. Washington, Lincoln, and Jefferson would take the levels on the eastern United States and Monroe, Mrs. Monroe, Madison, and Theodore Roosevelt would take the four other levels on the West. While the plan was being made on how to return to home to Texas, Tim's sister, Rachel, heard the controller of the game chanting "we can do this" over and over again. The voices sounded like her parents and brother.

She got so scared that she ran downstairs into her room as fast as a cheetah. When she calmed down, she went back to Tim's room and noticed the chanting had stopped. She wanted to fix the game but there were two problems: she was scared she would die if she touched the controller and she didn't know how to play video games.

Back in the game, Madison and his group went off to defeat the first boss battle so they could move to the next level. The first place they went was to San Juan Hill in Cuba. It wasn't that hard to beat the soldiers in the battle because of Theodore Roosevelt. Roosevelt said that he knew the weaknesses of the Spanish soldiers that they were fighting. Instead of staying in place and getting behind shelter, Roosevelt ran directly toward a huge cannon. The cannon was about to take fire and Roosevelt moved over to the right to avoid getting shot by the tank. Then he started running around it super-fast like a jet.

While he was running, he punched a bunch of soldiers and knocked them down and took their weapons and threw them over to Madison. The others were all watching in amazement. Then the others in Tim's group joined the fight against the Spanish soldiers. Once they defeated all of the soldiers, they went to invade the army base in Cuba. When they arrived at the base, they found the enemy general. The general had 100 soldiers with him. However, it wasn't difficult to defeat the soldiers since they were not very skilled. Roosevelt kicked the general off his chair, which set off a spell and advanced them to the next level.

***

The next place they went was the San Francisco Gold Rush. A group of robbers were trying to steel most of California's riches. But Madison's team wasn't going to let that happen. They found the mine and saw the robbers. Since Madison was a silent and shy man, he had to rely on Roosevelt to yell at the robbers.

Roosevelt shouted, "Excuse me, gentlemen! Yeah, I'm talking to you. My friend here wants to tell you something."

Then Madison said in a soft voice, "Will you stop steeling things that don't belong to you?"

The robbers said, "What?"

Madison repeated, only this time stating words from history, "I said, if men were angels, no government would be necessary... Obviously you are not angels. Will you stop steeling things that don't belong to you?"

Before Madison could say another word Roosevelt knocked every robber out cold.

"Bully! That's what Madison was talking about," said Roosevelt. Everyone congratulated Roosevelt and Madison for good team work.

Meanwhile in the North, Washington's group was suffering a rough winter at Valley Forge. Out of nowhere, a bunch of British troops fired at the American tents and camp. It was a surprise attack that was added in the game by Tim's sister by accident when she was checking the wires.

Washington said, "This wasn't part of history. Anyway, we are under attack." He then stated those famous words from history, "I hope I shall possess firmness and virtue enough to maintain... my leadership. Get your weapons and show me what you got."

But Lincoln said, "Why don't we just talk to the British and ask them to let us be." Washington said, 'That's not a bad idea. Everyone, hold your fire! Lincoln has something to say to the British." Lincoln was walking up a hill to talk to the British while they were trying to shoot him.

Then Washington thought, "Wow. Lincoln is about 15 feet away from the British and they couldn't even shoot him. They must have awful aim." When Lincoln put out his hand he started speaking words that changed history, "My fellow soldiers, the world will little note, nor long remember what we say here today… but we are on a mission to get back to our home and we need your help to find your leader. We have to speak business with him to let us…"

Lincoln carried on speaking and didn't stop until the British agreed to bring Washington's group to their leader. When they arrived they found a man with a crown and robe with jewels sitting in a golden chair. It was the King of England. He asked his soldiers who these people were.

One of the soldiers said, "This is Washington, Mrs. Washington, Lincoln, and Jefferson. They would like to speak with you privately."

The King said, "Well then, give us privacy." The soldiers had a feeling that they had done something wrong, since the King was not happy. They were scared and decided to run out of the room quickly. Then the King got out of his chair threw off his robe and revealed his diamond sword.

The King said, "Shall we?" and tried to attack Washington with the diamond sword. Washington pulled out his sword and blocked himself from getting hit.

The King fought aggressively, but George Washington

was a tall, strong man and quickly defeated the King, knocking his sword to the ground. The King wisely surrendered. Washington's group was now able to continue on their quest, but first they had to beat another challenge in the game. They had to name as much information as possible about Theodore Roosevelt. Fortunately, Jefferson was with them and was very smart.

Washington said to Jefferson, "Start talking about all of the information you know about Theodore Roosevelt."

Jefferson began reciting facts about Theodore Roosevelt. He said, "Theodore Roosevelt was born on October 27, 1858, in New York City. He was also our 26th President of the United States. Theodore's nickname was Teddy. When Teddy was a kid he was sick most of the time and he couldn't go outside. This made him work to build his strength. He would go to the gym, ride horses, hunt, and he even boxed. His mother and his first wife died on the same day on February 14, 1884."

"Before Teddy was president, he was the Secretary of the Navy and quit to become part of the Rough Riders. His unit was part of the Battle of San Juan Hill during the Spanish-American War. He became governor of New York in 1899. In 1900, he was picked to be vice president for McKinley and then became president when McKinley was assassinated in 1901. His foreign policy was 'Speak softly and carry a big stick,' which meant to be polite when you speak but have the power to make your argument meaningful."

Jefferson was on a roll, beating the video game. He continued, "During Teddy's term, Franklin and Eleanor Roosevelt married in 1905. Franklin Roosevelt was Teddy's fifth cousin. Teddy was Eleanor's uncle. In 1905, Teddy won the Nobel Peace Prize for ending the Russo-Japanese War. Teddy created five national parks to add to our country during his presidency. He was also the president with the most pets in the White House. Teddy died at age 60 on January 6, 1919 at his home at Sagamore Hill."

It worked. Washington's group was able to go to the next challenge in the video game. They arrived at Fort Sumter and had to swim all the way to the army base. When they got to the base, Jefferson said that the Confederacy would attack them in two minutes. It was 4:28 a.m. They would be attacked at 4:30 a.m. Washington saw a boat sailing towards the base. A bunch of soldiers jumped out of the boat and swam the rest of the way to the base to begin their attack. Washington screamed, "The Civil War has begun."

But Mrs. Washington stopped Washington from attacking. She said, "I don't think the Civil War will begin for a few years, darling." Then Mrs. Washington grabbed golden clothes from a drying rack and said to the soldiers, "Would you stop your attack if we give you these golden clothes?"

The soldiers dropped all of their weapons and promised that they would not attack. Mrs. Washington took all of the clothes off the rack and gave them to the soldiers. This delayed the Civil War and Fort Sumter was saved from being attacked by the Confederate Army.

***

Back in Texas, Rachel bought another manual for "Save the Presidents on Mount Rushmore" from the "Awesome Games" store. The manual taught her almost as much information as she knew about presidents. After completing the manual, she went to Tim's room to play the game. She pressed the start button and chose the settings option, but was having trouble with the password. Each time she keyed in the password it would tell her that it was incorrect.

While Rachel was trying to figure out the problem with the password, Roosevelt's group was arrested by a policeman in the game for no real reason. Everyone thought the arrest was just part of the history from the game. They put all of their heads together to find a solution to escape from prison. Monroe commented that if Jefferson were there, they would already have a solution.

Then Monroe said, "Everyone, I have an idea." James Monroe was charming and had a great personality. There was a policewoman guarding the prison. Monroe winked at her and in a charming voice said to her, "Excuse me ma'am, would it be okay if my friends and I leave this prison?"

The police woman started to blush and she opened the door for Roosevelt and his group. They were all shocked because Ant's dad was nothing like Monroe but did a great job of imitating him.

In Texas, Rachel was really annoyed because she couldn't enter the password correctly. She got so angry that she threw the manual out Tim's bedroom window. She decided to try it one more time. When she did, the video game listed a series of security questions. She had to answer them in order to access the password and game. The computer screen read: "Who was the real 12th president of the United States and for how long?" It also challenged her to explain some facts about George Washington and Barack Obama.

Meanwhile, Washington's group was about to fight in one of the worst battles in American history. It was the battle of Gettysburg. It was weird because when they were at Fort Sumter, it was a completely different month and the Civil War had never started. Mrs. Washington asked, "Didn't I stop the Civil War from beginning."

Jefferson said, "Mrs. Washington, you did stop the war from beginning in 1861, but it actually began in 1862." Then they noticed the Confederate soldiers coming toward them and Robert E. Lee was commanding them. But the Confederates were soon going to have company. All of a sudden Ulysses S. Grant came out of nowhere and behind him were 500,000 Union soldiers. This was strange because Grant was never at Gettysburg. But it didn't matter. A few seconds after Grant showed up, Roosevelt's group came with 1,200 police officers.

Washington knew that if they could win the battle this

would end the Civil War. Out of nowhere a cannon ball landed directly in front of Washington and blew up in his face. The Confederates started to celebrate because they thought that Washington was dead, but they were wrong. Washington's team also thought that he was dead, but when they looked closer they realized it was a Union soldier who died that looked like Washington. The Union soldiers and the team saw the real Washington standing behind all of the Confederate soldiers.

Washington took TNT out of the Confederates supplies and he lit it on fire. One of the Confederate soldiers noticed the TNT, but it was too late. Washington threw it at them. It exploded and the battle of Gettysburg began. Everyone started fighting, even Mrs. Washington. It was a crazy scene. At first it looked as if the Confederates were going to win but then the Union started to gain the advantage.

General Grant was firing cannon balls that killed many Confederates. Washington had an idea. He remembered how to make iron armor out of metal. He took one of the broken cannon launchers and molded it into iron armor. The Union soldiers were now the most protected soldiers on the battlefield.

***

While everyone was fighting for the Union, Rachel was putting all the information into the game in order to access it. She answered the question "Who was the real 12th President of the United States and for how long?" by typing in David Rice Atchison, Senator from Missouri and president for one day.

She continued to type almost every fact that she knew about George Washington. She started, "On February 11, 1731, the first president George Washington was born. Everyone thinks that he was born on February 22, 1732. However, while he was still living the calendar changed in 1753. He was a general during the Revolutionary War. After the war was over, he went back to his home in Mount Vernon. About six years after the war ended, people needed Washington to be their leader. Washington had to take the office because he was the only one that everyone trusted. When he decided to become president, he won by a landslide against John Adams, who would go on to be the second president.

Washington was sworn in to the presidency on April 30, 1789 in New York City. In 1792, Washington ran for reelection. He won again by a landslide. When his second term ended, he did not run for reelection. He went back to live in Mount Vernon. In 1799, on a cold and bitter day, Washington went for a ride on his horse. When he got back to his house, he had a cough. The next day he had a sore throat. Later in the day he started to have trouble breathing. He couldn't get liquid down his throat and he was starting to die. On December 14, 1799, George Washington died at age 67."

Rachel began to give information about Barack Obama and she needed to do it quick so that everyone could return home safely from Mount Rushmore. She started typing as fast as possible. "Barack was born on August 4, 1961 in Honolulu Hawaii. In 1964, when he was two years old, his parents Ann and Barack Sr. were divorced. In 1992, Barack and Michele Robinson got married. Their first child was Mila, who was born on July 4, 1998. Their second child, Sasha, was born on June 10, 2001. On January 20, 2009, Barack Obama became the 44th president of the United States."

It worked! After putting all of the information into the game, Rachel pressed the enter key and was able to put in the password. When she entered the password, the screen said, "What is the problem?"

Rachel responded, "My brother, my family, and my brother's friend's family are stuck on Mount Rushmore in your video game."

Then the game replied "Okay, I will try to find people at Mount Rushmore." About two minutes later the game said, "I did not find anyone on Mount Rushmore."

Rachel asked the game, "Can you search all over the video game?" There was a long pause. Nothing was happening. Rachel was getting worried.

Finally, a voice started to come through the controller and said, "I found the people you are looking for. They are fighting in the Civil War. Should I bring them back to Texas or should I let them fight for our country?"

Rachel said, "I think you should bring them back."

While Washington's group, Madison's group, and the Union soldiers were fighting against the Confederates,

Washington suddenly disappeared. Then Madison vanished shortly after. While Jefferson was figuring out the Confederates strategies, a big gust of wind picked up Jefferson and carried him out of the game. One by one everybody vanished from the battlefield and returned home to Texas.

Everyone who vanished from Gettysburg arrived in Tim's bedroom at 11:00 p.m. It was late and they all decided to get blankets and pillows and sleep on Tim's floor. It had been a crazy day!

Rachel got up in the morning and heard some noise in Tim's room. When she walked into his room she was surprised but happy to see everyone had arrived back safely. Rachel offered to make everyone breakfast seeing that they everyone was tired from all the challenges that they needed to accomplish in order to get home.

While eating breakfast, Tim and Ant were filling Rachel in on all of the different excursions they went on and how she would love to have seen them reenact history. Rachel made a pact with Tim and Ant that, when they graduate high school, she would take them on a road trip by car to Mount Rushmore and meanwhile they will leave video gaming to the side. Ant agreed with Tim and Rachel that reading might be the way to go and that video games are not all that they are cracked up to be.

So, next time you are thinking of messing with someone's video game, just stick your head in a book and let your imagination run wild.

THE HAVEN WAR

Shayna Silverstein and Mallory Thomas

A long time ago before the Earth was created, there were two ancient goddesses named Gadalious and Infernia. They lived in a world called Haven that was in the process of being destroyed. The two goddesses protected Haven.

Infernia was the goddess of the elements – fire, air, water, and earth. She was the child of Gaia and Uranus. Gadalious was her younger sister. Infernia once had a brother, but he faded away. Infernia's job on Haven was to create new resources. She had a pet elemental dragon, which was a holy animal. She loved her planet.

Gradalious was the goddess of transformation. She could transform into anything. Her holy animal was the unicorn. Her job on Haven was to put everything together and make sure everything was running well.

Haven was only the third planet after Uranus and Gimba. Haven was a natural resource planet that created stars and other planets. The planet was made up of four corners, which were also the four elements.

Haven wasn't always facing destruction. It used to be a happy place where animals roamed freely all day. One day Infernia was working on a guardian for haven. The plan went wrong and the guardian turned into an evil titan lord named Kronos. Kronos then created evil titans. Gadilious and Infernia were so worried about Haven's safety that they created gods to fight Kronos and his titans. Kronos was so powerful that he ate all the gods except three – Zeus, Poseidon, and Hades. The Havenians nicknamed the gods the "Big Three."

Haven was still being threatened by Kronos and his minions. Since Kronos was born on Haven, his power was tied to the planet. That also meant that, every once in a while, Haven created a planet that was full of evil titans and it needed to fight them. Every day, Gadalious and Infernia had to fight the titans because they didn't have time to make more gods.

Infernia and Gadalious asked the Big Three to help protect their planet. But the three gods declined the offer and said they were busy making a new planet called Earth. They said Earth was a planet for creatures called humans. Even though Gadalious and Infernia were devastated by the news, they understood that the Big Three were busy with their own planet.

The two goddesses then saw three ugly giants destroying the Fountain of Life. The Fountain of Life stored the souls of all creatures. Gadalious realized that the three giants were Reptilia, Hugamus, and Elysia, and were the ugly children of Kronos.

The goddesses used their powers to protect the Fountain.

Gadalious transformed into a dragon and Infernia went to battle with her fire spear. But the three ugly giants were ready. While two of them fought the goddesses, Hugamus kept on destroying the Fountain. In the battle, Infernia slashed at Elysia and struck a mortal blow. The ugly giant dissolved into dust (which is what all ugly giant monsters did). During the fight, Gadalious managed to burn Reptilia to a crisp. Infernia then shot an arrow of perfect aim into Hugamus's thigh, which, after a loud moan, finished him off. He, too, dissolved to dust.

To repair the Fountain, the two goddesses said a phrase in ancient Greek: "Polka chica ya he ya," they chanted. Many lives were facing extinction that day. The giants were only the beginning of the battle. Titans were attempting to bring Kronos back to haven. The ugly giants were only a distraction to keep the goddesses busy, while the titans prepared to invade Haven.

***

As Haven was busy with their war, on Earth the Big Three had created Olympus. Olympus was a place where gods and goddesses lived. Gadalious and Infernia were in desperate need of a hero for their war and had looked on their planet and on the new planet named Earth. The two goddesses finally gave up trying to find a hero and decided to create one. The god they created was named Aporis. He was the god of life and death. Aporis could just look at someone and make them die (if he wanted to). The god was not the biggest god, but not the smallest god either. Gadalious and Infernia were very pleased with what they had created. Maybe he could help them guard their planet.

The two goddesses asked other gods and goddesses to come and protect Haven. Some of them agreed to do so, but some did not. The gods and goddesses that said "yes" were Ares, Hestia, Athena, Apollo, Demeter, Garfis, and Janus. Ares's role on Haven was to lead the planet's army. Hestia helped the wounded in Haven's hospital. Athena helped make up new weapons to use in defeating the monsters and titans. Garfis, the god of energy, gave energy to the army. Demester harvested food and crops for the inhabitants of haven so they could stay healthy and prepare for battle. Janus would trick the tians into thinking he was a tian, and then he would kill them. The goddesses felt good about the army they had assembled. The planet was nearly ready to be defended.

There was one part of Haven, however, that Gadalious and Infernia did not control. It was Kronos Land. Since Kronos was born on Haven, he controlled part of the planet. The official name of Kronos Land was Domination. Gadalious and Infernia knew why Kronos had given his territory that name – he wanted world domination and was starting with Haven.

Many of the gods and goddesses had no specific role until the war threatened them. They simply fulfilled roles and were then known to be a god of that activity.

***

A week had passed and Haven was almost under control, until one day Kronos decided to come back to the planet. At first, he did nothing, but then he decided to destroy the Earth Corner. Gadalious and Infernia were devastated, so they organized an attack against him. In one hour, Haven's army had destroyed over 5,000 of Kronos's titans. However, they did not catch Kronos; he simply laughed and disappeared into space.

The gods knew why Kronos was heading to Earth. He was going there to destroy the other gods and goddesses so that no one could oppose him. Meanwhile, more titans kept coming to fight on Haven. The way titans were created by Kronos, but one of them was taller and stronger than the others: Hyperion. He was the titan of fire and was one of the four elements. The other elements were Atlas, Oceanus, and Kronos; together, they were known as the Overlords.

The Overlords – without Kronos – went to destroy the Fountain of Life. The goddesses who were there were Demeter, Athena, and Hestia. They fought their best and were able to stop the Overlords from destroying the Fountain of Life. They were helped by Gadalious and Infernia, who put a boarder around the Fountain to make it hard for titans or monsters to destroy it. However, the Overlords soon discovered the magical border, so they headed to the core of Haven, which was the place where the planet created stars and other, smaller planets. The Overlords wanted to try and use the core in order to make other planets where the titans could roam.

The Overlords accidentally ended up at a place called Malesius. Malesius created angels to protect planets. When the Overlords and titans discovered their mistake, they attacked the angels. Sadly, the angels lost the battle and most of them were destroyed. Those angels that survived the battle went to Haven to help with the war and to seek protection from the goddesses. Some of the angels that were trapped on Malesius by the titans were turned evil and forced to worship the Overlords and titans. The goddesses were very upset and realized they needed more help in battling their enemies, so they created children. Gadalious created two children named Shayna and Mallory Ivory. They were sent to Earth along with the children of other goddesses.

The fighting on Haven lasted for years. Millions of Haven's creatures were forced to go to war and many died. Haven's population was going down. The titans continued to fight and also destroyed Haven's resources. Haven was running out of everything and running out of options. Some of the residents of Haven and some of the Olympians lost hope and fled to the Earth. Apollo, Hestia, Athena, and Ares stayed at Haven to fight.

The Overlords were beginning to win the war and were getting more powerful. They again tried to go to Haven's core in order to destroy the planet. Gadalious and Infernia rushed to meet them at the core and, just as they arrived to defend it, the Overlords attacked the core. They didn't expect such a large reaction.

Haven never saw light again.

***

Over 150 years later, the gods and goddesses that had fled to Earth wanted to see how the war ended. Zeus led them back to Haven. They were all in shock to see how it ended. The destruction was worse than they had imagined. The bodies of Gadalious and Infernia were still on the battlefield near the core. They were not dead because gods and goddesses never die; they fade away. To fade away is to leave the living world and go somewhere else to a place no one knows.

With their planet destroyed, they had nothing to live for. Gods and goddesses exist for a reason. They are what it is that they do, and if there is nothing more to do, they fade away.

The other gods and goddesses took Gadalious and Infernia back to Earth to join them on Olympus. There they gave Gadalious and Infernia their final blessing, which was to go where they wanted to go. Nobody knows where they went. They turned into small specks of light and disappeared. It was exactly midnight on December 31, in the year 1,000 BCE.

The stories of Gadalious and Infernia inspired gods and goddesses as well as the people on Earth to believe in themselves. The two goddesses had fought and given their lives to protect the planet Haven and all the creatures who lived there. It is now up to each of us to imagine where they went and how their story continued.

COOKING RULES

Isabella Watson and Claudia Watson

The New Girl

"I have another big idea," said Elizabeth.

Her BFF, Sally, who had helped her put on the fashion show at her school last year smiled. "Here it comes," thought Sally. Every few days Elizabeth had another "big idea." But that was why Sally liked her friend so much. There was never a dull moment when Elizabeth was around. Plus, she had to admit, the fashion show had been a huge success.

It started off as a mess when the most popular but also the meanest girls in school – Katherine, Milla, and Tiffany "Taffy Candy" – made fun of them and said no one could design clothing and model outfits as well as the three divas. Katherine had won the fashion show two years in a row.

"But we sure showed them," thought Sally with a smile.

The whole school had shown up for the fashion show and ended up cheering wildly when Elizabeth and Sally surprised everyone by cutting the lights to build suspense for the big finale. From the dark stage, Henry, the quiet kid from class who happened to be a very good DJ, started pumping the music. The whole school went wild! Even Elizabeth's older brother John and his friend Big Bruce, two of the most popular boys from the upper school, got up on stage to strut their stuff!

But that was last year. Elizabeth had come up with many crazy ideas for school activities in the months since the fashion show last spring. But none of them had worked out.

Sally opened the front door wide and invited Elizabeth in to her house. "So," asked Sally with a mischievous smile, "what's the new plan?"

"We're gonna be famous chefs!" blurted out Elizabeth as she walked into the living room. From behind her back she pulled out two chefs' hats. They were tall and white. She put one on top of her head and plopped the other one on Sally's head. It was too big and slid down over Sally's eyes.

"Oh, no you don't. I'm not wearing that thing," said Sally from beneath the silly hat.

"Every chef wears one," was all that Elizabeth said. She turned and walked into the kitchen in Sally's house.

Sally shrugged her shoulders and followed, pushing the tall, white hat up and off her face. "So, I suppose we're gonna be chefs," Sally thought to herself.

Game On!

Miss Honey Jones had been Elizabeth's favorite teacher since she moved to the new school last year. It was Miss Honey who encouraged Elizabeth to enter the fashion show since she was a new student. She also helped with the lighting and staging for the popular school event. Elizabeth was so glad that Miss Honey had moved from the fifth grade to the sixth grade and was her teacher again this year.

"Okay, class," said Miss Honey. "I want all of you to be risk takers. Don't be afraid to try something new and don't be afraid to fail. Remember, if you never try something, you will never know if you are really good at it." The teacher asked everyone to try to do something new, something they had never done before and to not be afraid to do it. She asked for ideas from the class.

As always, Katherine's hand was the first in the class to go up. When Miss Honey called on her, the leader of the mean girls said loudly, "But what if we're good at everything?" The girl known as "Katherine the Cat" turned around in her chair and snapped her fingers loudly.

The other two mean girls were sitting behind her: "You know it!" said Tiffany "Taffy Candy" very loudly.

Milla Mumford also snapped her fingers and said something. No one knew what she said, however. Her nickname "Mumbles Mumford" was the perfect name, after all.

"Well then, Katherine" began Miss Honey, "you three should have no reason to hold back. What new things do you want to try?"

Katherine didn't hesitate long. She turned around and looked at Henry in the back of the room. "I think Henry could try being cool. That would be a change for him! And I will try not to laugh at him."

"And Katherine could actually try doing her math homework," Henry snickered under his breath. "Of course, that would mean she needed a brain." Elizabeth heard Henry's comment and winked at the quiet DJ. They had become friends ever since Henry agreed to play music for her fashion show last year.

Katherine shot Henry and Elizabeth a threatening look. She and her two mean friends had never gotten over the fact that Elizabeth won the fashion show. Elizabeth's idea to have all the kids bring used clothing and try mixing and matching them to dance music and lights had been a hit. Katherine the Cat had announced to everyone before the show that the idea was "stupid," but it turned out to be the hit of the year.

As Katherine's friends roared with laughter at the comment about Henry, Miss Honey quieted the class and instructed everyone to take out their iPads and write three new things they would try.

"What do you want to try, Henry," Miss Honey asked?

"I don't know. Maybe avoiding the Cat and her posse," joked Henry.

"In your dreams," replied Tiffany and Katherine at the exact same time.

"Now, now. Come on, everyone. Who has a good idea?" Miss Honey asked again.

Elizabeth slowly raised her hand. "I've been thinking. I'd like to be a chef. I thought we could all try cooking together as a class. Cooking is..."

"Puh-lease!" cried Katherine and Tiffany together, interrupting Elizabeth.

"Yea," mumbled Milla Mumford, "you can't even cook toast" (which came out sounding like "You can kudos").

"Duh, Mumbles," chuckled Henry. "You don't cook toast."

"Okay, Mr. DJ, how do you make toast, then?" asked Katherine with her nose crinkling up (which came out sounding like "Oh misty day of May tomatoes").

"It's easy – you TOAST it!" answered Henry.

Elizabeth and Sally laughed, but only for a moment.

As Miss Honey raised her hands to quiet everyone, Katherine looked straight into Elizabeth's eyes and said, "Game on!" Elizabeth's smile disappeared. She knew Katherine had not forgiven her for winning the fashion show last year. Now she would try to ruin another one of Elizabeth's ideas.

Fire and Smoke

Elizabeth's favorite cooking show was Pioneer Woman on the Food Network. So she went online to look up several recipes from the popular TV show. She found a few delicious recipes and asked her mother to purchase the ingredients at the supermarket. It was time to start improving her skills in the kitchen.

The two friends planned to make a grand feast for Elizabeth's family. The menu: Pasta carbonara with peas, bacon, and cheese; butternut squash soup with cream, chives, and parmesan cheese; diced avocado and tomato salad with balsamic citrus dressing. And for dessert, a chocolate, peanut butter pie on an Oreo cookie crust shell. Plus, there would be a special, scrumptious treat – strawberry, pistachio, and vanilla macaroons. Yum!

Elizabeth told her whole family to relax in the living room. She and Sally would make the meal and set the table. For starters, Elizabeth played beautiful, Italian music using Blue Tooth. The girls set out the ingredients and warmed the oven and skillet on the stove top.

A few minutes later, Elizabeth's mother announced, "Wow, that sure does smell good!" Elizabeth's mother also asked several times if she could come into the kitchen to help the new chef. But Elizabeth screamed, "No!" She wanted to surprise everyone. While the bacon was frying and water boiling, Elizabeth set the table with the family's best silverware and a big candle.

The butternut squash soup was on the stovetop and it smelled delicious. It was time to cook the peas and pasta. Elizabeth put them in the boiling water, then began grating the parmesan cheese. Sally was cutting tomatoes. Halfway done, Elizabeth realized she needed to mix the ingredients for the peanut butter pie and get it into the freezer. As she was kneeling beside the oven to get the mixing bowl out of the kitchen drawers, she heard the sizzle of water spilling over the side of the pot.

The water was boiling over and began spilling to the floor next to Elizabeth's feet. A few drops of the scalding hot water singed her foot and caused Elizabeth to scream and jump back. She dropped the mixing bowl, which crashed to the floor loudly. The sound caused Sally to spin around, knocking the handle on the pot of soup and sending the delicious, thick broth hurling through the air. Elizabeth fell backward to the floor and landed on her backside. The soup poured down on her like a hot, creamy rainstorm, drenching her hair and splashing across the floor.

The crash in the kitchen sent Elizabeth's mother and father racing in to see if she was alright. Rounding the corner, Mr. Phillips stepped into the soupy mess on the floor and slipped. Reaching out with his hand, he tried to stop his fall but grabbed the kitchen table. It did not work. Mr. Phillips pulled the tablecloth off the table and sent all the dishes and glasses flying across the kitchen in a huge crash.

Mr. Phillips landed near Elizabeth, flat on his back. As he slid across the floor, he bumped into Sally's legs and knocked her off balance. The tomato she was cutting and a knife flew through the air and landed dangerously near Elizabeth, but

Sally fell right on top of her friend. The floor was now covered with soup, glass, pieces of plates, bread, and everything else needed for a great feast... plus Sally, Mr. Phillips, and Elizabeth! Mrs. Phillips screamed in alarm as she came into the kitchen and saw the disaster on the floor.

Fortunately, no one was hurt. Except Elizabeth's pride. Mrs. Phillips managed to step over and around the three people lying on the floor and finally turned off the heat on the boiling water.

And then a napkin that had flown through the air and landed next to the pan with the bacon that had been sizzling on the stovetop caught fire.

Mr. Phillips slipped and fell again while trying to stand up. But his loud groan was muffled out when the smoke on the stove set off the fire alarm hanging from the ceiling in the dining room. Mrs. Phillips pulled the fire extinguisher from below the sink and sprayed the stove top, putting out the small fire and covering the mess in white foam.

Elizabeth's great dinner ended in disaster. Only Cocoa, her pet dog, enjoyed the meal. He licked up all the butternut squash soup on the floor while Mrs. Phillips tried to "shoo" him away from the glass on the floor.

"Not the best start to your culinary career," smiled Elizabeth's older brother John. He was standing in the dining room with a big grin on his face.

"Oh, boy," thought Elizabeth, "some meal that turned out to be!"

A Contest

That night, Elizabeth watched another episode of Pioneer Woman on the Food Network. She thought to herself that she could never be such a good cook. Elizabeth's mother and father tried to make her feel good by telling her not to worry. Her brother John joked that her food was delicious – for Cocoa, that is! The little, brown dog was sound asleep near Elizabeth with a belly full of fancy soup!

The Pioneer Woman smiled and talked as she cooked. She made it look so easy. And then Elizabeth heard the lady on TV say something that caught her attention. "I love to cook. The key is to have fun, no matter how hard the recipe. If you are having fun, the food will taste so much better." When Elizabeth looked up, the Pioneer Woman seemed to be looking directly at her, with a big smile and deep dimples in her cheeks.

She also remembered what Miss Honey had said about not being afraid to try new things. Elizabeth smiled as she thought to herself, "I bet even the Pioneer Woman burned her first meal and made a mess of the kitchen! My father still teases my mother about when they first got married and she burned a potato!"

And that quickly, Elizabeth ran out of the room to call her friend Sally on the phone. She had another one of her big ideas.

Elizabeth explained in an excited voice to Sally that she had thought of a way the whole school could cook together – the two of them would organize a cooking contest for the school. Like the fashion show, she would have disco lights, decorations, and Henry blasting music. The school wanted to raise money for the fashion show at the end of the year and was planning on having a car wash. Why not a cooking contest instead?

"It will be easy-cheesy," Elizabeth told Sally. The hard part would be getting permission from Miss Honey and the principal. Fortunately, when Elizabeth went to see Principal Stan in his office the next week, he called himself a "foodie" and said he was just as excited about the contest as Elizabeth! He agreed to help Elizabeth plan the menus and buy the food... as long as he was able to cook too.

The two girls got busy making the signs and using Face-Book to notify all the students and ask for volunteer chefs. Of course, Henry agreed to bring his DJ equipment and Miss Honey said she would set up the lights from the school theater. It would be a fun party, just like the big fashion show!

Elizabeth wanted her brother John, a senior in the upper school and the popular captain of the basketball team, to be the guest judge. She knew many students would come to the cooking contest just because John was there, especially all the girls. But he said no and then joked that he would help out by contacting the fire department!

Mrs. Phillips, however, made her son agree to help, saying, "You and your friends on the team can be the judges. After all, doesn't Big Bruce like eating even more than sports?" Mr. Phillips agreed to help buy all the cooking utensils. The parents were still feeling bad about Elizabeth's disaster in the kitchen and wanted to help.

It was a lot of work, but in four weeks the cooking contest was ready. Elizabeth had a big surprise planned for the event! She did not even tell Sally or her family. The only one that knew about it was Principal Stan.

The Big Event

The school cafeteria was decorated as if it was a dance. Round disco lights flashed bright lights around the walls and Henry made sure the beat was loud and catchy. There were five long tables in the center, one for each of the teams that entered the contest. Each one had ingredients and cooking supplies. Over 100 students showed up that evening and were seated around the five long tables.

Katherine the Cat and her two mean friends were team one. Elizabeth and Sally were at table five as the final team. Principal Stan was in the middle with his secretary as team three. Elizabeth's brother, John, walked to the microphone in front of the tables and welcomed everyone to the cooking show. The girls in the audience screamed like they were at a Katy Perry concert.

John read the menus that each of the five teams would be preparing. They were all simple – macaroni and cheese, popcorn, and quesadillas, except for Elizabeth and Sally's. No one knew what to make of their menu – it read: zany `za;

131

crazy tacos; Niagara Falls fun-do; and the panther surprise, which was named for the school's mascot, the fighting panthers. Principal Stan was going to try to cook cherries jubilee and bananas foster. This would require fire for the flambé, which meant John might end up having to call the fire department, after all!

"Three, two... one," John screamed! And the cooking contest began.

Sally began cooking the pizza dough and warming the tacos and taco beans. Elizabeth set up their table. She knew it was going to be a big hit with the students. She had thought of many fun and whacky ingredients to line up across the long table. The students could come up and make their own zany pizzas and crazy tacos. What's more fun than that?

Elizabeth set out small, decorated bowls of everything. She had them labeled: Section 1 was "Sugar-licious" and had M&Ms, sprinkles, and jelly beans; Section 2 was "Meat me at school" and had pepperonis, cheese squares, and chicken fingers; Section 3 was "Make your parents happy" and had tomatoes, broccoli, and apple wedges; and Section 4 was "You must be insane" and had bowls of Oreos, color-died marshmallows, and fortune cookies.

The five teams were busy cooking. Henry was playing music. Everyone was having a good time. John walked around to each of the teams and asked the kids questions about their recipes. When he asked about the Niagara Falls fun-do and Panther Surprise, Elizabeth would not tell him what they were. "It was a surprise," she laughed. All the students began inching up to Elizabeth and Sally's table to get a good luck at all the fun bowls full of ingredients for the do-it-yourself pizza and tacos.

When John asked Katherine to describe her recipe, she said "It will be as sweet as me." Even John rolled his eyes. Principal Stan was too busy concentrating on his flambé to talk.

After 30 minutes, the lights were turned off. John announced: "Okay, ladies and gentlemen. We are in the final countdown. The chefs had better be ready, cuz its time to stop cooking and see what they prepared! 10 - 9 - 8..." The whole audience joined in the countdown and, from his DJ set, Henry added a crashing drum beat to each number.

When the countdown got to "3" there was a huge crash. Everyone stopped.

The legs on Elizabeth's table had collapsed. All the fun bowls of ingredients had fallen, and piles of food had spilled onto the floor. All around Elizabeth, tomatoes and M&Ms rolled across the floor. The audience became quiet.

Elizabeth wanted to cry. So much work had gone into the show and the students were very excited to try her zany, fun concoctions. Henry stopped the music.

Surprise!

"Hey!" It was Henry yelling over his PA system. "Look..." The DJ was pointing to Katherine the Cat, who was trying to hide behind the curtain near Elizabeth's table. Miss Honey turned the lights back on and Henry jumped on top of a chair and pointed to the Cat.

"Caught you red-handed... or red-pawed," he laughed. Ha! It was Katherine who wrecked Elizabeth's table."

The students started to boo. They remembered when Katherine tried to ruin Elizabeth's show last year and they had all been excited to try the fun ingredients.

"Katherine..." Miss Honey began saying. But Elizabeth walked over to the microphone. Miss Honey handed it to her. Everyone quieted down.

"It's Okay. Come on, we're all here tonight to have a good time. Cooking is fun, right?" But no one answered.

"Alright," Elizabeth continued. "So we won't have crazy pizzas and tacos. But, are you ready for the Niagara Falls Fun-do and the Panther Surprise?"

But the students in the audience stayed quiet... until Henry screamed "She said: ARE YOU READY?" and then began playing a catchy beat. Miss Honey cut the lights again.

From behind the curtain, Sally and Elizabeth's parents pushed out two large carts on wheels. The first one had a four-foot-high chocolate waterfall. On the cart were fondue sticks and piles of strawberries, bananas, marshmallows, and other snacks to dip into the chocolate fountain.

Henry announced, "And now for the big surprise..."

Then the second cart appeared. It had a large Baked Alaska ice cream cake with a tall school flag sticking out of it. The panther mascot was on the flag. Lighted sparklers lit a circle around the huge treat. Over the PA system Henry played the loud panther growl, which was the school's trademark before their football and basketball games.

Walking beside the second cart was the real Pioneer Woman from the hit TV show. She carried a large tray filled with colorful macaroons. Elizabeth had invited her to the show. She was so impressed with the response to the cooking show that she asked for the microphone. The Pioneer Woman announced that she would make a large donation to pay for the school's upcoming fashion show. She also said that she was inviting Elizabeth to come on her show and cook with her. She then waved her hands in an invitation for everyone to come try the grand desserts.

The students started to cheer and ran to the cart. The line to try the tempting treats stretched the whole way across the cafeteria. Students were dancing and eating. The music was pumping. John spoke and asked the guys on the basketball team to announce the winner of the contest. He handed the microphone to Big Bruce, but Bruce simply mumbled and laughed. He had a mouthful of chocolate. So did all the other boys on the team. "I think we're all winners," laughed John, holding up a fondue stick with chocolate dripping down his arm.

Elizabeth walked over to her brother and took the microphone. "Thanks for coming everyone. And a special thanks to Principal Stan and the Pioneer Woman." The students applauded wildly.

"Now," Elizabeth continued, "I think we should donate all the leftover food to charity and have another one of these cooking contests…. because COOKING RULES!"

BYE-BYE, BULLIES

Bobbi Zimmelman

t was Heather's first day of sixth grade and she was really nervous. Heather had a feeling that middle school would be a lot more different than elementary school.

"Heather, get in the car. It's time to go to school," her mom called.

"I'm coming. And before you can ask, yes, I have everything," Heather replied.

Ever since kindergarten, Heather had always been the smartest kid in her class. She really hoped that she would have that same reputation in middle school.

"Bye, Mom. I'll see you at two o'clock," Heather said.

"Bye, Honey. Have a good day," her mom replied.

Heather got out of the car and went to find her locker; then it was off to her first class. Finally, after asking several people for help, someone actually helped her find her classroom.

"Hi, my name is Jenna. Are you new here?"

"My name is Heather and, yes, this is my first day," she replied.

"Well, here is your locker and then your class is just the second door on the left next to the lockers," Jenna said helpfully.

"Thanks. Can we sit together at lunch? Because... um, I don't have any friends."

"Of course," Jenna reassured her. "I'll even introduce you to some of my friends."

"That would be wonderful. I'll see you later," she said as she waved goodbye.

"See you later. Bye."

Heather started off toward her locker and class, hoping for a great first day of school. Jenna did the same thing. In homeroom, Heather's teacher talked about rules and what middle school was like. The whole time Heather was worrying, especially when her teacher talked about tests. It sounded as though the work in sixth grade would be a lot harder than fifth grade work. She tried to get that off her mind, though.

***

Finally, it was time for lunch, much to Heather's relief.

"So, how were your first three periods today?" Jenna asked.

"Good. How were yours?" Heather replied.

"Awesome. Well, these are my friends – Maggie, Ella, Jessica, and Dakota," Jenna said.

"Okay. Hi Maggie, Ella, Jessica, and Dakota," Heather said, kind of nervously.

"Hi, Heather. Jenna told us about you earlier today. By the way, I'm Ella," Ella said.

"Hi," said Heather.

"My name is Jessica and my sister is Maggie." Jessica introduced them.

"And I'm Dakota. It's nice to meet you, Heather. I hope your first year at middle school is good," Dakota said cheerfully.

"Well, it's nice to meet all of you. I'm really glad that I already have five friends on my first day of school," Heather said. For the rest of the lunch period, Maggie, Ella, Jessica, Dakota, Jenna, and Heather talked about what they were most excited about for the year. All of them were disappointed when the lunch period was over.

"See you at the end of the day," Dakota said.

"See you guys later," Heather replied. They all said goodbye, then headed off to their classes.

***

Heather was sitting anxiously at her desk. It was ten minutes until two, nine minutes, eight minutes… It felt like two o'clock would never come. Finally, it was one fifty-eight and her math teacher was writing the homework on the board.

"Brrring!" rang the school bell, indicating the end of the day. Everyone rushed out of the classroom, excited to go home. Heather was the last one out of the class. She packed up her things, said goodbye to her teacher, and then went to her locker where her friends said they would be.

"So, how was math?" Jessica asked Heather.

"It was good. Well, we didn't actually do much math. The teacher just talked about what math class would be like for us this year. Honestly, it was really boring," Heather replied with a sigh.

"How about we all walk home together?" Maggie suggested.

"Sure. By the way, Heather, Ella and I both live in the neighborhood The Falls," Jenna said.

"Oh, my gosh. I live there, too," Heather said excitedly. "Do the two of you want to come to my house?"

"Sure," Jenna said.

"I really wish I could, but I have swimming practice today. I'm sorry," Ella replied sadly.

"Okay. Maybe you can come another day instead, then," Heather suggested.

"Alright," Ella said.

"Should we start walking home now?" Maggie said.

"Yeah," Jessica replied.

The girls all started walking home, until Ella, Jenna, and Heather were walking to Heather's neighborhood. Ella said goodbye and it was just Jenna and Heather walking together. Finally, the two girls arrived at Heather's house.

"Mom, I'm home. And my new friend Jenna came with me," Heather said.

"That's great that you made a friend already. It's nice to meet you, Jenna," Heather's mom replied.

"Hi. Heather actually has four more friends, but they all live in a different neighborhood – that is, except for Ella," Jenna said. "Also, I'm in seventh grade. So are the rest."

"That's wonderful. I'll go make you girls a snack," mom said.

As the girls were eating their snack (a smoothie with fruit and ice cream) they talked about their day at school. Then they watched some TV and did their homework. When they were done it was five o'clock.

"I should go home now. It was great hanging out with you. I'll see you tomorrow. Bye!" Jenna said.

"I'll see you tomorrow, Jenna. Bye!" Heather said with joy.

Heather walked Jenna to the door and then went to help her mom with dinner. That night, they said goodnight to one another. Heather was so excited that night she could barely sleep. She was so excited to see her friends and go to her classes, which were a lot of fun for her now that she had several nice friends.

***

In the morning, Heather rushed to get ready for school. It felt like she would never get to leave the house. Finally, it was time to leave.

"Have a good day at school, Sweetie," mom said.

"Bye, mom," she replied.

"Hey guys. Where's Maggie today?" Heather asked.

"She's sick. Her fever is 100 degrees," Jessica said, with emphasis.

"Tell her that I hope she feels better soon," Ella said.

"Um guys, we should get to class. It's almost time for class to start," suggested Dakota. So all of the friends separated and went off to their classes. On the way though, something very unpleasant happened to Heather.

"Oh look here. It's little Miss Heather who can't even get a person in her own grade to be her friend. Instead she had to find seventh graders," Nikki teased.

Nikki was the biggest bully in the sixth grade. Her favorite hobby was to tease people. Heather couldn't think of anything to say back to the bully, so she ran to the closest bathroom. Luckily, it was the girls' bathroom and not the boys' bathroom.

In the bathroom, Heather locked herself in a stall and cried. She didn't even care anymore if she was late for class. But she couldn't show her face in school – at least not yet. She was really hoping that Nikki didn't follow her. Also, she was hoping that she didn't get into trouble for not showing up in class.

"Brrring!" the bell rang.

"Oh, no. I'm going to be late for class. I can't be late for class," thought Heather. She quickly splashed water on her face and then hurried to class.

When she got to room 108, she tried to slip in unnoticed, but that didn't quite work out as planned.

"Where were you, Heather?" Ms. Monroe asked.

"I... Um, I was in the bathroom. I guess I lost track of time. Sorry," she replied.

"Well, just take your seat and make sure not to be late again," Ms. Monroe said.

Heather sat down. Unfortunately, she was in the same homeroom as Nikki. That meant that for the first half hour of the day, Heather had to hear the snickering from Nikki's side of the room. Heather focused instead on lunch; she was so excited to tell Jenna and the others what had happened.

"So how was your second day here," Jenna asked at lunch.

"Good, but not all good. You know who Nikki is right? If you don't, she's the bully in my grade. She started teasing me before homeroom and now I'm really upset," Heather replied.

"You should tell your teacher or your parents," Jenna advised.

"No, I can't. I'm not ready to tell anyone. Well, other than you."

"Come on. You have to tell someone."

"No and you're not going to make me change my mind, Jenna."

"Fine. But I'm not going to say I won't tell the others."

"Fine, you win," agreed Heather.

"Yeah."

They ate the rest of their lunch in silence, with Jenna

sitting at the table and Heather reading her book. At the end of the lunch period, Jenna went over to Jessica to tell her about Heather and Nikki.

"Hey, Jenna. How come you never sat with us at lunch?" asked Jessica.

"I never saw you guys. Instead, I saw Heather, so I went to sit with her," Jenna replied. "She needed to talk to someone."

"Oh, okay," Maggie said.

"Speaking of Heather, she has a bully problem. Our worst sixth grade nightmare has turned into her worst sixth grade nightmare!" Jenna exclaimed.

"No. She can't have a bully; she's such a great person! Please say that you aren't telling the truth, Jenna," Ella begged, surprised and upset.

"It's true. I'm not kidding. Heather told me at the lunch table, that's why I never came to look for you guys," Jenna said. "I thought that if Nikki saw her alone, she would just tease her even more."

"Oh Jenna, you are such a great friend. We should go tell one of Heather's teachers," Dakota said.

"We can't. I already asked Heather and she said she doesn't want anyone to know about Nikki," Jenna replied disappointedly.

"But you just told us. Please tell me that she said you could tell us, because if you didn't…" Dakota replied.

"It's okay. Heather said the only people I could tell was you guys. Just as long as you don't tell anyone," Jenna said, cutting

Dakota off. "Anyway, we're going to be late for class, let's go."

So the five of them headed off for their class. Jenna was secretly wishing for one of the others to tell a teacher about Heather and Nikki. She realized that it was mean, but she didn't want Heather being bullied. She agreed with Ella that Heather was such a great person! Jenna tried not to get too distracted during science though. She was smart enough to know that if her teacher caught her daydreaming, she would assign her extra homework.

***

"Do you want to walk home together today, Heather?" Ella asked.

"Sure. Do want to come with us, Jenna?" Heather invited.

"Okay," Jenna replied. The three of them got their stuff from their lockers and then walked out the school together.

"So did you tell the others yet?" Heather asked Jenna, hoping for her to say "no."

"She did, and I just can't believe that someone would do that to you. You're such a great person, it just doesn't seem possible that this could happen to you," Ella said. "We have to come up with a way for your parents and teachers to see what Nikki is doing to you." Ella started thinking up ways for this.

"But I already said that I don't want anyone to know yet. Nikki will know that I told someone and then she'll just tease me even more. I just can't tell anyone," Heather said.

"You told us though, so you must be ready to tell some-one," Jenna said.

"I just don't want to tell anyone else, okay?" Heather said, her temper rising.

Jenna and Ella saw that as a sign to stop talking. The three of them walked the rest of the way home in silence. When Jenna and Ella tried to say goodbye to Heather, she just walked off.

"Heather must be pretty annoyed, if she isn't even talking to us," Ella said.

"I know. Even though Heather doesn't want us to do this, I know what we have to do," Jenna said.

"Yeah. Are you thinking what I'm thinking? We have to go back to school and tell Heather's homeroom teacher," said Ella. The two of them turned around and went back to school. They really cared about their friend, and that's what true friends do.

"Ms. Monroe, we need to talk to you," Ella said.

"Girls, if you need to talk to me, do it during school hours," she replied.

"But it's important. We have to tell you now," Jenna said.

"Okay. What do you want to tell me?" Ms. Monroe asked.

"Heather, from your homeroom class, is being bullied. Nikki, also in your homeroom class, is her bully. She teased Heather for not having any friends in her own grade and that's why Heather was late for class this morning. She was in the bathroom crying," Ella explained.

"Oh, okay. I'll have to talk to Heather and Nikki in school tomorrow," Ms. Monroe replied.

"Oh no," Jenna said under her breath.

"What's wrong with that? Did Heather not want you to tell me?" Ms. Monroe said.

"Kind of," Jenna said.

"I want you both to know not to tell anyone something behind someone else's back again. But I'm still going to talk to Nikki and Heather tomorrow," Ms. Monroe said.

"Okay. And it's fine with me if you tell Heather how you know this, because I know she'll realize that it was us who told you," Ella said.

Ms. Monroe, Ella, and Jenna left to go home. Jenna and Ella knew what was coming for them the next day during lunch period and they were not looking forward to it.

***

It was the next day, and Ella and Jenna were nervous for lunch period. They knew Heather would ask them why they told her teacher about the bullying when she told them not to do it. At the end of homeroom, Ms. Monroe kept Heather and Nikki to talk to them. "Nikki, it's not right what you said to Heather. She may not have any friends in sixth grade, but she loves the friends that she does have. I want you to apologize to her. Now," said Ms. Monroe.

"I'm sorry for teasing you, Heather," Nikki said, half-heartedly.

"I accept your apology. Just one question," Heather said.

"Yeah?" Nikki asked.

"Not you, it's for Ms. Monroe," Heather said. "Who told you this?"

"Ella and Jenna. They're good friends, Heather. You may not have wanted anyone to know about this, but they did the right thing telling me," Ms. Monroe replied.

"Just what I thought," replied Heather. She walked straight out the door to the cafeteria so she could talk to Ella and Jenna.

"Here she comes. Prepare yourself," Jenna said to Ella.

"I'm ready," replied Ella.

"How could you do this to me? I told you I didn't want anyone to know about Nikki. Why?" Heather said, annoyed.

"I'm sorry, but we just had to tell someone. We know you didn't want anyone to know, but we had to. We're sorry," Jenna said.

"Just don't even talk to me. I'm going to sit with Maggie, Jessica, and Dakota."

"Heather, we're really sorry. Please don't be mad at us," Ella explained.

"Fine," Heather said.

As if they knew what Heather was thinking, Jessica, Maggie, and Dakota came and sat with Heather, Jenna, and Ella.

"Did you tell her? Did she freak out? Freak out for me!" Dakota said with a smile.

"Dakota, what if she doesn't know yet, that would just make her extra mad?" Jessica asked.

"It's okay, Jess, I know about it," Heather said.

"Good. I didn't want either of them to give it away. So, I'm guessing you're not mad?" Maggie said.

"I'm not," Heather replied. "I have to go. I need to talk to Nikki," Heather said.

Heather walked over to Nikki just as Nikki was walking toward Heather. "I guess we were doing the same thing," Heather said.

"Yeah," Nikki said with a laugh. "Listen, I'm really sorry. Can we be friends? Please?"

"I was just about to say the same thing. It would be great to be friends," replied Heather.

"Awesome," Nikki said. They hugged each other and then they both walked over to Jenna, Maggie, Dakota, Jessica, and Ella.

Sometimes the best way to deal with something is to address it directly and sometimes people simply get off to the wrong start!

MIDDLE SCHOOL AUTHORS

OBLIVION

Adriana Bockman-Pedersen

Rynia was watching her feet shuffle along the wet leaves when she was overcome by the eerie sensation that someone was watching her. She spun around and squinted at the trees far off in the distance, but found nothing out of the ordinary. She shook her head and continued on her walk through the forest but was soon stopped again when she heard the sounds of horses' hooves against the forest floor. The barking of dogs reached her ears and she began running, afraid of who it might be.

Unfortunately, no human could outrun a galloping horse and thus Rynia soon found herself surrounded by the King's men. To her surprise, however, they seemed not to notice her as they flew past her on their horses and didn't look back.

At the last minute, the man at the front held up his hand and they all halted. He coaxed his horse around until he was facing Rynia. He looked her in the eye and her heart leapt in excitement and fear as she realized that it was King Endric, himself.

Rynia gathered the material of her long skirt and curtsied to the king, but he waved it off as if it was not necessary, "What is your name, child?" he questioned, unsmiling.

"I am Rynia, daughter of Myne, your majesty." Rynia replied. The way he was staring at her made her uncomfortable. She quickly looked away.

"Where are your parents, young one? A girl your age should be accompanied at all times. Such is the law." Endric inquired.

"Both are dead," Rynia replied simply "I have been on my own for several years now, Sire."

"Then why are you not at one of the homes for orphaned children?" One of the King's men asked.

Feeling guilty, Rynia avoided eye contact, "I ran away from the last one. I don't prefer to seek help when I don't need any."

"Have you a place to sleep? Do you have anything to eat?" the King asked.

Rynia shook her head "no."

"Come with us then," King Endric suggested. "I would ask that you join my family and I at the palace for a while. It would honor me greatly if you would accept. Genim, lend the girl your horse."

* * *

Rynia had never seen the Royal Palace before, yet there she found herself being escorted inside the gates by the King personally. It was the largest building that Rynia had ever seen, bigger than the apartment buildings that served as homes for the people who lived in poverty down in the village. The palace was built of white stones that had been mined in the far countries and the gates were made of pure gold. Towers loomed overhead, the flags of Faeryn flying proudly at their tips.

Rynia spurred her horse on and followed the King and his men to the royal stables where they left the horses to be groomed by the stable boy. The King took leave of his men and motioned for Rynia to follow him. Doors were opened to them by guards and when people passed them in the corridors they bowed quickly to the King and gave Rynia a questioning glance, but Endric seemed oblivious. They reached a sitting room where King Endric instructed Rynia to sit down and wait. He left her alone with the doors closed. She sat in silence and looked around the room. After a few short minutes the doors burst open, revealing a small group of servants.

A woman standing in the front approached Rynia, "What is your name, child?"

"I am Rynia Myne. But I prefer to be called Rynn."

"Well then Rynn, we have much work to do before you can meet the rest of the royal family. Nawaër, come take her measurements. She is going to need a new dress before the day is through. Fyra, start heating water for a bath. This girl is much in need of one. Would you style this rat's nest that she calls her hair, Gawaia? And do something with braids; the Queen likes that. We need to make her beautiful before the day is through," the lady ordered the other maids and then muttered under her breath, "We have our work cut out for us."

One bath, a hundred pinpricks, and thirty hair tugs later, Rynn was prettier than she had been in a very long time. Nawaër had made her a dress of evergreen silk, embroidered with silver leaves at the neck line and the sleeve cuffs. It was cut low around the neck where they had placed a pearl necklace. Gawaia had twisted her dark brown hair back into a complicated sort of bun, where diamond clips held it in place.

"Are you sure that I'm aloud to be wearing these things?" Rynn asked hesitantly, as she stared at herself in the reflecting glass.

The women laughed, "They were made especially for you, my dear!" Fyra continued, "The King chose to take you in, which was a spontaneous decision, but I suppose he missed the sounds of children running through the halls. If you are going to live in the royal household, then you have to look the part. These were the King's orders."

"Well," Nawaër clasped her hands together "I think it is time you were introduced to your new family."

"Temporary family," Rynia corrected "He only asked me to stay a while. I'm still not sure why."

The women just laughed and escorted her out the door. As they walked, Rynia began to feel more and more nervous. She wondered whether the Queen and her sons would accept her and she began to fear that the King was just playing a cruel joke.

Just like every other girl in the world, Rynia had dreamed of being a princess at some point or another. The beautiful gowns and jewelry had appealed to her when she was younger and had been living in Runnim, the poorest side of the town. But as she had grown older, she had realized how fortunate she actually was. She had begun to notice how the royals were constantly frowning and learned that the King had many duties that he had to fulfill, including the decisions that impacted the entire kingdom and everyone's lives. He made the decisions to tear down work places, causing the men to be jobless and their families to go hungry. It had become less of a pleasant daydream and more of a nightmare.

And now she was about to meet the royal family.

***

Rynn took a deep breath as the double doors opened, revealing the royal family in heated discussion. Gawaia cleared her throat to get their attention. Queen Arhiona turned her head abruptly, an expression of surprise etched on her beautiful face. "Come in," She invited Rynia. Fyra and Nawaër pushed her inside the room and then shut the door behind her, leaving Rynn alone with the royals. "Come forward, my dear, and let me look at you."

Rynn took a few tentative steps toward the Queen, who looked Rynia up and down. "I can see why you chose her," she said to Endric. "My Dear, I am sure that you are wondering why you have been invited to live in the palace." Rynn nodded and Queen Arhiona continued, "Why don't you sit down and all will be explained."

As it turned out, Fyra had been right. The Queen had two sons who were now grown; thus, she missed the days when they were young. She also desperately wanted a daughter, which was why Rynn had been brought to the palace. They wanted to take in an orphan and make her a Princess. After Queen Arhiona had told her story, Rynia found herself feeling sorry for the Queen, and she decided that she would be happy to help fulfill the family's dream. She agreed to stay at the palace.

Rynn had been staying in the palace for a little over a week and yet she was already used to the comfortable lifestyle that had become her own. Once a day, she had sword fighting and archery lessons, skills she had wanted to learn for a long time. She wore different clothes, had the choice to bathe any time she wished, and was served hot meals every day. It was the life she had secretly wished for, despite her stubborn pride, which had driven her to live alone without help ever since her father had died.

She was at archery practice when one of the Princes came running out onto the lawn, his hands held above his head so that she saw him and didn't shoot. "Rynn," he addressed her.

She set down her bow and turned toward him, "Is something the matter?"

"No, quite the opposite actually," Prince Kaedon said

smiling widely. "There is to be a dance here at the palace this coming weekend. Many people of importance will be there and you are the guest of honor."

* * *

The week couldn't have passed quickly enough. By Thursday morning, Rynia had greeted hundreds of guests and welcomed them into the palace. She had a gown ready to wear to the ball and had been assisting Fyra and Nawaër with the decorations. However, on Friday evening, just after supper, Rynn was walking back to her chambers when she overheard raised voices from the room she walked past. She backed up and pressed her ear to the door, but the voices where still inaudible. She eased the door open, making sure not to make her presence known.

Two men were standing in the darkened room – one that Rynn did not recognize, the other she knew to be the King's nephew, Prince Ethilium.

"I wouldn't recommend it so soon, my Lord. You should give the plan more time." The man took a step toward Ethilium.

"As my advisor, I merely have to take what you say into consideration. But as the Prince, I will make my own superior decisions when I do not trust your council, Grenick," Ethilium said threateningly.

"But to overthrow the King of Faeryn is too large a step for you to take at this time. You have no great armies to command and not nearly enough funds to carry this through, even if you came out the victor. You would need the resources to take over the entire country, not just to kill the King." Grenick retorted.

"Do not speak of these plans so loudly or so help me I will have you executed! You may have forgotten, but we are in that very same King's palace and his guards are milling about the corridors ready to defend him." Ethilium's voice was dangerously low.

"Yes, my Lord, I apologize," Grenick replied cautiously.

"I will follow through with this; I cannot wait any longer than I already have."

"But Sire," Grenick protested

"And if you speak of this to anyone..." Ethilium was interrupted by Grenick nodding vigorously and assuring him that his lips would stay sealed.

Rynn closed the door carefully and rushed back to her room. She knew that she should alert someone, but she heard foot steps behind her and was afraid that it could be either of the men. So she locked the door behind her and went to bed, though she didn't fall asleep for several hours, thinking how to tell the King about what she had overheard.

***

The next morning was filled with chaos and Rynia never found the right time to tell the King about his nephew's diabolical plan. At three, she was whisked back to her chambers to get into her gown. It was a royal blue that complimented her eyes and a gold sash was tied around her waist. Gawaia gave Rynn a sapphire necklace and twisted her hair into a half up-half down style.

When Rynn saw her reflection in the glass she barely recognized herself, compared to what she had looked like just a few short weeks ago. Her mind was completely distracted and she forgot all about Ethilium and Grenick, at least until she was informed that she was to be escorted by Prince Ethilium himself.

"No, I can't go with him," Rynn objected when Fyra told her.

"I know you don't really know him but he really is a nice lad," Fyra said.

"But…" Rynn started as she was pushed out the door. Ethilium was standing there waiting for her, which made her wonder if he had heard anything. If he had, he didn't show it.

"My lady, Rynia," He addressed her and held out his arm for her to take. He was dressed elegantly in a deep purple tunic and a gold embroidered cape. His boots clicked along the stone floor as they walked.

Rynn avoided his eyes as they walked in awkward silence. She didn't want him to realize that she knew anything and was afraid that he would see right through her if she tried to hold a conversation. They were admitted into the ball room where the King beckoned Rynia over.

"King Endric, I have something to tell you." Rynia said urgently "The other night I…"

Endric interrupted her, "That is going to have to wait, my dear. I have to give a speech." It took a few moments, but he got the attention of the bustling crowd. "I have an important announcement to make. Although it has been just under two weeks since we came upon the child in the Clairen Woods, we have grown to love her and feel as if she was always a part of this family. She has brought happiness back into our home and we can't thank her enough for that. Thus my wife and I have decided that we would welcome her into our home permanently, if she would have us?" He looked right at Rynia waiting for her answer.

Rynia's heart soared when she heard his last words. She would no longer live as an orphan and would have a real family. "Yes, yes of course!" she cried excitedly and flung herself into the King's arms.

All the guests cheered and Rynn smiled at them. She couldn't hold back her excitement. Then she remembered Ethilium.

"I have something I need to tell you," she whispered to Endric as the guests continued what they had been doing before.

"I am terribly sorry, Rynia, but my nephew seems to want to speak with me. Would you mind waiting until we're finished?" Endric asked. He walked away without waiting for her answer.

Rynia watched in anxiety as the King left the room with

Ethilium. She picked up her flowing gown and rushed after them. She followed them quietly out to the courtyard and hid behind a pillar. She was getting awfully good at spying.

***

"What is it that you wanted to say, Ethilium? My daughter wished to speak with me," the King asked.

"She is no daughter of yours! Rynia Myne is but an orphaned child who tricked you into making her a princess. She has no right to live here at the castle," Ethilium challenged his uncle.

"She has more right to this family than you do if you continue speaking to me in that manner. The girl has a good heart and she needs a home. Kaedon and Beldwin have taken to her as well. She belongs here," the King retorted.

"She belongs here just as much as a rat belongs in a stew," Ethilium said angrily. "I can't believe you have let her into your mind like that. Can't you see that she is manipulating you?"

"I would watch your words, nephew, or I will have guards escort you from the premises," King Endric said, his voice dangerously low.

"Of course, uncle. It wasn't my place to say. I apologize," Ethilium said. "Perhaps I am simply jealous of this girl who gets to join your family. I would give anything to live here."

"You are forgiven, Ethilium. But I don't want to hear any

more of that sort of talk." The King clapped his nephew on the back.

In a flash, a silver dagger caught in the moonlight. Rynia ran from behind the pillar, "No!" She shouted in horror. She ran at Ethlium who was frozen in shock. She pulled the King's sword from his belt and pointed it at Ethilium.

"You think you can defeat me, little girl?" Ethilium chastised her.

"I could try," Rynia said boldly and swung the sword at him. Her maneuvers were clumsy, for the sword was much too large for her to handle.

Ethlium's broad-sword came down on her hard and he held it there. He forced her to walk backwards until her back was against the well in the center of the courtyard. With a mighty shove, she was flung into the dark hole. She felt the sensation of falling as the black enveloped her.

And the last thing she saw before losing consciousness were the blinding lights of oblivion.

MORE THAN A GAME

Pablo Jaramillo

There he was, silently getting ready to amaze the hundreds of thousands of people at home watching this live. Everyone in the stands was watching, excited as ever. He was about to do it – Michael Jordan was getting ready to dunk. He backed up and sprinted to the free throw line and leaped. The crowd was silent. It seemed as if he was in the air for a minute. At the same time, all 32,000 jaws of the people watching at the arena dropped. It looked as if it was taken out of a video game. Michael Jordan had just jumped from the free throw line to dunk the ball – it was the first time this feat had ever been done. At that moment, everyone knew who would be the winner of the 1988 dunk contest.

Jordan remains an inspiration to many basketball players today. His story is very courageous and full of perseverance.

***

Michael Jordan was born in Brooklyn, New York. When he was just a toddler, he moved to Wilmington, North Carolina and attended Emsley A. Laney High School. He played all kinds of sports at his high school. He was on the baseball, football, and the basketball teams. Interestingly, Jordan had tried out for the varsity basketball team, but only made the JV team because his height was an issue. However, he was not fazed by the coach's decision. He made the best out of his JV season and racked up multiple 40-point games. By his junior year, he was ranked in the top 10 high school players in the United States. Jordan went on to the University of North Carolina at Chapel Hill and was named "Freshman of the Year," averaging 13.4 points and a 53.4 field goal percentage.

Jordan was so trusted by his college coach, Dean Smith, that Smith drew up a play in the NCAA championship for him to take the game-winning, three-pointer. Jordan released the ball and North Carolina had become the NCAA champs in 1982. It was an all-around interesting game because the championship had been played against Georgetown, which had another great player in Patrick Ewing, who went on to play for the Knicks in the NBA and later became Jordan's rival. Jordan was selected to the NCAA All American Team in his sophomore and junior years.

Jordan left North Carolina one year before his graduation, so that he could enter the 1984 NBA Draft. He was selected third by the Chicago Bulls after Hakeem Olajuwon, who went to the Houston Rockets, and Sam Bowie, who went to the Portland Trail Blazers. The reason the Trail Blazers did not select Jordan when they had their pick was because they already had a point guard with similar attributes as Jordan – Clyde "the Glide" Drexler.

The Bowie pick by the Trail Blazers was later recognized as the worst pick in North American sports history. Not only did they pick Bowie over Jordan, but Bowie had a terrible injury that caused him to lose a season and limited his career. In Jordan's first NBA season, he averaged an amazing 28.2 points per game. He was very warmly welcomed into the NBA and became a fan favorite even when the games where not in Chicago.

Two years after being drafted, Jordan went back to finish his last year of college and get his degree in geography in 1986.

***

"Honey! Come downstairs!"

"I will be there in a minute!" I proclaimed. I finished reading the last paragraph and folded up the newspaper and left it on the bed. "Hey honey, what's up?" I said to my wife, Yvette.

"Michael, are you going to play golf with the boys today?"

"Do you want to do something special?" I asked.

"No, nothing in specific," she said.

"So, then I probably will go play."

I devoured the breakfast and hopped in the car with my clubs and hat. I drove to the golf course a couple miles away, turning on the radio to ESPN; they seemed to be talking about me. Steve Kerr was talking to Clark Kellogg about the same thing I read in the paper. They were talking about my early years and also about the dunk contest.

It was February 6, 2014. This very day 26 years ago I won the dunk contest with the free throw line dunk. I had totally forgotten about it. It makes sense that the story of my early years in the league was on the front page of the papers. I miss my NBA career.

I arrived at the golf course and called my caddie and friend, John. I walked into the shop to rent a golf cart and as soon as I stepped in; everyone began to congratulate me. I thanked everyone and said that I love the fans. A kind man at the pro shop rented me the cart for free or as long as I wanted. My friends Alex and Robert finally got to the golf course.

We played a full 18-hole game. As we were leaving, we decided to go grab something to eat. We got into our cars and went to The Big Meatball. It is actually called New Jersey Boys, but we just call it the big meatball because it has a dish that is a huge meatball with parmesan cheese inside. We all ordered a big meatball. My pal Robert offered to pay, but I told him that I would take this one because he bought the last one.

We finished our meal and I signaled to the waiter to come over with the check. I gave the waiter the card and he walked off to the card register. He seemed surprised about something; he kept on swiping the card. He shook his head and walked back to our table.

He looked me in the eye and told me that my card had no balance on it. I told him he must have been kidding.

In desperation, I took the card and walked over to the machine to personally swipe it. At this point, I felt my skin getting hot and sweat dripping down my cheek. After being one of the best paid, wealthiest people in the world, I was about to be broke.

I felt like a disaster. In desperation, I looked at Alex and Robert to see if they could help me out and pay the dinner for tonight. I didn't say a word other than "thank you" until I got into my car. I felt as if my voice would get weak and I would tear up if I tried to explain things.

This day had never even come to my mind. Now that I think about it, I had wasted a lot of money in the past year or two. I bought my wife that Maserati she wanted. I bought all of my children 24-karat gold gifts, including a Rolls Royce Phantom for all of them. They even had their names written in diamond on the side.

I knew I was going to lose everything if I did not do something about this issue very soon. The first person I always called when I needed help was my eighth-grade basketball coach. Brandon Mcthay was a kind, go-to friend of mine. He was now part of the NBA as the head coach of the Miami Heat. Brandon, along with Coach Marcus, had taken my game to the next level.

Marcus and Brandon heard my story and gave me some guidance. I remembered and asked Brandon about his previous job with Under Armour. Brandon said he would give them a call whenever he got the chance. Brandon gave the company a call and they said that they needed a coach for a ninth grade basketball team near the suburbs of San Diego. The team practiced in the recreation center a couple minutes from my house. Since their old coach quit this job, I was officially named the head coach of the organization.

***

I got to the gym and met the players. We got into ball handling, form shooting, defensive positioning, and shell defense. The players were all very disciplined and very respectful of me. They always answered, "Yes, coach" or "Yes, sir." Under Armour decided to give me a sponsorship in return for my coaching the team. Our first team tournament was on this Saturday. We all got to the tournament and began our pregame warm-ups.

As I was observing the other team, I noticed that they were much taller than our team. However, I felt confident in my boys. We got into the huddle and I said some words of encouragement and, in a matter of seconds, the game had begun. We lost the tip off and they lobbed it to the middle and dunked the ball. We pushed it up the court and Tony made a three pointer. The game kept on having multiple lead changes. It remained close to the very end: It was the fourth quarter with 41 seconds left. We were down by three.

We dribbled up the court as the scoreboard showed 11 seconds. I called "timeout" as we got trapped in a corner. I drew up the same exact play Coach Dean Smith had drawn up for me to hit the NCAA championship-winning shot. I showed them how to run it. Charles came off of the pick and looked for the off-ball screen for Maxine set by David. Maxine caught the ball and fired. It rimmed off the hoop and went out. We lost the game 98-96.

***

The whole team hung their heads as they walked out of the gym. I saw that they were all sad, so I smiled at all the players. Troy asked me why I didn't look mad.

I answered to Troy, "Troy, you boys just lost by two points to a team with an average height of six feet, seven inches. Our height average is six feet, three inches. You all just left your hearts out on the court and I can't be more proud. This proves that it doesn't matter how tall you are, nor does it matter the clothes you wear, or from where you come. What matters is how much love and mental strength you feel for the game. Troy, I can see that you're sad and that makes me happy. That makes me happy because you don't just brush a loss off of your shoulders; no, you let it eat at you. This is why I am smiling, Troy. All of you players on this squad will soon be going to college."

I had their attention so I continued, "Yeah, this job pays

well and all, and I got my house back but couldn't buy all my cars again. But that's honestly not what matters to me anymore. I am not as rich as I was before, but I feel like I am richer on the inside. I have so much love for you boys. I feel like you 11 young men are my sons. Not only am I teaching you to become better players, but I am also teaching you to become better people."

The players all cheered. I think they, too, learned some important lessons. I have learned something from the coaching job, too: You cannot go buying everything you want. You have to live a balanced life and spend your money wisely. I am so glad that fate took me on this path to this team because I have learned and taught so many very valuable things that will help the team grow up as good people and basketball players.

And that matters more than fancy cars and clothing!

THE LOST TIME MACHINE

Jakub Pawlowski

Were you ever interested in your family history? A little boy in Europe named Johnny was; that is, before he found a time machine that would change his life!

On a nice, sunny afternoon, Johnny and his family went to visit his grandparents in a small town not far away from his home. Immediately after he got there, he received a gift from his grandfather. Johnny's parents were talking with his grandparents while he was quietly playing with the toys he had received as a gift. They were little, toy soldiers with two different colors to tell which was good and which was bad. He had never been so interested in little figurines like this, until one day he asked his grandfather where he got them.

***

Johnny was not that interested in stories, but he liked to hear about the military and the life of soldiers; after all, he was an eight-year-old. His grandfather had told him that, one day after World War II, he and his brother had gone to explore the woods, beaches, and fields to see if there were any old helmets or guns they could find. Although they tried not to wonder away from their home too often, they could not control their curiosity that day. Sure enough, they found an old tank that had been destroyed. For years, that tank was their hideout where they pretended as if they were driving the tank.

Johnny became very interested in this story; he would do anything to have such an adventure like his grandfather had when he was a boy. Johnny asked where the field was that grandpa was talking about, and his reply was that it is not far from the house. So, his grandfather and father took Johnny to see whether or not the old tank is still there.

"I remember that it was next to a big tree, but I am not sure if the tank will still be there because it has been a long time," said his grandfather. Unfortunately it was not there. It had probably been taken out to the junk yard before Johnny's father was born, but that did not keep Johnny from looking for more adventures. He asked his grandpa if he had any helmets that he had found when he was young. Fortunately, his grandfather had an old helmet he had found in the woods.

When Johnny put the helmet on his head he noticed that it was a little too big and it had a big crack in the middle. But he still wore that helmet every time he came to his grandpa's house. He always asked his grandpa and his father to walk over to that field, and they often had long talks about his grandpa's old adventures.

As Johnny grew older he became more and more curious, so he decided to walk the fields alone thinking of where his grandfather used to go. He would admire the birds chirping beautiful songs, the vast golden wheat fields, and the wind blowing softly on his neck. He felt like he was in Heaven. He could not get enough of this peaceful and quiet land he walked on. In fact, it was hard for him to believe that there had been a war fought on that beautiful land to defend and save his country. Because of this thought, he had often wondered if any of his family fought in the war.

Johnny joined the Boy Scouts to see how boys of his age helped during World War II. Being a Boy Scout was a little like being in the military and the Scouts had a lot of experiences having to do with nature. He learned all about secret codes, signs, and old techniques used to track animals and people or find your path back home.

This was all Johnny thought about and every time he went to his grandparents he would share what he learned with his grandfather and ask him more questions about his adventures.

***

Johnny and his parents arrived to his grandparents' house where they were staying for two nights. So Johnny once again asked his grandfather questions; this time he asked if he had any old or strange notes he had found during his childhood, but all his grandfather had were old helmets, rusted guns, and some used bullets he had found in the dirt. Johnny wondered if he would find old bullets next to the tree or nearby, so with no time to loose, he asked his grandpa if he knew how to make a homemade metal detector.

With the metal detector finished, Johnny was now able to go look for old bullets or other mysterious things. With a little spade, he had marched outside to go on an adventure. His mother called out and said that dinner was at 4:00 p.m. Johnny looked at his watch and saw that he had one hour and it took about 15 minutes to get to the big tree, so Johnny decided to run as fast as he could in order to have more time exploring.

While Johnny was running, he had crossed a dirt road leading away from the village his grandparents lived in to the city. When he got onto the beautiful fields, he stumbled on a rock. Johnny got up and whipped off the dirt from his pants and shirt and then looked for any bruises or cuts. Fortunately, nothing was broken or bleeding.

However, Johnny was sad to see his metal detector broken. But when he looked back at the rock, he noticed that it was not a rock; rather, it was a little dome shape. With great curiosity he wondered what it was that had tripped him. He quickly pulled out his tiny spade and began to dig. It was a little hard to dig because he did not want to damage the object. A little while later he saw what he had tripped over. He was awestruck when he found an allied helmet and under it was a strange cylinder-like object.

Johnny quickly dug out both items and looked at his watch. It was only 3:30, but Johnny decided to rush home and open the cylinder. He put the old helmet on his head, his broken metal detector in his backpack along with the cylinder, and, with his spade in his hand, sprinted home. Johnny wondered what was inside the cylinder, but he was so excited to have found something that he bet had to be great and full of history.

***

When Johnny arrived home, he said hello to his family and quickly ran upstairs to the room where they were staying overnight. His grandmother called to him and said that dinner would be ready in about 15 minutes. Johnny quickly jumped on his bed and took out the cylinder, carefully opening it. A little dirt had fallen on the sheets, but that was okay because it was an exciting historical discovery. When he opened it, old papers fell out. With great care, he unfolded the first paper and discovered that inside of it was a black and white picture of a big family with a lot of siblings and another photo of a young man wearing a military uniform.

With great caution, Johnny examined the photos and set them aside. He then moved on to the writing on the old paper. Johnny tipped back his helmet because it was falling on his

177

eyes, and he needed to see the writing. The writing was in cursive and he could not make it out, but he was able to read that they letter was written by a man: "Nicolas Stefanicki," read Johnny out loud.

Johnny was in great shock; his last name was John Stefanicki. He was choked up. No words were able to exit his mouth. He quickly but carefully folded the paper and put it back in the cylinder, then fixed his helmet, and ran downstairs to the guest room where his grandfather and father were talking about politics. Without saying a word, he cleared the coffee table and placed the can and helmet on it.

"Is everything okay?" asked his father.

"I tripped over this helmet and under it I found this can." Johnny's grandmother and mother had come into the room and saw the dirty helmet and can on the table. Johnny opened the can and gave the photo of the man in the uniform and the photo of the family to his grandfather.

"Do you know who he is?" asked Johnny softly. Johnny, his grandmother, mother, and father saw tears coming down his grandfather's face. Johnny's parents and his grandma were confused, but Johnny knew what was happening. He quietly explained everything to them and took out the note that was inside. He asked his father to read it out loud, and that note was from Johnny's grandfather's father, who had placed the note in the cylinder after he had written it to his wife – the mother of Johnny's grandfather.

The photo of the family was Johnny's grandfather, his

siblings, and his mom and dad. "This must mean that the helmet must belong to my great grandfather" said Johnny.

After a couple of minutes, everyone sat at the dinner table and ate. During the meal, Johnny's grandfather talked about how his dad used to tell stories of what he had gone through and what he had done, but he never said anything about a note he had left.

Great memories that had once been lost were brought back into the family after so many years. Johnny had great luck in finding that time capsule. Had it never been found, then he would have never found out about his great grandfather, who fought in the war for his country and for his family.

Johnny could not wait for his next adventure and, hopefully, another discovery!

WOLF WATERS

Sam E. Perez

It was an eerie, quiet night. The wind whispered through the town; leaves tumbled softly through the streets. It was so deserted and cold that it would send shivers down anyone's spine. It was almost dark, and the town's residents were closing their doors and locking their windows. After all, dusk is when the scary creatures and spirits came out to play. If you were not from this town, you would think that all these people were crazy. However, the people of this town know what happens when the sun goes down – they had learned the hard way. Welcome to Wolf Waters.

It all started one Monday morning when Mia Tourell moved into the quiet, little town of Wolf Waters. Within a month of turning 18, she moved the 1,250 miles from Los Angeles, California, needing a new start. As she pulled up to her new driveway, the crunch of the gravel brought her back to the present. She had the sneaking feeling someone was watching her. She was right; her new neighbors were peeking out their windows and staring at her behind their partly opened doors. She looked at them and they quickly shut their doors and windows.

"What is the matter with them?" Mia wondered. She hopped out of her car and wrapped her arms around herself. Chills rolled down her spine as the temperature suddenly dropped. Shaking off her paranoia, she walked to her old Chevy and popped open the trunk and pulled out several boxes to carry inside her new house.

After hauling the boxes up the brick steps to the front door, she set them down and pulled out her shiny, new key. She fumbled to put the key in the door while balancing an extremely heavy box. "Just what the heck did I pack in here anyway," she muttered under her breath.

"Here, let me help," a voice whispered in her ear.

Mia jumped and turned around to see a guy about her age with brown hair and blue eyes standing there. "Sure," she whispered back, unsure of his real intentions.

He chuckled and pulled the key out of her hands. The lock turned over effortlessly as he said, "Jake, the name's Jake Grand." He nudged the door open with his boot, bent down, and grabbed the boxes from the ground.

"Mia, the name's Mia Tourell," she imitated.

Jake smirked and walked into Mia's house. She looked around for the first time. It was much larger than she had thought. Sure it was dusty, but it held a sort of old world charm. Long, red velvet drapes covered the windows, blocking out all means of sunlight.

"A vampire must have lived here," Mia joked. Jake spun around sharply to look at her but then relaxed, winked, and chuckled along with her. She was not sure what it was, but something about Jake gave her the creeps.

Mia walked around and placed her hands along the red, velvet couch, and found it amusing that it matched the heavy drapes. The walls of the house had an ugly, faded, floral wallpaper that felt dry and brittle to her fingers. She made a mental note to look up "How to Remove Wallpaper," the next time she was online. She continued on to the dark, mahogany staircase. It really was beautiful, she mused.

As Mia ran her fingers down the banister of the stairs they picked up dust, which she carelessly blew into the air while she spun around in circles admiring her new home. She did not even realize that Jake was still there. He cleared his throat and Mia turned back around as her cheeks flushed with embarrassment.

"Where do you want these?" he said with no emotion on his face. Mia had not had a chance to really study his face, but now she noticed that he had small, crystal-blue eyes and dark, chocolate-brown hair. He was rather pale, but he was perfect looking; it was as if he was too perfect to be real. She shook the silly thoughts from her head and pointed to the couch next to him. He carefully set the boxes down and looked back into Mia's eyes. Jake's eyes looked vacant, which scared her. It was as if there was no soul lurking in his body. Just as she was starting to get really uncomfortable, his hands curled into fists and a smirk found its way onto his face. His eyes glistened in the dark and his eyebrows furrowed in a vile kind of way.

"It's almost dark," he whispered after what felt like forever. Mia's face fell in confusion, 'So what?' she thought. "It's time to come out and play" he snickered. She gasped as he zipped through the room and out the door with an almost superhuman speed.

***

Mia ran after him and out the door, but he was gone, just like that! "What did he mean!" she wondered, feeling confused and worried. She sighed and slowly turned around to walk back inside. Maybe this town was too weird for her.

Suddenly, a scream echoed through the street. Mia's eyes went wide in fear and all the blood drained from her face. She raced back into her house as fast as she could and closed the door behind her. "What was that?" she thought. Her legs trembled as she leaned against the door for support. She ran a hand through her long, curly, brown hair and slid down the wall onto her bottom.

After a few minutes, she let out the breath she had been holding and rubbed her temples. She hoisted herself up off the floor and stood up shakily. She walked over to the couch where the boxes were. She grabbed them and set them down on the floor. Pulling her sweater around her, she snuggled into the couch cushions, closing her eyes for the night.

Mia awoke to the sound of banging and shot straight up off the couch. She straightened her crinkled shirt and patted her jeans. Mia sighed and pulled her long hair up into a messy bun. She hesitantly walked over to the door, trying her best to be quiet, especially after last night. Holding her breath, she peeked through the peephole. When she realized it was only a little, old lady wearing garden scrubs and worn gloves, she let out a sigh of relief. Something caught her eye though; the woman looked startled or afraid. Mia cautiously opened the door, stepped outside, and closed it behind her. She folded her arms across her chest and tucked a stray piece of hair behind her ear. "Can I help you?" Mia asked.

"You are new?" The shrill, little woman asked.

"Y-Yes, why?" Mia questioned while raising her eyebrows.

"Don't forget to lock your doors, otherwise the scary creatures will come out and play," the woman said creepily.

Mia gulped and nodded her head. Although she did not want to be rude, she ran inside and slammed the door in the woman's face. Swiftly turning around and peeking out the peephole, she saw that the old woman was already gone. Mia locked her door and sighed. She walked back to where she had slept and bent down. She started unpacking the boxes, when her stomach grumbled angrily. "I guess I am hungry," she whispered to herself. Standing up, she grabbed her car keys, phone, and walked over to the door and hesitantly unlocked it, then walked out, forgetting to lock it behind her. Mia got into her car and headed toward the nearest supermarket.

After about 20 minutes, she found a Publix and walked inside, heading straight to the deli. When she got there, she suddenly realized that no one was around. The store was deadly quiet, and Mia could hear the nervous inhale and exhale of her breath.

***

"Hello? Anyone here?" Mia yelled. She checked her watch and it said it was about five o'clock. "How did it get so late?" Mia wondered. She shrugged, looked around the deli, and, seeing no one around, said to herself, "Don't mind if I do." She hopped behind the counter and picked up some roast beef, provolone, lettuce, tomatoes, green peppers, and white bread. After she made her sandwich, she bit into the delicious, savory sandwich. "It is not nice to steal," a cold, menacing voice said behind her. She whipped around, dropping her roast beef sandwich in the process.

"You scared me!" she yelled.

Jake chuckled, "It is still not nice to steal."

"I would not call it stealing, more like fending for myself," she said while scanning the store.

"Sure," he said sarcastically while rolling his eyes.

"Well, now look what you've done," she said angrily, pointing to her sandwich that was lying on the ground in one big mess.

"Not my problem," Jake shrugged while walking away. Mia rolled her eyes and turned away from Jake.

"He is bad news," she thought to herself. Remembering where she was and wondering where all the people were, she called out to Jake, "Hey, what kind of store has no employees in it?"

Without turning back to look at her he said, "If you know what's good for you, you'd stop asking questions and get home before the sun goes down." With that chilling statement, he walked out the door leaving her to wonder again what he meant by that.

"This town is getting weirder by the minute," she said. Grabbing a soda out of the cooler and a bag of Doritos near the register, Mia dropped a five-dollar bill on the counter and quickly hurried home. She did not know what Jake was talking about, but she was not going to take any chances either.

***

Mia sprinted out of the Publix and ran to her car. The wind whipped around, even stronger than before. The crisp air nipped at her nose and blew pieces of hair into her face. Mia wrapped her arms around herself and hopped into her car. The ignition on the Chevy started up and made a deep rumble. Mia put her seatbelt on, put the car in reverse, and hit the road.

On her way home, Mia could not help but notice the people scurrying into their homes, locking their doors and closing their windows. "What are they afraid of?" she wondered.

Mia quickly got out of the car and ran toward her front door. She scrambled around in search of her keys and pulled them out of her pocket, inserting them in the keyhole. Turning the key, she unlatched the door and rushed inside. When looking at what was in front of her, Mia's mouth was gaping at the sight. The couches were ripped to shreds, the floor was trashed with all of Mia's clothes and possessions, and on the wall was something clearly written in bright, red paint. "You have been warned, it could have been worse; lock your doors," Mia read out loud as her fingers and legs trembled.

She fell to the ground and whimpered. Her whimpering turned into full sobs. "What am I going to do, someone is stalking me?" Mia cried. She took in gulps of air as the tears cascaded down her cheeks. "Maybe I should take the warning," Mia whispered to herself as she looked at her trembling hands through a haze of tears. She took a deep breath and stood back up, wiping at the few stray tears remaining on her face.

Mia checked her watch and it read 7:30. Her eyes widened and she darted around the room checking all the windows and doors, making sure that they were locked. When she was done checking the windows and door, she sighed and prepared to try and get some sleep. Mia was truly considering moving back to Los Angeles because all of these weird and strange events and creepy, unfriendly people were just too much for her handle.

***

In the morning, Mia awoke startled and confused. She looked around the room in confusion. What was once wrecked and a mess was now clean and neat like it never was touched before. "What? I swore this was a mess just yesterday?" she thought in confusion. She sat up from the couch that had been her bed for two nights in a row. Mia opened the large, thick curtains that were keeping the room in darkness. As she opened the drapes, the light poured through, soaking the entire room with warmth and large rays of sunlight.

Everything seemed normal and quiet. Giving her latest experiences with this town, it was a little too quiet. She walked back toward the door; her stomach growled in protest. Rolling her eyes, she remembered the bag of Doritos and the soda, and grabbed them off of the floor where she left them the night before. The bag made a high-pitched noise and crinkled when she opened it up. The smell of nacho cheese swirled around the room, making her taste buds water. She bit into one of the chips and her stomach grumbled with content. As she munched on the chips, she walked out of her house and unlocked her car to carry in the rest of her moving boxes.

As Mia grabbed the boxes, she observed that the sun was already setting. "But that can't be right?" she whispered while looking down at her watch. Sure enough, the watch read 7:30 and she lifted her eyebrows in confusion. "How could the time move so fast between the walk from my door to my Chevy?" she wondered. Knowing that most things in this town have been strange, she rushed inside with the last of the heavy, taped boxes. Once inside, she closed the door with the back of her foot.

After putting down the last of the boxes, Mia walked into the living room, sat down on the couch, and sighed. She pulled the cellphone out of her back pocket, needing to hear her mom's voice, but noticed the phone had no cell service. "Great, just great," Mia murmured while putting the phone back in her pocket. Feeling frustrated and alone, she leaned back on the couch cushions and closed her eyes to rest.

Suddenly there was a high-pitched scream from outside that sent Mia bouncing off the couch with fright. She put her hand over her racing heart, thinking, "Tonight is going to be a long one." As she rose off the floor, she heard a creaking on the mahogany stairs behind her. Chills traveled down Mia's spine and the hair stood up on the back of her neck. She closed her eyes and took a deep breath, not wanting to turn around, but needing to know who or what made that sound.

Standing at the end of the dusty staircase was Jake. Mia gulped in large breath of air and stammered, "W-What are you doing here?"

"You left your doors and windows open, that's what I am doing here," Jake responded in anger.

"It was you who wrecked this place!" Mia yelled. She was furious, why would he do this?

"Oh, you can thank your old neighbor for that one," he exclaimed with a smirk on his face. She realized now that the old woman had been trying to warn her about Jake all along.

"You," Mia gasped, walking backwards away from him as fast as she could, tripping over the couch.

"Now it is time to come out and play." Jake whispered, looking around and pointing toward the windows. Out of nowhere, fat little monsters with long, pointy nails and scaly skin came through the windows, glass shattering in all directions, broken pieces of glass fell to the ground while some ripped through the heavy drapes. The monsters screeched, and Jake laughed maniacally. She screamed and ducked behind the red, velvet couch. She crouched and put her hands over her ears in the way a toddler would to block out the scary noises.

The monsters roamed around her house, destroying and breaking everything in their path. Mia started crying and screaming.

"I told you to lock your doors, Mia. You never know who could come in and play," Jake said jumping in front of her. He lunged for Mia just as she squeezed her eyes shut, hoping for it all to go away.

***

"Ahhh!" Mia screamed with all her might, waiting for Jake to hurt her. Nothing happened. She opened her eyes to see that she was not crouched behind the red velvet couch, but sitting in a chair. Confused, she said to herself, "Where am I?" Mia looked around to see shelf after shelf lined with books of all different shapes, colors, and sizes. Mia then looked down and saw that she was sitting in a chair pulled up to a desk and took a closer look at what was in front of her. "Urban Legends and Myths: The Legend of Wolf Waters," she read out loud. "It was all a dream?" she whispered, sighing in relief.

Everything came rushing back to her; Mia was a freshman in college and she had a research paper due on urban legends, so she had gone to the library to get started on it. She ran a hand through her hair taking deep breaths. The reality of what just happened brought immense relief, but at the same time confusion. She must have muttered something under her breath again, as a woman nearby whispered, "Miss, please be quiet, this is a library." She turned to see who it was and saw the old woman from her dream wearing a nametag and holding a pile of books.

Mia quickly got up from her chair in shock. She shook her head, "It was just a dream, it was just a dream," she kept telling herself. She had to convince herself there was no reason to be scared of the old woman. Not wanting to take any chances and not in the mood to work on her paper anymore, Mia collected her books and put her sweater on to leave. "Well, at least this nightmare gave me something to write about," she chuckled to herself.

"You're doing a paper on urban legends too?" a man said from behind Mia.

"Yes," she said in agreement while turning around.

Standing there was a guy with small, crystal-blue eyes and dark, chocolate-brown hair. He was rather pale, but he was perfect looking, as if too perfect to be real.

Mia was hit with déjà vu. She shook it off and grabbed her bag and pushed her chair in.

"Do you go to the college right across the street?" the guy questioned, while Mia continued to study his face.

"Yes, do you?" she answered with worry in her voice. She could not help but think she had met him before. As she walked toward the bookshelf where the book belonged, she noticed the guy still following her.

"Yes I do," he said confidently.

Realizing that she was being silly, she shrugged her shoulders and introduced herself. "Well, my name is Mia Tourell." she said, putting her hand out.

"I know," he smirked, and walked away.

ECHOS OF FLAME

Rachel Stauffer

"May Ellen! What is this?" Miss Crockett scolded as she ripped the paper from beneath my pen. I hadn't heard her approaching; usually I am much better at hiding my work from her.

"It's poetry, ma'am." I explained as I had a thousand times before. I hung my head and stared at my too-tight-hand-me-down black button shoes. "And my name is May Ella, not Ellen." The girls sitting next to me pretended not to notice the scolding.

Miss Crockett promptly ripped the paper to shreds. "I will call you what I want, May Ella." She dragged my name out, like it tasted sour on her tongue. "I've told you countless times, you are to be working, not writing silly poetry." She spat as if explaining herself again was not worth her time, but was gracious enough to do so. "Am I right, girls?"

The girls at the neighboring sewing machines didn't even look up from their work as they chirped, "Yes, Miss Crockett."

Miss Crockett looked pleased with herself, straightening her back as she always did when we girls addressed her. Then she dumped the many pieces of shredded poetry on the concrete floor of the factory. "Now, pick up your mess." She demanded. She spun around and clomped off to oversee the other departments and do whatever else managers do.

As I bent to pick up the minuscule pieces, the other girls at the surrounding stations leapt up to help. This sort of thing happened often, so they knew exactly what they were doing. Quietly, they helped pick up the paper and put it into their aprons, their movements practiced.

Mary Goldstein, a tiny, curly brunette, only 11 years old, was one of the youngest at the factory, and was always first to help. I smiled at her. Mary had always been like a sister to me. Her Star of David necklace dangled around her neck as she bent to pick up the pieces of paper.

It was Jennie Levin, a 19-year-old beauty, who broke the silence. "I hate this place!" she exclaimed. Jennie was never afraid to speak her mind. All five-foot, six-inches of her stood defiantly over the pile of scraps. As she stomped her foot for emphasis, her short black bangs, which had been precariously balancing behind her ear, fell into her electric green eyes. She had always been outgoing, even with her hair. None of the rest of us would ever dream of wearing our hair so childishly with bangs. But somehow, Jennie pulled it off.

"Jennie! That was an incredibly rude thing to say" huffed Fannie Launswold, who was one of the eldest girls at 24 years old. "Where would you be without Mr. Blanck and Mr. Harris? Homeless? Starving? You should thank your lucky stars that you have enough pay for a roof over your head and food in that big mouth of yours." She shook her head disapprovingly. She and Jennie had never gotten along.

"Big mouth? I have a big mouth? I'll have you know that my father would not be too happy to hear about that!" Jennie pulled her fists up to her pretty, but grimy, face and said, "C'mon! Are you scared of a little girl like me, hmm?"

Fannie paid her no mind, but Emily, another girl who was about my age, rose to her defense. "You say that again and I'll…" Emily started to threaten.

But Fannie tugged on her braids, pulling her away from Jennie and cutting her off. "That's enough, all of you! You're all behaving like children." Fannie's intense blue eyes scolded each of us individually.

They all handed the scraps to me; I would try to rewrite it later. We sat back at our machines and continued to work, even little Mary. I could hardly focus; I was too busy plotting my escape.

***

That night, after all the other girls had gone home, I packed my few belongings. I was living at the factory because Miss

Crockett, the factory manager and overseer, agreed to let me stay at night in exchange for working extended hours. Unlike most of the girls, I was an orphan. When they went home for the day at five o'clock, I stayed and slept on the eighth floor of the Asch Building (which was the floor I worked on), with only a threadbare spare towel to keep me warm. This, of course, was much better than sleeping outside, where the threat of kidnappers and the weather was not too great. But that night, I did not sleep. I gathered my journal and pen, which I was told was my father's before he died, and made sure I had my anklet on, which my mother made for me as a baby. It was almost silly to check. I never took it off.

I crept into Miss Crockett's office, which is supposed to be locked, but she gave up on doing so long ago. Quietly, I opened her drawer in hopes of finding her usual dinner leftovers. To my delight, I found an unopened bottle of Canada Dry Ginger Ale (ginger ale was my favorite) and a Hershey bar, the new kind with the almonds (just looking at it made my mouth water). I shoved the snacks into my makeshift sack that I had fashioned out of my apron and dashed out of the office. Now, I was prepared.

I had no idea what time it was, but I estimated it was sometime in the early morning. Miss Crockett and the girls would arrive just before dawn, so I had to hurry.

Shuffling out the side door, I peered around. No sign of life on either Greene Street or Washington Place, the two streets that intersected just outside the building. It must be really early. I thought to myself. I had no idea where I was going, only that I had to be long gone by the time Miss Crockett realized I was gone and thought to look for me.

I thought about running, but I decided it was best to draw as little attention as possible. It's curious enough that a 16-year-old girl was out so early, and all on her own! I decided to follow the sidewalk and see where it took me. Some kind person would see me eventually, right?

After walking for quite some time, the March air had caught up to me. I tried to distract myself from the cold by staring at all the buildings, making up stories about the people who might work there.

Just then, I bumped into someone.

His papers flew everywhere and I scrambled to help gather them. "I am so sorry sir; I should have been paying attention," I apologized profusely. Looking up to see his face, I noticed it was not a man at all, but a newsboy who looked not much older than me. I handed him his newspapers, not taking my eyes from him.

"No, it's fine Miss. I'm sure it's my fault." He looked up to meet my gaze and his mouth fell open slightly. I wasn't sure what he was looking at that made him so surprised, so I turned around to look. There wasn't anything there. He hadn't been looking at me like that, had he?

He swallowed slightly, rising from his stooped positon. "What's a young lady like yourself doing out so early?" he asked, his deep hazel eyes hadn't stopped staring at me.

"Oh, nothing," I lied as he extended his arm, gesturing to help me up. We were standing on the sidewalk, my hand still in his, gaze still locked.

"Um," he stuttered, pulling away. "I'm James. James Clark." He held out his hand for a handshake, which was awkward and seemingly unnecessary considering the amount of time we were holding hands in the first place. But I obliged and shook his hand regardless.

"I'm May Ella Fontaine." We shook hands. The silence that followed was very awkward, mostly because I got the sense that he was still staring at me. I suddenly became aware of my freckles, something that had not ever bothered me in my entire 16 years of life, but was making me self-conscious at that moment. *That's silly.* I thought. *There is nothing wrong with your freckles.*

"So, are you always out this early? Do you live around here?" James asked, his gaze shifting to the surrounding buildings, giving me a great view of his jawline. "No, I live and work at the Triangle Shirtwaist factory, down in the Asch Building." I paused, and then added "I'm an orphan."

"Yeah, me too." He replied, looking back at me. *Am I really this short, or is he really that tall?* "Oldest of seven."

"Really? Seven?" I asked.

"Yep. All boys too." *I'm convinced. His hair must be made of gold.*

"Wow. I'm an only child. I think, anyways. I mean, there's really no way of knowing, unless you count my friend Mary from the factory; she's just like a sister," *Shut up May Ella! You're rambling!*

"Well, anyway, you should probably get back to the factory. It must be close to five now." James advised.

"Right," I said. "The factory." My face fell with disappointment. It was silly to think I could really run away; how could I leave Mary and the others? I had to go back before Miss Crockett noticed that I was gone. However, I would keep the snacks... how could I possibly pass up some Ginger Ale and Hershey chocolate? With almonds!

James nodded respectfully and hustled on his way. In the darkness of the early morning, I saw something fall out of his pocket. Reaching down to grab it, I noticed it was a marble. Not just any marble, but a nice, collectable marble. It was blue and shiny... it must have cost him a whole $20 for that thing!

"Hey, wait! You dropped your marble!" I called out, but he was already long gone.

***

Sitting at my sewing machine, all I could think about was James and his marble. I would have to return it; it was very expensive and I would feel horrible if I didn't. But he was a newsboy, right? He would come around again the next morning. I made up my mind that tomorrow I would wait outside for him to come. *To return the marble, nothing more.* I told myself over and over, though I could not get myself to believe it.

Early the next morning, I walked to the same spot where I had seen him the day before. Rolling the marble nervously between my index finger and thumb, I waited for him to arrive.

Sure enough, there he was, clad in his checkered flannel, cargo pants, and newsboy cap with stack of newspapers. I waved at him, "Good morning James!" He looked slightly surprised to see me again, but broke out into a smile.

"Hi, May Ella!" He threw a paper at a doorstep. "It's good to see you out here again." Whoosh! Another paper.

We talked much longer that day, mostly about his terrible boss, Mr. Rossi, who yelled at everyone in Italian, and the other Italian immigrant boys would have to translate for him. This made me laugh, which was something I hadn't truly done in quite some time. I told him I could translate for him, too; I had learned a lot by listening to the other Italian girls who worked near me at the factory. He told me that he would be happy if I did.

Just as he was about to continue his route, I remembered the marble. "Wait, your marble! You dropped it yesterday." I stopped him, producing the shiny blue marble in my palm. He smiled at me. "You can keep it, May Ella Fontaine."

***

I saw James several times afterward and every day for a whole week! I loved the way my name sounded when he spoke it aloud. I had always thought that my name was choppy and that my French last name was weird and awkward, unlike the Italian names of my friends that seemed to flow off the tongue. I even found myself writing poems about him.

Each day he told me about his six brothers: William, Paul, Louis, Joe, Raymond, and Henry, who was barely two years old. I told him about Mary, and how she had been my family when I had no one else. We talked about our jobs, being orphans, and so on, and we found that we had so much in common. Every day I would wake up early to see him. And it made me happy – happier than I had been in a very long time.

It was the morning of March 25, 1911. Nothing had seemed out of the ordinary. I had woken up early to see James and nearly pranced out the door to see him. He was delighted to see me, as usual.

"May Ella Fontaine!" he exclaimed as he did every morning. He wrapped his arms around my waist and swung me in the crisp March air. Setting me down, he could hardly contain his excitement.

"Oh, May Ella, you'll never believe it! You see, I've been thinking about us, and, well, where do I start?" He was grinning from ear to ear, his breath a cloud through his pink lips.

"James, what are you talking about?" I asked through a laugh. He was usually happy to see me, but never quite this giddy.

"Well, I don't know how else to say this, but..." He stopped for a split second. "I want you to run away with me."

My heart stopped for a second. That was not what I was

expecting at all. Sure, I had thought about it before; I would never have met him had I not tried to run away in the first place! But with him? That was an entirely different story. Sure, maybe I wanted to, but was it even a good idea? What would Fannie think? How could I leave Mary? Where would we go? Would he take his brothers? All these questions swam in my head making it hard for me to think straight.

"Run away?" I asked timidly. My voice was very small all of a sudden. "Now?"

"Yes! You're always telling me how horrible it is at the factory, and it's not much better working for Mr. Rossi. Oh, May Ella! Just think of the possibilities! We could get on a train out West, or maybe we could find a place in the sub-urbs. Heck, we could sneak on a ship to France and see your homeland. Maybe we could find the rest of the Fontaines. I'm almost 18; we could even get married soon! Can you imagine getting married in London? May Ella, we must run away, don't you see?" He was out of breath by the time he finished.

I must say, the idea intrigued me, but it was too much, too soon. Getting married? I was only 16, even though I doubted I would ever find someone more perfect than James Clark.

"Look, James, it's a fantastic idea, it really is. But you have to see the big picture. What about our jobs? What about Mary? Your brothers? We can't leave them, how could we possibly?"

"No, May Ella, we wouldn't have to. We could take them with us! And you could write poems to sell; you're amazing!

We could make it work." James put his hands on my shoulders. "Don't you want to?" His eyes implored as he stared clear into my soul. *I do! I do want to James, more than anything!* My heart screamed at me to tell him, but my head told me no. I couldn't do it, not yet at least.

"Let me think about it." I told him, pulling away and turning to go inside.

***

And think about it I did. I thought about it all day. It was an all-consuming thought until one word broke the deafening silence. "Fire!!"

I hadn't even realized, but smoke was pouring into the room. Girls were starting to panic as flames lit some fabric on the other end of the room.

"What's going on?" Mary asked in the confusion. "May Ella, what's going on?!"

The fire was spreading faster than I could comprehend what was going on. "Someone dropped a cigarette!" I heard someone shout. "I bet it was Miss Crockett! That mean old hag is trying to kill us all!" The girls were screaming in panic as the fire raged across the room. I was frozen in place, unable to move or think.

Just then, a weak stream of water spewed around the room. Miss Crockett held an old hose, trying desperately to put out the fire. But I knew it would not work. The hose was older than time; it was almost entirely rotted and the valve was rusted shut. Miss Crockett gave up and tried to usher the girls towards the staircase, and ultimately, the exit. We were on the eighth floor and the stairs would have taken forever. Besides, the door down there was usually locked. Suddenly I felt a shove from behind. It was Fannie, desperately shoving girls towards the elevators. We had to run through a tight corridor to get to the elevators, and being as small as I am, I nearly got trampled numerous times.

Fannie was bringing up the rear, yelling in Italian for us to stay calm. Of the four elevators, only one worked. The operator insisted that it could only take 12 at a time, but Fannie demanded that we must try. Ultimately, Fannie forced twice that amount in the elevator.

I was toward the back of the line and the heat was rising. My heart pounded in my chest. *I'm going to die.* I thought. *We are all going to die.* But it all happened so quickly; my brain had hardly enough time to react. Not even enough time to cry or anything.

"Miss Launswold!" called the operator. "The heat is too intense, I can't run it anymore!"

Fannie went ballistic. "What do you mean? We've only run it four times!" The operator just shook his head. "I'm sorry ma'am, it simply can't be done."

But Fannie was already shoving girls towards the fire escape. I heard Jennie protest, "What are you doing?! That fire escape will break before we even get ten girls down!" Fannie paid her no mind; she was too focused on the task at hand. Mary clung to me so tightly I was afraid she might cut off the circulation in my hand. My heart was doing overtime and the heat was melting my face. The screams of my friends echoed through my ears, making me want to scream, too. But I had to keep it together, for Mary's sake.

Fannie was shoving girls down the staircase, five at a time. I almost tripped as she forced me and Mary down the stairs. I could feel it starting to give, so I pushed Mary in front of me so that she would have a better chance of making it down. That was my fatal mistake.

The force of the shove broke the stairs and Mary went tumbling down.

"Mary!" I screamed desperately as her body hit the ground below with a sickening thud. Several others fell down, as well. I had barely finished screaming her name when Fannie and Jennie started pulling girls off the stairs.

"C'mon girls, let's go! We have to move, the fire is raging! Let's go!" they yelled.

Now I had lost it. Sobs were choking me and tears were blurring my vision. Jennie pulled me back into the inferno and I had lost all sense of feeling. I was utterly numb. Fannie pushed me, Emily, and another girl about my age named Kate toward the window.

"The window?" Emily shrieked. "You must be insane!"

Fannie didn't stop moving as she explained, "The fire department is down there with a net. You three go first. Just jump!"

Emily, Kate, and I all stood on the window sill, death gripping each other's hands. "On three?" asked Kate. Emily started to count up but I had already jumped. Pulling them with me, we fell, screaming, to the city street below. As we collided with the net, it tore, rendering it entirely useless. I landed funny on my ankle, but I was otherwise unharmed. Emily was yelling, "It's broken! It's broken!" But it had no effect. Firefighters pushed us out of the way as girls fell from the windows by the dozens, several of them burning alive as they streaked through the air. Eventually I saw Jennie, plummeting from the eighth floor, arms folded, to her certain doom.

The firefighter's ladders were completely useless; they only reached the sixth floor. I was sobbing hysterically as a fireman wrapped me in a blanket and tried to calm me down. I barely heard what he said. All I heard was one voice. "May Ella!" And then I blacked out.

***

When I woke up, I was in a hospital, James and a nurse hovering over me. "What happened? Where are the others? Are they all ok?" I asked frantically, my words piling over one another.

The room was silent and all James did was hand me a paper. The headline was, FIRE AT THE TRIANGLE SHIRT-WAIST FACTORY KILLS 146: SURVIVORS ARE FEW AND LUCKY TO BE ALIVE.

I stared at the paper for a long time. Did that really happen? Did I really survive that? Then it all came flooding back. Tears gushed down my face. James held me for God knows how long. What I had seen would never leave me; it was seared in my brain forever. I had gotten off with a broken ankle, but 146 girls weren't so lucky – and they were 146 of my friends. How would I move on?

I knew I had to go on. I owed it to the girls. They wouldn't want me to stop living, certainly not Fannie Launswold, who was a true heroine that day. I thought of Jennie Levin, who died with her arms folded, who wouldn't go down without a fight. And I thought of Mary Goldstein, who will forever be in my heart. My only hope is that this tragedy will not go unremembered, and that we, the Triangle Shirtwaist girls, will be remembered dearly.

Note: This story is written in memory of the 146 who died on March 25th, 1911, during the Triangle Shirtwaist Factory fire.

THE TOWN OF GOLDENLEAF

Victoria Stone

Wind whistled through the trees and rain splattered the forest floor. A dense layer of fog covered the leaf-strewn ground and the moon illuminated the pathway. Brooke shivered and tightened her grip on her flashlight. Oh, why had she agreed to that bet? A bag of Snickers no longer seemed like a fair trade for walking through the dark, scary forest.

Brooke had heard the stories her friends always told, but never believed them. She had always thought she was mature, that she would never believe in some childish myth, and yet here she was, flinching at every small sound. As she started walking forward again, she felt something holding her down, and she tripped. Brooke screamed and tried vainly to crawl away from whatever was grabbing her foot. Then Brooke craned her neck to see her attacker and was relieved to see a tangle of branches from a dead bush.

With a sigh, Brooke untangled herself and stood up.

"I'm such an idiot," Brooke muttered to herself and continued walking. Then suddenly she stopped, feeling as if she was being watched from off to the right. She slowly turned around, holding her flashlight in front of her like a weapon. A twig snapped and the wind started to pick back up. The place where the sound came from was covered in shadow. Brooke slowly walked forward.

"Is anyone there?" she called out, but there was no response. "Violet, Troy, stop trying to scare me, it isn't working," Brooke tried to say bravely, but her voice trembled and gave away her true emotions. She took a hesitant step forward, and as she neared the shadowy area she thought she could make out loud hard, labored panting...

"Boo!" came a loud voice from behind Brooke and she jumped, hitting her head on an overhanging branch.

"Yeah right, you definitely weren't scared, ha!" Troy laughed and Brooke reddened in embarrassment.

"I was not scared!" Brooke insisted and rubbed her bruised head.

"Yeah right, that's why you jumped and hit your head, scaredy-cat!" Violet laughed, punching her friend lightly in the shoulder.

"Why are you guys here, anyway?" Brooke asked, changing the subject.

"To make sure you were not eaten by a werewolf," Troy smirked.

"Oh, you guys are just horrible liars! I know you came here just to scare me," Brooke sighed.

"Maybe," Troy answered mischievously.

Violet added, "Alright, let's go. We gave you enough of a scare already, so let's leave the forest together."

***

The trio of friends walked forward, and at first they walked with confidence and assurance. Not long afterward, however, Brooke and her friends started to feel uneasy and frightened by the eerie forest. The trees, which looked beautiful, tall and proud in daylight, looked like shells of their former selves in the dark and fog. They had lifeless, grey finger-like branches that seemed to snag on every piece of clothing the children had on.

The wind picked up once more, making a sound that resembled a howl. Brooke shivered. "How much farther," Brooke asked, hugging herself tightly.

Troy looked back at her, "I don't know."

"I think we are lost," Violet added, looking around in confusion.

Brooke growled, "Oh, that's just peachy!"

They walked slowly and nervously, looking around with wide, frightened eyes. Brooke suddenly stopped, hearing footsteps behind her. "What was that?" Brooke whipped her head nervously back and forth. A loud, mournful howl echoed through the trees.

Troy froze, "Did you hear that?"

"Umm, guys," Violet whispered, "you should take a look at this." Violet was pointing to a tree that had five long scratches down its center.

Brooke looked at her friends with horror, "Stop trying to scare me. I know you set this up."

Violet's eyes widened, "Why would we do something like that? No, I promise we didn't." Troy nodded in agreement, but Brooke still looked doubtful. "We have to go or else whatever is in this forest is going to come!" Violet predicted impatiently.

No one moved, though. They were all staring at the clump of trees that hid what they thought would be a monster. Then as they watched, two green eyes shone from the trees.

A hairy monster came out. It would have looked like a man, if not for the fur covering his face, legs, and arms. He was wearing a short-sleeved shirt and shorts. He lifted his hand to shield his eyes from the light of the three flashlights.

Brooke, Troy, and Violet screamed. The three children ran through the trees, trying their best to not look back. When they finally broke the tree line, Brooke's mom ran over to them. She quickly noticed their horrified faces and trembling hands.

"What happened? You three look like you've seen a ghost!" Brooke's mom said worriedly. Not one of the children could speak; they were still frozen in fear.

"Were-werewolf!" Violet finally screeched.

***

No one in their small town, Goldenleaf, believed them, not until two days after the incident. That was when a man ran into Goldenleaf from the forest. He was holding the limp body of a fawn.

"Vampire in the forest! Vampire in the forest!" the man spluttered and held the dead animal up for everyone to see.

"Look at these fang marks! A vampire bit this fawn and left it to die!" The man screamed and pointed madly at the two punctures on the fawn's neck. Immediately, everyone remembered the children's story and although Troy, Violet, and Brooke had recovered, the incident was still fresh in people's minds.

"Oh! This town, it's full of monsters!" yelled a woman from the crowd of people that had come to see what was happening. Immediately, the people started talking all at once with panic and fear in their voices.

"No! It might not be anything. Let's not all get scared of something that may or may not be real," a man's strong voice snapped the crowd out of their panic.

"Yes, we should not jump to conclusions from such small and unproven evidence. Just to be sure, be careful in the woods. I am not warning you of monsters, but of the more likely wild animal in our forest," a woman added. Some in the crowd seemed to agree with what the man and woman were saying, although many still looked doubtful.

Seven days after the incident, two teens snuck into an old, abandoned house on the edge of town. "Aww come on, stop being such a baby! There's nothing in there anyway," Josh had sighed.

"Yeah right, then why are we here?" Emily asked.

"To show we aren't like those other babies that are afraid of all those supernatural occurrences happening. Seriously Emily, I mean come on, you know it's all fake," Josh responded with a roll of his eyes.

Emily crossed her arms, "who knows. A lot of people believe it and, even if the house is not haunted, it's old. It can collapse and crush us. We shouldn't go," Emily insisted.

"Hmm, maybe you are like one of those other babies. Fine, stay here, but I'm going in there," Josh said and, to prove his point, he started walking toward the house.

Emily hesitated for a second but then followed her friend as he walked into the house.

The door of the house was slightly ajar, but the two teens did not think much of it. The door, strangely, had to be pushed inward and it made a horrifyingly loud, "creak!" Everything inside seemed to be from the nineteenth century. A chandelier with candles instead of light bulbs hung from the ceiling. A faded green sofa and a red and brown rug were placed in the middle of the room. Wind blew in from an open window, causing the curtains to fly, but not causing the grey mass of dust and spider webs that covered everything in sight to move. Just the steps of the two kids stepping into the room sent plumes of thick dust flying into the air.

Emily and Josh coughed but did not move. Finally the

dust settled but for fear of the same thing happening, they did not take another step into the room.

"Now what?" Emily asked Josh as a cold feeling settled in her stomach.

"I don't know. Let's see what we can find," Josh said and walked forward, making dust fly into the air.

"No, wait. Don't…" Emily started to say, but was stopped by her coughing fit.

Covering her nose, she ran forward to walk beside Josh, who was already reaching a wooden staircase.

Then suddenly, just as Josh started to lift his foot to go up the stairs, the door slammed shut. Josh and Emily froze, staring at the door in horror. After the initial shock faded, Josh set his foot down and stood up straighter.

"Must have been the wind. Come on let's go," he said.

"Josh, I have a bad feeling about this. I think we should leave," Emily told Josh nervously.

Josh sighed and shook his head. "What, are you scared?" Josh snickered.

Emily's eyes widened in astonishment; Josh had been so rude today and he was not usually this way. "What's wrong with you? Yeah, I'm scared, deal with it. I am leaving," Emily growled.

Josh frowned and said honestly, "Emily, I was just joking with you. If you want, we'll leave."

"Yes, thank you. Let's just not step on the… Did-did you

see that?" Emily's voice went from relieved to horrified in a second.

Josh looked around in surprise, "What's wrong, Emily? I didn't see anything," he said.

Emily pointed at the chandelier with a trembling hand. It was floating in mid-air and moving slightly from left to right. Emily had not seen anything holding up the chandelier before, but had guessed that she could not see the chain from her angle at the time. Josh ran up the stairs quickly as he saw the floating object and Emily followed him, trying not to look back. When Emily and Josh were about to reach the top of the stairs; something landed on top of their heads.

It was a spider web that stuck to their hair, complete with three hairy tarantulas.

Emily let out a blood-curdling screech and ran back downstairs, throwing off the tarantula on her head. Her hands were now sticky with spider webs, but she did not bother wiping them off. She also did not seem to notice the dust rising from the ground underneath her as she ran.

Emily finally reached the door and pulled it open quickly. She did not stop even to catch her breath until she finally made it to her house. Josh made it there a few minutes after she had arrived. He looked as horrified as Emily; whose face was pale and sickly looking. The teens explained their misadventure to their parents, who in turn, told others. It was now well known that in the same town where a werewolf was sighted and evidence of the existence of a vampire was found, there was also now a haunted house.

***

But that was not all! Ten days after the werewolf incident, another strange thing occurred.

"Please come! My grandmother's skin is getting red and she has a fever!" a boy screamed at everyone at the town's small meeting place.

Immediately everyone feared the worst – another impossible event. Filled with fear and curiosity, they followed the boy without question. When they arrived at his grandmother's house, they immediately noticed a small, old woman lying on a bed. The poor woman's face was red and painful-looking. Even her nose seemed to be covered with blood. Her arms and legs were also scarlet and swollen.

"Not something else! Oh, we live in a monster-ridden town! We are all going to die!" a woman screeched as she left the room, "Everyone for themselves!"

The rest of the people that had come to see the boy's grandmother stood there frozen in shock; looking from the poor, old lady to the door where the woman had vanished.

"You have to help my grandmother, please!" the boy pleaded with desperateness.

A man looked at the boy coldly, "Mrs. Jackson is right. We need to fend for ourselves. Who knows if your grandma is contagious? I am sorry for your problem, but I cannot help you."

And with that the man left and two more people followed him.

"Cowards!" a man spat at them as they left.

The boy looked on with worried eyes, "Can you please help my grandma?"

"Yes, I will. At the time of our greatest need, we must stick together, not go our separate ways. Working together we can accomplish more, so why not work with each other instead of against each other?" a woman said.

The people who remained agreed, and because of the woman's words a wonderful thing happened. The townspeople of Goldenleaf worked together to solve what they called, "impossible or supernatural occurrences and dangers."

***

The first thing they did was go into the forest looking for the werewolf. They searched for days until finally, the same children that found the werewolf the last time, found him again. They had also gone on a search party with their parents and Brooke's neighbor. But this time they did not run. They just stood there, frozen in shock. They had been told that they were crazy at first, and even now that the other people believed them, they did not believe themselves.

The werewolf looked at them with sorrow and shame. His

green eyes did not seem to glow like a fierce wolf's anymore. Now it seemed like his eyes glistened with unshed tears.

"I am sorry. I know I am a monster," the werewolf/man said tearfully and looked away. He sounded like a regular person, although his voice was much smoother than any man Brooke had met. Brooke immediately felt ashamed that she had run from this poor man. Monster or not, he seemed to have feelings and Brooke knew she had hurt them.

"No, I am sorry. I shouldn't have judged you by how you look or by what you are, or rather what I think you are," Brooke said honestly.

The werewolf smiled sadly, "Don't worry, you are not the first, nor will you be the last. Oh, and in case you were wondering, I am not a werewolf. I have Hypertrichosis. It is a rare disease where you have excess body hair all over your body. I can understand your confusion though, if you thought I was a werewolf. After all, Hypertrichosis is informally called "werewolf syndrome." My name's Keith, by the way."

Brooke felt even more guilt at the man's words. Everyone had thought that the hairy figure she and her friends had seen was a werewolf. No one had even thought about the possibility of a regular man with an unusual disease. Not one person, including herself.

"I'm sorry, Keith, I had no idea. I just have one question, what are you doing here in the forest?" Brooke asked.

Keith smiled, "Here, I am alone and free. No one really judges me because not many people come here. No one knows my name, so I can wear comfortable clothes. Everywhere else, however, I always have to wear a jacket with a hood and pants to hide my condition."

Brooke nodded and smiled back, "I understand. Goodbye and have a great day."

The next supernatural occurrence they solved was the fang marks in the fawn. They performed an autopsy on the fawn and discovered that it had died due to poison. The poison was identified as a copperhead snake's venom. Although it was unusual for a snake to bite a fawn on the neck, the town's people accepted the explanation. It seems the snake had bitten the fawn while it was resting on the ground.

It also turned out that the "haunted house" had been used as an actual haunted house attraction in the 1920s. A combination of a wheel and tilted sticks was what made the door close once weight is applied at a certain point. The chandelier was suspended in what seemed like mid-air by a transparent string. The fake tarantulas and spider webs were also set to fall when weight was applied at a certain step.

The woman with red skin was taken to the hospital. A doctor there diagnosed her with Erysipelas, a condition that caused a fever and her skin to become swollen and red. The woman stayed in the hospital for a few days but she healed quickly and without any signs of what happened to her.

Solving these unusual occurrences brought the town together. Everyone realized that working together and not panicking is best. Plus, things aren't always what they seem to be.

UPPER SCHOOL AUTHORS

DREAMLAND

Katherine Berlatsky

The stars outside the farmhouse were obscured by clouds; the full moon's glow was only barely visible. Rain pattered on the roof, dripping through the leaks and into the well, making an odd echoing sound as it merged with the water underground. Lightning flashed, glinting off the lightning rod, allowing the weather vane to be momentarily visible. A crow cawed in the darkness, the flutter of its wings disappearing into the thunderous, thick clouds. Another lightning bolt struck, this one hitting the rod which guided the electricity underground and into the water reservoir that connected to the well.

For a moment, a sort of glow seemed to emanate from the well – and then it was gone. Inside the house, the grey cat sat on a windowsill, its tail flicking back and forth all through the night. The next morning the sun was out, leaving as the only evidence of the previous night's storm the wet grass and the steady dripping of water off of the cottage's roof.

***

The old woman who lived there – Liana – woke up at daybreak to the tabby cat sitting on her chest, meowing. With a groan, she pushed it off her body and stood up, her back creaking. She shuffled to her bedroom door and pushed it open, catching a glimpse of the black cat as she ran down the hall. Liana made her way through the kitchen and to the front door. She picked up the wooden bucket that was next to the door and stepped outside.

Liana shivered. The air was brisk and a cool breeze blew through the clearing in the woods where her house stood. Steadying herself, she walked the 25 feet or so to the well and hooked the bucket onto the string. Using the crank, she lowered the bucket into the well, grimacing at the effort it took her to bring it back up. Unhooking the bucket, she walked slowly back to the house, careful not to spill a drop.

The old woman took a sip and then placed the bucket back by the door, frowning. Was it her imagination, or did the water taste faintly of iron? She shook it off, and by the end of the day she had stopped noticing it, despite the fact that the concoction was slowly strengthening…

***

That night, she lay in bed listening to the noises outside as she always did, letting them lull her to sleep.

***

Twenty years younger, the woman stood on the edge of the cliff, arms spread wide. She spun, round and round, letting the wind play with her hair. She laughed and laughed and laughed, not even noticing as lightning struck behind her. It broke the stones on the cliff, stone that had stood strong for thousands of years, and it was only as she started to fall that she stopped laughing and started to scream.

A familiar face appeared over the edge, staring down at her, but she couldn't quite place it. It captured her attention for a moment until it withdrew as if it had never been there.

Liana could see the grey of the cliff rushing past her as she fell, and feel the air pulling her apart, driving the rain like needles into her skin. The ground was getting closer and closer. She closed her eyes as she drew nearer, overcome with fear. But her hopes and fear didn't stop her from slamming into the ground. Nor did it stop her bones from shattering, driving themselves through her skin as the rain washed away her blood. Suddenly the rain and the wind were gone and she was lying on her bed.

Shaking, Liana opened her eyes to see a man with the same face as the one on the cliff standing at the foot of her bed. She screamed and scrambled to sit up. "Who are you?"

she asked, her voice trembling with a mixture of fear, adrenaline, and confusion.

The man only shook his head and walked away, stepping through the wall, shadows curling around him. Liana stood up, tried to follow and to understand what had just, impossibly, happened, but the ground shook and she fell back into the bed. She was panicking now as lightning hit the ground right in front of her, causing a rift in the ground under the house.

A red glow was pouring out of the gaping hole and Liana, scarcely knowing what she was doing, stood up and tentatively walked over to it. The crack was much deeper and much wider than it really should have been, seeming to extend to the core of Earth itself.

Climbing the walls was… something. Was it fire? It was. And it was getting closer. Liana could feel the heat on her face. Rushing out of the room and to the front door, she grabbed the bucket and ran back to her room. She poured the water over the flames, but it seemed to only act as an inflammatory, and the flames grew higher. Frantically, she looked around, searching for anything she could use to stop its growth. But now the flames were on the floor. She jumped onto the bed, thinking only of the impossibility of the situation, but the fire was eating through her bedstead, her blankets, her sheets.

Now Liana was standing on the bed. The fire began to burn through her toes, and she could see the charred flesh hanging off the bone. In no time, it was on her heels and she was screaming; the red heat was climbing up her legs and the flesh was bubbling. She couldn't stop the pain as it reached her knees, climbing up to her stomach. It was destroying the soft flesh, briefly revealing organs before devouring them as well. Liana couldn't stop screaming as it reached her chest, and her heart was on fire; she could see it burning until the flames obstructed her vision. She knew she was going to die, and the blackness was coming in, a welcome relief, and...

***

Liana woke up, choking on her own sobs; but she was on her own bed and in her own room. It took her a moment for her eyes to adjust to the darkness around her, but when they did, she thought she could make out a dark shadow on the edge of her bed, looking like a second blanket. And with a certain stretch of the imagination, it appeared to be moving slowly...

Lightning flashed outside her window, bright enough to allow Liana to see that the shape in the darkness wasn't one being. It was a roiling, disgusting mass of spiders and, standing behind them, was the same man as before. She tried to stay calm – after all, it was only another dream – but the spiders were getting closer, and now there was enough light for her to see them. They were big and furry with sharp teeth and giant, red eyes, and now they were on her toes.

She pulled her feet back, trying to dislodge the spiders, but a couple of them clung on and were moving faster, up her leg.

Trying to ignore the spiders, which she felt sure weren't real – no, make that not really real – Liana looked at the man, who was watching amusedly. "Who are you?" she asked again.

"No one of consequence," he said, gesturing at the spiders. As if moving as one, they surged forward, crawling up her stomach. She shuddered – it was impossible not to – mantra of, "Not real, not real, not real" going through her head.

"Please," she said.

"You'd rather I didn't," he said, waving once more at the spiders. They were on her face now and, no matter how hard she tried, she couldn't deny their presence any longer. Liana opened her mouth to scream. But she choked as one of the spiders crawled into her mouth and down her throat. She couldn't breathe.

Every time Liana gasped for air, the spider forced itself farther down her throat, and even though there was still some conscious part of her that knew it was a dream, the rest of her was asking, What if? What if? as its furry legs tickled her throat.

The rest of the attackers had retreated, becoming shadows around the man and then disappearing. She could feel the spider crawling in her ribcage now. It was approaching her heart and she stood up, retching, but nothing was helping. The man was watching and laughing. Liana could feel the spider walking on her heart – literally on her heart – and it was raising one thin leg, about to poke it down through her heart. It happened! She could feel the leg driving through her heart, creating a tiny hole.

Liana tore at her chest, stabbing at it with her glasses, desperate to get it out. There was a hole in her heart, getting bigger, pouring blood. She gasped, her throat suddenly filling with blood as the spider's leg made it all the way through her heart. She screamed as she collapsed onto the floor. Her consciousness was slipping away as blood poured from the wound in her chest. Her eyesight was blurring and failing. Liana knew she was gone. The image of the man blurred as he appeared to stand up and then disappear.

And then everything was black.

***

And she opened her eyes, safe in bed.

Liana was on her back for some reason, which was odd in itself, as she never slept on her back. But because she was on her back, she could see the hole where her ceiling had been. It was now gone. In place of it was a huge black cloud in the sky. Lightning flashed and she felt a drop of rain on her face.

Another dream, she thought. For a moment, when she had first opened her eyes, she had thought that it was reality. It seemed real. Another drop. And another. Soon, it was pouring and somehow her hair was dripping wet. But Liana wasn't complaining – this dream wasn't nearly as bad as the others. She continued to think that way until she looked over the side of the bed and saw the water rising.

Her bed began floating, which was odd, but she knew the effect wouldn't last for long. Liana sat up and turned sideways, placing her feet in the water. It was, to her surprise, neither hot nor cold, but a pleasant enough temperature. But the temperature wouldn't matter if she drowned. The room was filling with water and soon it was up to her knees. She slid off the bed and into the water. As Liana stood in the room the cold water reached up to her neck.

Liana began treading water and was suddenly aware of the man next to her. She didn't look at him, afraid that if she acknowledged his presence, he would make it worse. They treaded water next to each other in silence for a moment, before the voice of the man broke the silence.

"I'm surprised you haven't asked again."

Still not looking at him, she replied, "What would be the point? You wouldn't answer anyway."

"I will this time," he promised.

She took a moment, concentrating as the water rose, and then said, "Who are you?"

"My name is Nico. I'm stuck in the dream world, just like you. I'm here to offer you help."

"Some help you've been giving me lately," she said and then gasped as she was briefly dragged under the water. Liana reemerged, coughing.

"It was necessary. But this is important," the mysterious man said.

"I'm listening."

"In the next dream, you will see a door. In order to get out of the dream world, you must get through the door. Otherwise, you're stuck. Forever."

Liana considered that final word and her fate for a moment. She didn't trust the man, obviously. But what harm could it do? "Okay," she said finally. "But one more question: Why I am here in the first place?"

"Lightning in your well. There was an odd chemical deposit, the last instance of which was over 100 years ago. And that one was in my well."

Liana nodded, sensing that it was a bad idea to ask any more questions. The water was nearly at the ceiling as she allowed herself to drown, sinking slowly to the bottom of the room as her lungs constricted. Liana felt her chest burning, fighting not to come back up. She could feel her body slowing reaching the bottom and, with a last burst of willpower, closed her eyes.

***

Liana opened her eyes again and realized that she was on her bed. She looked to her right, then to her left, saw the door and stood up. It was more of a glowing portal type of object than a door, but she stood up and stepped toward it, confused that nothing was trying to stop her.

Liana paused in front of the object for a second and then lifted her hand, allowing a single finger to pass through. She

fell to the ground, eyes closed, and then opened them again –
she was on her bed.

Liana smiled. As jubilance overcame her, she turned her
head and looked out the window. Outside, lightning flashed.

LOCKED OUT

Kayla Blake

t had been four years since the three delinquents had seen civilization. They were in desperate need to have a decent conversation about the weather, sports… something. Four years of having the same conversations, seeing the same barren wasteland, and not knowing what was going to happen at any given moment had taken a toll.

Bucky, the oldest of the three, was naturally in charge. His name resembled him well because he was very stubborn and, like a lot of stubborn animals, was known to "buck." Sam was the next oldest at 17. She was slowly going crazy, but was still somewhat there. Ben was the youngest at the mere age of 14. He was Sam's little brother and considered the baby of the group by her, and even though he wouldn't admit it, he was glad that he was the youngest because he didn't want the responsibility of being in charge.

To get you caught up to speed, let's go to the very

beginning… or at least three weeks ago. It began as a normal day. They woke up at 6:30, departed for the school bus at 7:00, arrived to school at 7:15. It was a strict schedule that had consequences if someone was seconds behind.

Bucky was 18 years old and in the last year of school. All three of the teens attended Brighton High School in Brighton, Colorado. At school, the trio was not well-known but they knew each other and that's all they really needed. So, everything was normal up until the second tardy bell rang.

Ben's Log

There was violence all around. It was like a scene out of an action movie with flames the size of Colorado itself engulfing me and my classmates. Smoke clouded my visibility. Through the confusion, I thought I heard pounding on the door, as if someone was trying to come in and help us escape, but my brief minute of hope was soon deflated as I soon realized the sound was my heart beating within my chest. Not a second could be lost, so I tried to find an exit.

What I didn't realize was that the smoke had gathered in the middle of the room now, creeping its way down to floor level. I found myself entering a completely different world that looked like nothing I knew, except for the familiar smoke and a few stray ashes floating around. Not much could be done and escape for me and my soon-to-be-dead classmates seemed out of the question. Feeling alone and tired, I began to slowly slide down the back wall of the classroom and slowly fell into a calm slumber. Giving up completely, I felt like a failure and thought that I would rather die a failure than to live with the knowledge that everyone knew about my lost efforts.

Sam's Log

It happened all so fast that I could not comprehend a single event that had occurred. All I could remember was that I was taking out a pencil for the morning's daily bell-ringer when all hell broke loose in the back of the classroom. It was sort of a fiery explosion. Concrete from the walls flew in all directions and there was no time to try and figure out what caused the explosion. After hearing the painful, sharp ring in my ears, I began to come back to consciousness. Complete fear took over all of the muscles in my body; I was rendered speechless and somewhat paralyzed.

What I do recall was that there was a swift pain in my left leg, but then it left as quickly as it had shown up. Bucky was over me saying something, but my ears were still trying to work so I couldn't understand him. I knew it was urgent though, because Bucky never had such a look of panic on his face. For a second – just for a second – it looked like it was guilt that I saw flash through his eyes. But that's preposterous, why would Bucky feel guilty about this? It's not like it was his fault.

Bucky's Log

I swore that I would have Sam and Ben out of school by the time the explosion hit, but it came early. How was I supposed to know that the attempt would come ten minutes early? It was set up last weekend, when I found myself working with some bad company. The name of the group was WDLS, which stood for "We Don't Like Society." The whole idea of the group was to get back at society for making all our lives selfish and convincing everyone that they had to follow the norm because they shouldn't want to be a lone wolf.

I was heading home from Whole Foods with some fruit for my mom for her party tonight. All of her "health geeks" were coming over. It was always a lame idea to me, but it kept my mom occupied and not hovering over me, so I dealt with it. But, as I was coming down the road, I was stopped by a bunch of kids in masks and black outfits.

My first instinct, of course, was to run the rest of the way home, but then I heard one of them speak to me – it was a girl. I restrained myself from running, because they were new to me and seeming interesting. I never thought a girl could be the leader of a group like this, but it now makes sense to me. Girls are picked on the most by society. They always hear how they aren't skinny, tall, or pretty enough to be popular, so who better to start a group against society than a female?

I thought I would stay and hear what she wanted, but I didn't plan on joining this group – my mom would punish me if I did. The mysterious girl started off by introducing the group and the purpose behind it. It all made sense to me. What caught me off guard was that she was a young girl and so were the others – probably between the ages of 13 and 17. They asked me to help them set off an explosion at Brighton High School this week.

How could I respond to that? Heck, how would a normal person respond to that? I thought about running home, but wouldn't that be cliché? My guess was that she had thought about this possibility, and probably had someone who could chase after me and catch me before I could even reach the next mailbox down the street. So I stuck it out and pondered what my excuse was going to be for not helping them. It varied between not knowing how to make a bomb (which she probably already knew) and claiming I knew a cop that could arrest her. Giving up on all my excuses, I finally told her straight up that no, I wouldn't do it. I was so nervous that it felt like I was going to have a small heart attack while waiting for her response. I was preparing for a nasty remark or threat, but it was worse. She said "okay" calmly and walked away.

I knew the mysterious girl was going to set off the bomb anyway, but at least I knew the date and time because she had already told me. I could get Sam and Ben out before it occurred. On the other hand, I had been stupid enough to not think that she would change the time or the date of the explosion.

Ben's Log

I hate hospitals. They're the worst. I wasn't going to last in here more than a week and then I would probably have to be put in the section of this hospital for the insane. There were tubes wrapped around me so tight that at night I had nightmares that boa constrictors were squeezing my whole body until I couldn't breathe; and then I would wake up. The doctors would come rushing in and try to calm me down, but half the time I would still be flipping out, not because of the nightmares, but because of how much I want to leave this place. The doctors said I had another two weeks for recovery, or more if I couldn't stabilize my blood pressure. As a precaution, when I'm well enough to walk, they said they would send me to therapy classes to lower my blood pressure.

I kept trying to remember, but I had no idea how I got out of that burning building and into Brighton Medical Center. The nurses wouldn't tell me who brought me here. They kept saying, "It's too dangerous, he can never know." What does that even mean?

One dreary Monday morning, the main doctor came in. I called him Dr. Smiles because he always had a goofy grin on his face, and told me that today would be the last day and then I would be sent to a laboratory to be studied. This news didn't bother me as much as it should have, now that I look back at it, because they had told me earlier that something was placed inside of me and more testing needed to be done.

They didn't have the technology required to study me, so they planned on sending me away after I recovered. The laboratory was set up somewhere in the desert, which I figured was a very discrete location. I hoped that whatever they were going to do to me, it was not going to hurt.

Sam's Log

I was told that I was in Brighton Medical Center and that Bucky and Ben were here as well, just on another floor level. I so desperately wanted to see them and make sure they were okay, but first I had to make sure that I was okay. Apparently the explosion that went off in the school was right next door to the classroom that Bucky and I were in. I guessed that I was probably in worse condition than anyone in the school because the floor gave way under me, and since I was on the bottom, everyone landed on me when we hit the floor. I don't know how I comprehended what all the doctors were telling me, because I was in a coma. I was in a coma for about two weeks. And the doctors said that if I'm going to wake up, it would have to be soon and it may be in a different location. They planned to send me to a laboratory in a desert somewhere to be monitored around the clock.

I didn't want to go. I wanted to go home to see my parents and friends, but obviously I didn't have much of a say at that moment – I guessed that I had to be a part of their scientific study. I hoped I could make it through the ordeal. I also over-heard them say that my mom died in the explosion while attending a PTA meeting. If I was ever going to wake up, I was going to be motherless.

Bucky's Log

I felt terrible and really wished I was dead. For all I knew, everyone else was dead. I probably wouldn't wake up to any friends still alive, so what was the point? Some fingerprints on my backpack were found and they were linked to the girl who asked me to make the explosion happen in the first place. That little monster put her hands all over my back-pack. I didn't think anything of it before; I just thought she was holding my backpack so I couldn't run away. Because of her, I was to be sent somewhere discrete in some desert. I would be part of an experiment to see if I really did cause that explosion. By my SAT scores and semester grades, they should have been able to tell that I wasn't the one who did it. I couldn't assemble something that high tech.

They also wouldn't tell me if Sam and Ben were alive. They thought it was dangerous for me to know, because they thought the explosion was to hurt those I knew in the first place. I was dragged against my will to the laboratory and had no idea what was going to happen to me. I hated to admit it, but I was definitely scared.

Sam's Log

I was loaded, without care, onto a giant helicopter. I knew they were taking me to the laboratory. But I couldn't I wake up! Somehow, however, I could hear all that was going on around me. It was so frustrating.

It took a while to get to the laboratory. I don't know exactly how long it was, but it was long enough for me to count to sixty about forty times before getting bored. I didn't even know how to tell if I was awake or if I was sleeping, but the next thing I knew I was being unloaded into extreme sunlight and carried through a desert. My guess was that I was being taken to the mysterious laboratory.

Ben's Log

I did all that I could do to try and stop them from taking me. I just wanted to go home and pretend none of this happened... that Sam didn't die. The doctors finally told me that Sam was in a coma and had recently passed. It was the most devastating news I'd ever heard. Why did that stupid explosion have to happen? I swore that, if I ever found out who did it, I would rip them in two.

Bucky's Log

I was drugged (kidnapped basically) and taken to the laboratory. I didn't know this was legal without a parent's consent form or something like that. To think of it, I hadn't seen my parents since the explosion. But anyway, the journey on a helicopter to the lab was long. I remember thinking that I needed some good luck in order to survive.

Ben's Log

The laboratory looked exactly like one of those children's hospitals that looked all happy with brightly painted walls and pictures of hot air balloons, but the reality was that people probably died there from research or testing. I was told to stay in my designated room, but as soon as I was able to walk again, I vowed not to just sit still all day while waited for them to come cut me open like a cow being sent to the market.

I was walking down a hallway, when all of a sudden there was a group of people who rushed inside with someone on a gurney. I assumed it was someone who was hurt badly and hoped that maybe this wicked place would also treat people and not just experiment on them. But as they came closer, I got a good look of who was on that gurney. I truly believed that I had died and then come back to earth.

It was Sam. But it couldn't be. The doctors had told me that she was dead. How could this be? I was so stunned that I barely felt one of the wheels of the gurney run right over my foot. Although the pain should have been excruciating, it wasn't because of the pure shock of what had just taken place. Sam wasn't dead.

Bucky's Log

I didn't care if I was already at the laboratory. I fought hard, as if we hadn't even left Brighton Medical Center yet. They were not taking me in that building to experiment on me. There was only one possible way that these people would get me in that laboratory, and that would be if I was dead. I felt pain in my left thigh and then black spots danced around the rims of my eyes. I knew exactly what they did. They put a tranquilizer dart into my leg.

Sam's Log

Immediately after the sunshine faded, I could hear yelling and feet pounding. Around corners and through doors, I was being pushed on a gurney. I then felt pricking and prodding, and realized I was being hooked up to machines that I had never seen or heard of before. It wasn't painful; it was more like discomfort.

My heart started beating faster and then silence. I don't know how I felt so scared when my heart just stopped. I shouldn't have felt anything at all; I should have been dead. But this wasn't the case. Instead, my eyes shot open and I could see again, then my heart slowly started beating.

Ben's Log

The next thing I knew, a bunch of scientists ran up to me and then dragged me back to my room. They put me on the bed and tied straps around my stomach, legs, and arms like I was a cold-blooded killer. Funny thing was, they were the ones doing the killing.

Bucky's Log

I was thrown into a sort of cell. Since I woke up with no one around me, I had to settle for letting my anger out on the wall. I was mad, sad, and confused all at the same time. I had killed Sam, injured Ben, and probably just got sentenced to death. All in all, it was a rough couple of weeks.

Sam's Log

After I awoke, I was put on a stabilizer and was told that in just a few days I might be able to walk again. After being in a coma for a couple of weeks, you really start feeling thankful that you are able to communicate. They told me that once I could walk I would be sent to the main council room for questioning. I had no idea what that was about, but I thought it had to do with the whole "explosion thing" at the school.

Bucky's Log

No one came into my room for a few hours, so I just sat in the corner and zoned out. I tried to leave this horrible world behind and go into a better place, but the memories were so haunting. A scientist finally came up to the bars and said something. I was still zoned out, so I didn't comprehend what he said. Then he came inside the cell and yanked me up. He told me there would be a meeting in the council room in a few days and threw me back to the floor. I didn't try to comprehend what he just said because I was already dead, wasn't I?

Ben's Log

After they got me to calm down, they told me there would be a meeting held in the council room. I didn't know what that meant or what it would be about, but maybe I would be able to see Sam again. That's all I really wanted. Even though I persistently asked the scientists where she was, they always simply say that they didn't know. I know for a fact the person I saw was Sam and all I wanted to do was see her.

Sam's Log

It was time to go to the council room for the meeting they have been telling me about for the past week. Apparently it was a big deal. The first thing I remember noticing when I got to the room was that there was already a little boy in the room. He was sitting in the pews already. I walked up to take a seat next to him, and when saw him clearly I realized it was Ben! I couldn't believe that he was here. I was so happy, but then I wondered why he was here.

Ben didn't even notice I was there. I ran up to him and gave him a big bear hug. Ben jumped and struggled to get away, but then realized it was me and soon his attempts to escape halted. Then the back room opened and in the midst of the doorway stood a tall, handsome boy. It was Bucky and, at that moment, I began to cry. I hadn't realized how much I missed my friends.

Bucky's Log

I walked into the council room for the meeting, but what I walked in on was unsuspected. It was Sam and Ben hugging. What were they doing here? I thought Sam had died! Sam's not dead! This was great news until I realized that she was here at this horrible laboratory and so was Ben. I ran up to them and hugged them until we couldn't breathe anymore. But the slamming of a gavel cut off this happy reunion. I knew that the meeting was about to start.

Court Council

"You three have been bought to HARL – Health and Research Laboratory – because something is different about you. I would like to ask a few questions about the explosion that went off at your school," said the judge in charge of the Court Council. The biggest of the three kids got an anxious look in his eye and his feet began squirming. Obviously he knew exactly what I was talking about. "I don't know if you've heard but you were the only survivors of that explosion," I continued. By the confused looks on their faces, no one had told them.

"Yes, you were the only survivors and we believe it was because an explosion was not the only thing that took place that day at your school. After the explosion went off, a toxic gas was released in the school. Although you had injuries, you did not die. We have brought you all to HARL to do research on your bodies and try to find out how you survived this toxin. However, this toxin was not only released in this explosion, it is now being released by some forms of cars and other objects used in everyday life. We here at HARL believe that you are a new generation that has adapted to this new toxin and we want to know how you do it. So we have composed tests to see what makes you different. These tests will be difficult and may involve sacrifices that have to be made. So be brave and do what you do best: survive."

Bucky's Log

During that whole meeting I was stunned by every word that was said. We were the only survivors! So now we will have to do tests? GREAT! Not looking forward to this, not looking forward to this at all.

Sam's Log

How could we be the only survivors? What makes us so different? I was never one of those different girls that stood out. I was always kind of shy and blended in with the crowd. And what about the tests the court council was talking about? Will they be hard? And what did the councilor mean by sacrifices having to be made? I'm afraid.

Ben's Log

I was so happy to see Bucky and Sam, but I really didn't want to have to undergo testing at all. I'm not different. It was just a miracle that I survived, that's all. I wanted the scientists to know that there's nothing special about me.

Ending

The three children were put into a large box, which was then shot out into the middle of the desert. What was the point of this? This was their first test. The scientists believed that they probably wouldn't last too long. Somehow the three friends survived. They ran up to the side of the walls and started pounding their fists on them. They didn't know why they were trapped inside this box, except that it was somehow a test for them.

Little did the three children know, but the world had been destroyed by the toxin. They were placed out in the outside world, while the rest of society had that survived was inside the laboratory with the scientists, living and watching these three young children to see how they reacted to being outside with the toxin. If the children survived, they would be studied in order to understand why the outside air and toxins didn't kill them, how to evolve, and if a cure was possible. But for now the kids would have to survive on the outside with the rest of the world observing them from inside the box.

MY STORY

Olivia Buzzanca

walk in a room full of cubicles and people typing as fast as possible to finish their work. This was never my ideal occupation, but for now it will have to do. My new boss shows me to my very own desk surrounded be a sea of others. Did I make the right decision? Is this what I want to do? I search desperately in my mind for the answers to these questions, but I can't seem to find them.

Just the other day, I was thrilled to get the call back from my interviewer and, at that time, I had immediately responded, "Yes, I would love to start on Monday!" I was just happy that I might have the chance to live a normal, everyday life that had always seemed like a nightmare, but now felt like a dream. I sit down in front of my computer and I complete the work that my boss set before me.

I think about the name my parents gave me, Alissa Ann Jones, and I find myself typing this name into my computer and seeing the pop-up on my screen that reads "no results." This is exactly what I thought would happen and I am pleased to know that she no longer exists anymore.

I take a quick bathroom break to freshen up after hours of work. As I walk in to the restroom, I get a taste of gossip from a pack of girls walking out. "She must be the new girl," I hear. I only make out inaudible murmurs and faint laughter as they move further down the hallway. I glance up in the mirror and see an unknown girl staring back with big, blue eyes and dark brown, pin-straight hair. She acts the part of being a confident young lady who has recently decided to move to the Big Apple. I laugh, because I know the truth about her.

I think about the plane ride with my parents that happened months ago and the long walk through the woods after it crashed in Pennsylvania. I was alone and the only survivor in the "accident." I blamed myself for their deaths and remember my previous job. To my parents, we were taking a nice family vacation to the Sunshine State – Florida. It wouldn't have been a vacation for me though, because I would have been constantly in fear of my life. Florida would have been more of an escape from who I thought was my boss. It is now obvious that he knew my plan and took full advantage of that. He wasn't trying to kill my parents; he only wanted to get rid of me.

This is my story.

***

I worked for the witness protection program and my former boss had discovered I had grown attached to a family that we were helping. The first thing a new employee of the witness protection program does is sign a document saying she or he will not take part in any of the clients' lives after helping them. It didn't seem like much, but I guess I thought wrong. I knew it was risky, but they needed my help, and by doing this I risked my own family's lives. I never imagined myself in hiding, but I knew exactly what I needed to do. I needed to start a new life: A new appearance, job, lifestyle, and friends were part of this package deal.

In a daze, I walk back to my cubicle and sit down. The end of my first day is near and I see my boss out of the corner of my eye. He stands at the entrance of my cubicle, "So how was your first day?" Thankfully, all my work was completed and I showed it to him with pride.

I go "home" to my one bedroom apartment. All night I am reminded that I live in New York City, thanks to the never-ending sound of traffic outside my bedroom window. My room is bare, with a light, nude color on my walls, and dark wood flooring. I decided to equip my apartment with only the true necessities for the most basic kind of lifestyle. The blander I am, the less people will notice me. That is a basic idea that the witness protection program uses.

The traffic is dying down now, which makes it easier to fall asleep.

The next morning, I awake to the same noises from earlier in the night. I hop out of bed and pin my hair back to keep it out of my face. I quickly get ready for another day that will hopefully go as smoothly as yesterday.

I walk downstairs after locking my apartment door and double check it multiple times. If there is anything I have learned over my years, it is you can never be too cautious, especially now. I motion for a taxi outside of my apartment and see one stop a second later. I hop in without hesitation or fear of all the possible outcomes of this taxi ride.

"Where do you need to go," the taxi driver asks. I open my mouth to reply, but he seems as though he knows the answer. Where is he taking me? He looks back and a corner of his mouth curls up into a wicked smile. My heart is beating about three times faster than it should be and my stomach drops when I realize he is a former coworker. I don't know his name, but I am sure of it. They found me! Of course they did; it is part of their job to be able to find someone in hiding. I search for an escape route and think about throwing myself out of the moving car, but that would only make matters worse for me.

Instead I ask, "Where are you taking me?"

He responds, "Mr. Rodgers has been waiting for you."

There is a sudden lump in my throat and I want to scream and cry in terror. Mr. Rodgers is the name of my former employer who I have dreaded seeing since the day of the plane crash. The taxi stops in front of a building that is made of purely black glass. I inhale sharply and take a step out of the taxi. Can I still run? No.

A man stands outside of my car door. He is a tall, intimidating man, who has eyes that resemble a black hole. They are the eyes of a killer and a truly awful man that I used to look up to – Mr. Rodgers. He greets me with "Hello, Miss Wells." How does he know my new name? I chose the name Rebecca Wells because I thought it would be a safe name to choose. He holds out a hand and I take it, knowing there is no way out of this situation. We go up an elevator until we reach the 27th floor and begin to walk down a long hallway of closed doors. What is behind them?

He looks at me and says, "I believe we have some things to talk about." This statement is accompanied by an ugly smirk that I had wished I would never see again.

"Please come in Rebecca, or should I still call you Alissa?" My entire body tenses up and I can't move, yet alone answer the discomforting question. My mind starts to play flashbacks of all the times I have had with the man that stands in front of me, who I had claimed to know so well just months ago. One stands out and is continuously playing over and over again in my head.

***

It was years ago and I was interviewing for my job at the time. I had walked into a large building located in Washington,

D.C. and was immediately intimidated by everything, even the receptionist. Then, I tried to gracefully glide into Mr. Rodger's office. Even before I said anything, he knew everything about me. I was so shocked because he practically knew more about me than I knew myself.

I snap out of my flashback and remember where I am, which is standing in front of the man who wants to kill me for such a stupid reason. We walk into a room with a long table in it meant for about 20 people, but today it is only for the two of us. I sit down as he stares out the dark window and there is only silence for a few more moments, until out of nowhere he plainly says, "I know your secret, Mrs. Jones, and I want to say I was utterly shocked to find that it was you out of all of my workers." What is he talking about? What is my secret?

He continues, "You just seemed so innocent and that made me want to trust you, but now I see that I can trust no one but myself."

"Sir, can you please tell me what it is you are talking about?" I respond.

He narrows his eyes and gives me a stare-down like no other. "Don't play stupid. I already know," he says.

"Know what?"

"About four months ago, I found out that I had someone in the office giving information to enemy organizations," he takes a deep breath and starts again. "Or, a double agent, as you would call it. I had a group of my most trusted workers help me figure out who, out of our 200 employees, it was. Mrs. Jones, everything came back to your name."

I can't believe that he thinks I am a double agent. There are so many strange people in the witness protection organization that I would think would be more suspicious than me. Then it hits me; my parents were killed because of false information.

***

Mr. Rodgers walks out of the room after he realizes I have no response to his false claim. I hate being wrongly accused for the smallest things, let alone being wrongly accused of being a double agent. He comes into the room with a group of people now and I suspect that this is the team that came to the conclusion that I was the double agent. He walks back out of the room.

I can't believe that I thought I was on a "kill list" just because I grew attached to a family and didn't think that there was a bigger reason behind it. They all sit down around the table and I see why this large table would actually be of use today. They are all stone-faced and would look frightening even to a person walking past them on a busy New York City sidewalk. They set out candid pictures of me on the table and I look at them with sad eyes that I hoped would change their minds about their claim.

It does not; instead, they all look attentive and eager to explain the whole situation to me. In return, I give the same reaction back to them to show them this means war and a fire lights in my eyes. This isn't how I will go down, not without a battle that they all will remember.

"I have been waiting to meet you, Mrs. Jones," a tall slender man says and, as if rehearsed, they all agree by shaking their heads at the exact same time. I feel like I am surrounded by a pack of wolves out for blood. Mr. Rodgers isn't in the room and I find that strange. The same man, who must be the leader of them all, starts again, "Do you see these pictures," and I shake my head, "Please let me know when you are willing to speak," he says.

My breathing gets faster and I quickly say, "Yes, I do see the pictures, but I am unsure as to why these images are evidence of any false claim you have made of me." My sharpness throws them off and the nod they give me symbolizes a "game-on" attitude.

"I know you very well and know that you are not a double agent, but Mr. Rodgers doesn't know and who do you think he would believe? A nobody that has worked for him for only a few years or a large group of his close friends that have been his partners for many years. I am terribly sorry that you were the unlucky one chosen to be the victim in this framing, but it had to be someone and you fit the part. You see, we are all, in fact, double agents that needed a cover."

It is taking me a while to fully understand that I have been a victim of framing and now am most likely going to be killed, but then a miraculous thing happens. Mr. Rodgers walks into the room again and, this time, his lips are pressed in a thin line and he looks like he might cry. I am so confused about the matter before me, but know he has been secretly listening to this conversation. He looks at me and mouths the words, "I am sorry."

Mr. Rodgers removes the sad expression from his face and turns his head to the group of people with a menacing look in his eyes and it is obvious what will happen to them.

I try not to think of that day or the people who were a part of it. I walked away free with a new life and haven't looked back. I went back to my cubicle job and accepted the fact that a normal and boring life would be best for me. For once, this is the life that I truly want.

THE DIVIDED STATES OF THE AMERICAS

Olivia Eames and Tim Eames

The year is 1965 and I have heard this story from my mother so many times. World War II has been over for 20 years and peace now envelopes the world, albeit a peace enforced by capital punishment and harsh laws that are carried out by the secret police.

The end of the Second World War was swift and proved to be a devastating blow to the Allied Forces. It was well known that there was a race to create the first nuclear bomb, a weapon so powerful it could render a country completely defenseless and bring it to its knees.

The Japanese and the Germans created the first atomic bombs almost simultaneously and beat the United States in the atomic race by a full six months. Hitler decided to prove the power of his new weapon of mass destruction by using it on the thorn in his side for the length of the war – Great Britain, and the city of London in particular. The Emperor of Japan chose his target – the city of Las Vegas in the United States. It was September 2, 1945 and a coordinated attack brought to an end one of the most horrific wars of modern history.

Both the British and Americans were forced to surrender in the wake of such loss of life and the threat of additional bombings. This created a land grab by both the Germans and the Japanese. The Germans controlled all of Europe and Russia, the Japanese controlled the Pacific and China; the largest spoil of the war was the United States.

The United States was divided into two: the Germans controlled the eastern states and the mid-west, while the Japanese controlled the western states and the Rockies, with a buffer zone between the two, which ran from North Dakota to Texas.

As you can imagine, there are many people who were not very happy with this outcome and they began to organize against it.

***

My journey began in the summer of 1965. I was nervous. The movie was already 25 minutes into its run time and my contact had not arrived. It was another propaganda movie being shown of Julie Andrews and Christopher Plummer working in the factories, making the mighty industrial machine that was the Divided States churn.

As I started to doze off, a man in a black coat buttoned to the neck walked toward me and sat down on my left. He was wearing a hat that was pulled down low. He removed his hat and leaned back in a simultaneous movement. From his hat, he removed a business card with the emblem of an eagle embossed on it. The contact handed it to me in silence, nodded, and left the movie theatre.

It was too dark to see the message written in pencil on the reverse side of the card, so I gave the messenger a count of 50 to mingle with the returning workers on the streets of Boston before I rose and walked to the bathroom in order to decipher the message on the card. It was a simple code, but one that had proved to be elusive to the Gestapo. I was to meet my new employer at warehouse 13 on the south docks of Boston Harbor at 7:30 p.m. I had time, so I stopped at Tresca to enjoy a nice meal of lobster and mussels.

I arrived early to the meeting point. It allowed me to scope out the building for potential threats. After 45 minutes, I was convinced that I had not been followed. I walked confidently up to the front door, pushed it open, and made my way to the back of the warehouse. I was looking for the owner – a Mr. Lamont. I found him in his small but clean office that overlooked the whole operation. The facility was part of a large packing and distributing center for the rare minerals mined in the Blue Mountains that were so precious to the new overlords.

Lamont was pouring over a map of the interstate highways of the Divided States as I approached. He was surprised when he noticed my presence and said so in a torrent of profanity that was as colorful as it was descriptive. It took all my diplomatic skills to calm the man down and begin a frank discussion. I presented the card that I had received from the stranger in the movie theatre. He was still suspicious and rightly so; there was a bounty on anyone who would dare to dissent and there were many people who made their living from the secrets of others.

After much back and forth, we came to an agreement that was satisfactory to the both of us. Lamont gave me a key to a GMC truck that was parked in delivery bay nine downstairs, an envelope with money, and a map with an address on it that appeared to be in the middle of nowhere. We made our way downstairs and I climbed into the driver's cab of the GMC and started the engine. All the while, Lamont was giving me last-minute instructions. His final words were "don't trust anyone, don't stop, and wait at the coordinates for a man whose code phrase would be 'It's raining again in England'."

***

All of a sudden, the loading dock exploded in gun fire and many of the workers in the warehouse died under a hail of bullets. I had one choice and one choice only; I slammed the truck into reverse and floored it.

Both the truck and I bounced about 10 feet in the air as I crashed into and ultimately over the small Volkswagen that a solider hastily jumped from. I was now stuck. I put the vehicle in drive and mashed the gas pedal. It jerked forward and I was free from the other vehicle and heading down the perimeter road that would take me out of the docks. Explosions sounded and a gun battle on the docks ensued as dock workers shot back at the Gestapo. In the commotion, I was able to escape and pass unnoticed on to the main freeway I-90 that heads west from Boston.

My heart had finally stopped pumping quite so hard and the adrenaline was subsiding, so I was able to evaluate my situation. I had a full tank of gas, a pack of cigarettes, a large roll of German Marks as money, and my official papers that allowed me to move about the country as a delivery boy. All in all, it was not too bad. The freeway opened up ahead of me as the night rolled on. It was going to be a long haul to make it to the neutral zone by six o'clock tomorrow night. The night dragged on and the miles ticked down.

By early morning, I had driven almost 400 miles and badly needed to stretch, eat, and refuel the truck, in that order. A sign came into view; it was for the Himmler Plaza, just north of Ohio. I guided the truck into the plaza and panic raced through my body. Ahead of me was a road block on the off ramp to the plaza, flanked by two oppressive looking Tiger Tanks and a dozen armed SS guards. The traffic began to back up and the soldiers would either wave the vehicle on or motion for it to be driven down the slip road for an inspection.

It suddenly occurred to me that I did not know what was in the back of my truck. For all I knew, it could be guns and contraband. I dove into the glove box in the truck looking for a clue of what I carried, but there was nothing. I was quickly approaching the blockade. "Stay cool," I said to myself, "stay cool." I have papers and whatever I had in the back of the truck would not be grounds for treason on first inspection and maybe, just maybe, I would be allowed to pass by without an inspection.

There were two small cars ahead of me and both were allowed to pass, I got my hopes up as I approached the barrier and the mean-looking lieutenant. I was motioned to stop and did so. The man asked for my papers and I silently passed them to him along with my work authorization card. He took them and studied them. The officer looked at me and then my papers several times, before returning them and saying that they looked to be in order and I could proceed to the plaza. I thanked the officer and put the truck into gear and began to move forward.

I looked in my side mirror as I moved forward slowly. There, I spotted a man in a long trench coat emerge from the sentry hut adjacent to the barrier. He barked an order to the lieutenant, whose face went quite pale. He immediately ran forward after my truck, banging on the side.

"Stop, stop, stop," he shouted! I was of two minds; I could

either accelerate away and around the corner, and ditch the vehicle and run for it, or stop. I decided to stop. The turrets on the tanks had begun to swing in my direction and it was obvious that I would not get far before I was blown to smithereens. I complied and brought the truck to a stop.

***

"We will inspect your truck," the lieutenant exclaimed.

There was more commotion behind me as the other soldiers directed traffic to back up and make room for me to maneuver the truck down the slip road. The slip road was short and bathed in bright lights. I was the only vehicle in the inspection bay. My stomach began to churn again as I thought about what could be in the back of the truck. I stopped the truck as the officer approached. He requested that I switch off the engine and come to the rear of the vehicle.

In the commotion at the dock and in the hard driving since then, I had not had time to even consider that the back of the truck was locked. I started to panic as the officer requested the padlock be removed and the door be raised. I didn't have the key. I excused myself and returned to the cab. I removed the keys from the ignition; there were two keys on the key ring, a good sign. Standing next to the officer at the rear of the truck, I offered up the key to the padlock. He instructed me to open it. I inserted the key and turned it. It fit exactly into the chunky lock and it snapped open with an audible clunk.

I was now committed, I removed the lock sheepishly and raised the door...

CASTOR THE BRAVE

Jett Hollister

n the olden times of the medieval kingdom of Dracbarrow, the kingdom prospered under the ruler they now call the Great King. Such a name was given to the leader, not only due to the success the kingdom enjoyed under his rule, but also on account of his peculiar secrecy in not revealing his real name. The Great King took power after his entire family was murdered and, 20 years later, suffered the same fate. This would throw Dracbarrow into anarchy and terror as the kingdom struggled to regain its footing.

***

"On your feet, peasant," yelled the warden. Reluctantly, the prisoner followed the order and rose to meet the warden's neck, since the prisoner was still young and not tall enough to look him straight on. As he followed the warden to The Pit, he analyzed his surroundings. The prisoner had been planning this moment for weeks.

"Three guards, one stationed at each doorway," he whispered to himself quietly as he was led to the chamber of punishment. His crime had been starting a fight with other prisoners. Of course, that was just what he needed to get put in The Pit and initiate his escape. Refocusing on his situation and using the dim candlelight from the table in the corner, he could make out the profile of the guards: one dozing off in the doorway to his left, one on his right, and just what he had been hoping to see – his way out of this hell hole. He had learned that the chimney was the only way out of the top-security prison. He was quite relieved to see it, considering he had never been in this area – he was going completely off of other prisoners' accounts.

When the warden stepped to the left to whisper something to the guard, the prisoner realized this was the time to strike. He stabbed the warden with the sharpened arrowhead he had made earlier from a rock and bolted straight for the chimney. But just as he began to climb up, someone grabbed his leg.

The prisoner hadn't always been a fugitive. When he was younger, he went by the name Castor and was a joyous citizen under the rule of the Great King. But, when the Great King was murdered, it threw the kingdom of Dracbarrow into turmoil and changed Castor's situation. Ulric, the King's successor and murderer, ruled tyrannically and ordered the capture and murder of all who worked closely under the Great King. This included Castor's parents, as they were very close to the Great King; his dad was the Great King's right-hand man. This order led to the death of Castor's parents and also placed Castor in prison at the age of 14.

As Castor began climbing up the tight chimney to finally escape the prison after four years in captivity, someone grabbed his leg: the warden. With a bloody shirt and a look of death in his eyes, Castor knew that the warden wasn't going to just capture him. Castor came to a sudden realization that it was either kill or be killed. Although he was much smaller than his foe, who was nearly seven feet tall, he utilizing his smaller size to his advantage by ducking quickly to avoid the warden's fist. The warden's blow sailed over Castor and right into the cobblestone chimney, inches away from Castor's head. Castor sent his right elbow into the warden's knee, sending him to the ground. While the warden lay grimacing on the stone floor, Castor seized a silver candleholder on the table in the corner of the room and delivered a knock-out blow that went straight to the warden's skull.

Luckily, the other guards had fled when he initially stabbed the warden, but Castor had no time to waste. The fleeing guards had rung the alarm bell and he had to get out of the prison before any others showed up. Fairly fit from training every day in his cell, climbing the chimney was not too much of a struggle for Castor. He reached the top rather quickly, but what he saw outside the prison walls made his stomach drop.

***

Guards were everywhere. This was not part of the plan. He was supposed to slip off of the roof and hide within a hay trailer going out of the prison. With guards perched on rooftops in response to the alarm, he had no choice but to take the only other way out: through the front door. Quietly slipping down the chimney, Castor located the warden's limp body. Hearing the guards' swift footsteps down the hall, Castor made quick business of stripping off the uniform of the warden and hiding the warden's body inside the chimney. Even donning the warden's uniform, Castor was nearly spotted as he slid down the steps to the main floor.

The vital part of Castor's disguise was remaining calm. Guards at such a high-security prison could sense someone's fear and even see it in their eyes. If he could stay cool, Castor believed he would be in the clear.

However, just as he turned into the last corridor and saw the main entrance, he hit another major roadblock. A group of nearly 20 men was gathered at the entrance, blocking his escape. Even though he felt as though his heart was beating out of his chest, Castor stayed calm and carefully assessed the situation. What he needed, he decided, was a distraction. His eyes yet again locked on to a candleholder that held a lit candle. It was next to velvet curtains that draped the windows beside him. Slowly, he lifted the candle to meet the curtain and, within seconds, the curtain was fully ablaze. He did this to two other curtains and, upon putting the candle back, yelled, "Fire!"

All but one of the guards rushed to the site of the flames and Castor was able to slip past them with ease. He strode to the entrance, confident enough in his disguise to walk right by the remaining guard. Just as he began to think of a way to leave the grounds, a hand firmly grabbed his chest and stopped him from advancing.

***

Ulric had a great distaste for anyone still alive who had close relations to the Great King. So, he made their lives worse than death. Castor was unfortunate enough to be one of those receiving such treatment. Held in the most brutal prison in Dracburrow, he was underfed, overworked, and treated as a slave. His four years spent in the prison turned him from a carefree adolescent to a hardened man. This way of life did not only make him harder, but gave him an unrelenting hate toward Ulric. Castor had long ago decided he was going to kill Ulric once he escaped, or die trying.

Suppressing his immense fear, Castor turned to meet the guard.

"What are ye doing, mate?" the guard questioned. Good, Castor thought, he thinks I'm an actual guard.

"I'm, just, uh, going to check on the horses, sir," Castor said a bit too quickly. But, the guard waved him off and Castor breathed sigh of relief once he was out of earshot.

The prison was located a few miles outside of town and

was surrounded by a moat nearly 10 feet across, and was infested with alligators. The prison was located in a dense forest, inhabited by man-eating beasts, even the thought of which sent shivers down Castor's spine.

The current departure of hay trailers was his saving grace. The caravan of farmers took their hay to and from the prison to feed the horses and would secretly give him transport to the town. He snuck into the back trailer and waited out the ride.

When Castor hopped out of the trailer, he thought he was in the wrong place. This was not the town he left four years ago. There were no street vendors, people walking down the street, or even people to be seen. It looked like a ghost town. Upon asking a shop owner, Castor learned that this was Ulric's doing. Castor asked the man if he knew the whereabouts of Ulric.

"He's in his castle a few miles from here, actually," replied the clerk. Castor was surprised and nervous, but a bit content that Ulric was so close. He decided to depart around midday for the castle and took strength from the belief that, with Ulric dead, all of the Dracbarrow's issues could be resolved. Castor made care to prepare for his encounter with Ulric; he was quite possibly the heaviest-guarded person in the land. Ulric borrowed a silver dagger from the store clerk and, when the sun was at its highest, made out for the castle. Castor could not help but feel frightened as he attempted to assassinate the current king of Dracbarrow.

The castle consisted of four towers, all connected by a wall that surrounded a courtyard. Within the courtyard was Ulric's quarters and many of his palace guards. As Castor approached, he saw a loading area along the side of the wall for goods coming into the castle. Surprisingly, there were no guards there. It helped that no supplies were being unloaded at the moment. Castor quickly slipped into the loading area and into the main corridor. Castor could not help but admire the aesthetics of the corridor. Adorned with gold-plated inscriptions and marble statues, the hall was breathtaking. He quietly slid down the hallway toward the heavily-guarded courtyard.

To his dismay, he discovered Ulric on his throne in the center of the courtyard, surrounded by guards. Castor played out every scenario in his head. He concluded that if he were going to save Dracbarrow from Ulric, he was not going to be leaving the castle alive. Castor could not wait, for Ulric was leaving that day and Castor would never have such a chance again. Before he could think any further, he strode out from the corridor and toward Ulric. As he walked to the king, guards began to follow. The closer he got to Ulric, the faster the guards pursued Castor.

"Your reign is over, Ulric," Castor shouted from nearly 10 feet away.

By now the guards and Castor were running at a sprint.

All around him, Castor heard the guards yelling, "Stop him!" and "Halt!" But Castor knew he couldn't stop, or all he had been through would be in vain. As he reached Ulric, he drew his silver dagger and prayed. As he plunged the knife into the man that had caused him such pain and grief, he did not feel satisfied; instead, he wept for his soul and for his family.

Castor slowly felt the world being pulled from his grasp as a guard impaled Castor with his sword. Castor looked down at himself and saw blood. Thoughts of all he had endured raced through his mind as black engulfed his vision. Within this darkness, he saw his parents.

"Mom, Dad," cried Castor.

"It is okay, son," they said. With those words, Castor released his tight grip on life that he held on to for so many years and followed his parents into the afterlife.

***

Word of the assassination of Ulric spread throughout the entire kingdom, and Castor was hailed as a hero. The story of Castor the Brave would be carried on throughout generations and into the Golden Age that followed the reign of Ulric. As for Ulric, he was remembered only as a corrupt king and cruel man.

FIFTEEN. . . AND DRIVING THEIR PARENTS CRAZY!

Courtney Kleino

Finally, 15 years old! Fifteen is the age that is greatly antic-
ipated by 14 year olds and often dreaded by their parents.
Fifteen is the age when teenagers are given the opportunity
to finally feel the taste of freedom, even if that taste is more
like a nibble. Fifteen is also the age when parents realize that,
in just a few short months, their child will have an even bigger
taste of freedom. This is the freedom, excitement, and independence that come from getting behind the wheel of a car.
This realization is heart-attack material for most parents! This
is just one of many ways teens "drive their parents crazy!"

I know all of this information first hand, as I have just
turned 15. I have been anticipating getting my learner's
permit for the past six months. I have been counting down
each month with regular reminders to my parents regarding

my plan to get my permit the day of my actual birthday. Of course, this is because I wanted to get my real driver's license on the day I turn 16, as the law requires that you must have your learner's permit for 12 months before applying for a real driver's license.

My advice for all 14 year olds is to begin studying and take the required tests as soon as you can. I thought starting the course on drug and alcohol awareness and reading the Rules of the Road /Signs booklet the day before my birthday would be enough time to prepare. Well, it was not! There were a lot of things to read and learn, and it ended up taking a couple of days to review the course material and take the online exams.

My birthday is on December 30, and the DMV was closed on New Year's Day. So, I actually did not go to the DMV until three days later on Friday, January 2. We planned to get to the DMV before they opened to avoid a crowd. When I got to the DMV with my mom, there were already at least 50 people in line ahead of us.

As we waited in line, a man in a banana-colored polo was checking to make sure everyone had the correct documents. As he made his way down the line, passing the lady in the cat shirt in front of us, he finally was ready to check my documents. Knowing I was there to receive my learner's permit, he asked if I had passed the drug and alcohol test and the road rules/signs test. I proudly confirmed that I had successfully passed all the tests and I had all of the required identification with me. He then proceeded to tell me that the online test results are not always sent to the DMV office immediately. He said that we would have to wait until we got inside and our number was called to find out if the results were in the system.

So, we waited nervously for another 30 minutes, wondering if I would actually be able to get my permit that day. I started to panic when I realized that it was a Friday and the DMV would be closed over the weekend, which meant that I might have to wait until Monday to get my permit. I know it is only another two days, but for a 15 year old eager to get a permit, two days is an eternity. When we got to the first check-in desk where they give you a number and instructions on where to wait, we asked if they could verify if my test results were in the system. Typically, they don't verify the tests at the check-in; but thankfully, we got a really nice lady who helped us. Much to my relief, my test results somehow were there and we could proceed to the next waiting area.

After only waiting for 10 minutes or so, the unenthusiastic lady behind the desk called my number: D110. She again verified that I had met all of the requirements and my mom paid the fee. After being asked a number of what seemed to me to be pointless questions, the lady finally took my picture. She seemed a bit impatient with me as I made sure my hair was in place to prepare for the picture. I am not sure how she did not understand the importance of this picture that will be on my learner's permit and I.D. for the next 12 months and serve as a memento of this very important milestone!

Of course, I devoted extra time that morning to carefully applying my make-up, styling my hair, and selecting my outfit in anticipation of taking this picture. As it turned out, I was not too thrilled with the picture, but I don't think anyone really likes the picture on their driver's license. Regardless, I was absolutely delighted to be getting my very own official I.D. and learner's permit. It will surely be my most prized possession for the next 12 months.

The lady with minimal personality proceeded to tell me that I was the first person in 2015 to obtain my license at that DMV office. She asked that I take another picture in front of a background screen with driver's licenses on it so they could put it on Twitter. I am not one for public display or humiliation, but my mom said "yes, she will do it" without hesitation. So, I took another picture with a big smile on my face. I then practically skipped out of the office in anticipation of driving right away. Unfortunately, my mom did not let me drive home because she did not feel I was ready yet.

***

Each of my parents had previously taken me to the mall parking lot on a few Sunday mornings to practice staying in the lanes, regulating my speed, stopping, turning, and parking. I did pretty well during my cruising sessions at the mall parking lots. There was just that one time when my dad told me to stop and I put the car suddenly in park instead of using the brake to stop. My dad was not a happy camper at all! But, all in all, he admitted that I was getting the hang of this driving thing. However, I had not yet actually driven on the streets with other cars, stop signs, and traffic lights.

My mom is a bit of a worrier, so she was more than happy to relinquish the first outing on the streets to my dad. I immediately ran into the house to proudly show my dad and my younger sister my new learner's permit and ask my dad if we could go out to practice driving. He agreed without hesitation and my younger sister quickly jumped in the back seat to join us.

I thought to myself, "What is the worst that could happen?" Dad was sitting right next to me and there were barely any cars on the streets. I would be fine; this would be a breeze!

Okay, the right side is the brake; wait, no, it's the left. Where are the turn signals again? Yikes, maybe I should just stick to riding my bike?

As we pull out of the driveway, my palms were already sweating, but I was determined that my face would not show my fear. We coasted along the street at only 25 miles per hour. My nerves had settled and I started to gain more confidence. I had a little trouble with maintaining the speed limit. My sister was videotaping me from the back seat and offering unsolicited driving tips. Even though she is only 12 years old, somehow she thinks she is an expert driver since she has driven a golf cart before!

***

The next day, I was riding in the car with my mom. Once again, she refused to let me drive because she said that there was too much traffic. She suggested that I watch and learn from the passenger seat. She repeated what she chants every time we talk about driving, "Safety is the most important thing. It is a big responsibility to drive a car."

So, I quickly become bored, thinking this is not what I expected it would be like to learn to drive. I then started day dreaming about the perfect car! I envisioned this beautiful, shiny brown Jeep, fully loaded with all available options. It would have seats that stay cool, a state-of-the-art sound system, a state-of-the-art navigation system, and it would have a special feature that lets drivers know when it is clear to merge.

Then I started to further fantasize about how nice it would be to have a car that drove all by itself. The car could be programmed to automatically go where you want to go without the need for anyone to steer the way. Passengers wouldn't have to lift a finger. They could take a nap, watch a movie, and text freely without the chance of getting in an accident. There would be no more fights over calling "shotgun" to sit in the front passenger seat, no need to worry about using your phone while in the car, and no fear of learning how to drive. Life would be great – it would be like having a personal limo without the need for the limo driver!

I quickly awakened from my day dream when my mom asked if I wanted Starbucks. Surprisingly, she lets me drive home. She stopped the car and switched seats with me, with a tense look on her face. I could already tell she was nervous before I even pulled out of the parking lot. I made it onto the street without a hitch, confident in my driving skills. We coasted along without any stress. My mom told me that I needed to merge, but I was not sure what she meant.

Then all of the sudden, my mom screamed "MERGE!" and then she screeches "STOP," while squeezing my arm. She failed to tell me that the lane that I was in ended and that I needed to gradually merge over to the other lane. Now, I was stopped on the patch of grass adjacent to the street and had to wait for all the cars to pass before I could get on the road again. Remembering all I had learned over the past couple days, we finally made it home safely. However, I was thinking that we might want to leave the driving lessons to dad!

***

For every 15 year old who is nervous about driving, the best way to learn how to drive, in my opinion, is by practice. The experience of learning to drive a car is actually similar to the gradual steps we all took to learn to ride a bike. You start off with training wheels, then your parents hold your bike steady while you steer, and then you actually ride a few feet by yourself. You falter and even fall a few times, but you get back on the bike and keep trying. With more practice, you ride a little farther each time. Once you learn to balance and ride steadily on the bike, then you have to learn how to watch out for cars and dogs in the neighborhood.

In time, you are allowed to leave your driveway and ride from your house to a neighbor's house. With more practice, you gain experience and confidence on the bike. Gradually, you are allowed to venture farther on your own, as your parents feel it is safe for you to do so. Now, I ride my bike with ease and don't ever have to think about the basics of keeping balance or steering straight.

So, just like you were enthusiastically learning to ride your bike, try driving the car whenever you get the opportunity. You will gain confidence and experience by driving often and taking different routes. You will actually need to remember and follow all the road signs and road rules that you learned in the agonizing online course.

Driving may look easy, but it is harder than it looks. You have to get the experience of driving in different situations, on different roads, in different conditions, and at different speeds. You need to learn to watch out and anticipate what other cars might do. You also have to learn to watch in front of you and also look frequently in your rearview and side mirrors. Remember, driving is a huge responsibility, so drivers need to be focused and calm. You will learn to be a safe driver with lots of practice and you might even create funny memories that you will share when you teach your own kids how to drive.

Ironically, my 79-year-old grandfather who helped me learn to ride my bike when I was much younger, was in a car accident on the same day that I got my learner's permit. He is quite proud to have earned an excellent driving record for his entire life without a single ticket or previous accident. However, he was found to be at fault when he was attempting to do a U-turn and hit an on-coming car. Fortunately, no one was hurt and the cop did not give my grandpa a ticket. But, his car was totaled and the insurance company has raised questions regarding his ability to continue to drive safely. I have seen the look of fear and anger on his face as his competence is being challenged and his "freedom and independence" are being threatened. It makes me sad for him, because I cannot imagine losing the freedom of driving after you have been a good driver and independent for so many years.

***

I like being independent, which is probably why I like driving so much. All of our lives, we depend on our parents for food, shelter, money, and rides. I am a pretty mature, responsible, and calm kid. I take the privilege and responsibility of being behind the wheel seriously for my own and other's safety.

Over the past 15 years, I have earned my parents trust by making good choices and showing that I am responsible. I have not quite driven my parents completely crazy by my constant requests to drive and my newly-acquired driving skills. Admittedly, they are still a bit nervous when I get behind the wheel, but they agree that I am getting better and better with practice. I do know that my parents trust that I will drive cautiously, not be distracted with text messages or friends while I drive, and avoid any danger that would potentially harm others.

I get the fact that I am responsible for the safety of others in my car and on the road when I drive. I also realize that, once I get my real driver's license and my own car, I will have additional responsibilities like keeping the car clean, filled up with gas, and keeping up with the regular maintenance schedule. For now, however, I will enjoy my taste of freedom and gradual independence while I am still 15.

Driving is a lot of fun, but I realize that there is also a lot of added responsibility that comes with the privilege of my newly earned independence!

THE RINGMASTER AND THE FORGETFUL ROBIN

Bailey Maher

Dark. Why was it so dark? There was nothing but the sound of a distant chiming, like that of a music box. Why was she even here? Where is here? She tried to move, but couldn't. Then she heard it – a soft murmur of voices. They were far off and muffled. It was like they were speaking through cotton balls. It was aggravating – why couldn't she hear clearly. It's a horrible feeling, not being able to speak, to hear, to move.

Then, all at once, like getting pulled out of water, her eyes shot open and she was panting a mile a minute. With wide eyes, she stared up through the treetops at the starry sky. She tried to steady her heavy breathing. However, she was so focused on the task at hand that she missed the presence watching her. As she clutched her throat, a smooth voice rang in the quiet night air. The voice sounded light and cheery as it asked her "Are you awake, love?"

She could detect a British accent even though her mind was frazzled. "Uh, yes, sir. May I ask where you are?" she asked.

"I am here," said the voice, coming from her left. "I am there," said the voice again, this time from the right. "But alas, that is only my mind. For my body is right behind you, dearie," said the joyous voice right behind her left ear.

She turned quickly to face the man with the playful tone. When she turned, her wide hazel eyes clashed with a pair of bright blue ones. She blinked once. Twice. Three times. This man had to be the most beautiful man she had ever seen, and he was a bit familiar. His eyes were a mesmerizing shade of cerulean and looked like little oceans in his eyes, an ocean she felt very at home with.

***

A wide and charming grin lit up on his face. Sharp canines added to the originality of his wolfish grin. Long, golden locks reached his shoulders. His complexion was like porcelain and his face was painted in likeness to a parrot. But what was most unique about the familiar gentleman was his attire.

He wore a bright navy suit and a top hat of the same color sat upon his gold head. His hands were gloved and, in his right hand, he held a jeweled cane. He tilted his head to the side, blond locks falling into his eyes, and spoke.

"Why were you sleeping in the forest?" he asked with an animated expression, as he held out a gloved hand.

"She wasn't asleep," said a tiny voice in the back of her mind. "I, I don't remember, sir," she said shakily while taking his now-outstretched hand.

"Hmm, that's quite alright, love, but might I ask for your name? Do you remember it?" he asked and ran his thumb along her knuckles.

"Um... my name? Name... I - I forgot sir," she admitted as she sifted through her blank mind.

His eyebrows furrowed slightly and his bright, young eyes washed over her with an upset look. Yet his smile stood strong. It made her chest pang for the "stranger." And then he spoke again. "Well, would you like shelter at my abode?"

She looked up at the ominous dark forest and then back at the glowing man. "I would like that very much Mr..."

He perked up. "Ah, you may call me Ringmaster."

"Thank you, Ringmaster."

He chuckled a little hesitantly and said, "Do not thank me, Rosette, I do not deserve it. Now, come along, love. Let's meet the rest of the family."

She smiled and walked with him through the dark forest, only later realizing that she never told him her name. They walked for an hour or so, while having very different conversations. When they reached a clearing in the lush forest, the Ringmaster turned swiftly around, skipped behind her, and held a gloved hand over her eyes.

"What?" she asked reaching up to remove his hand from blocking her vision.

"Shh! Dearie, it's a surprise!" he laughed. They took a few more steps before he twirled around her with a glowing grin and said, "Welcome to the Miracle Circus!"

And a miracle it was.

***

The entire area glittered in the nightlight like a star. Royal purple tents were made of velvet and were held up by embellished purple rods that towered above the ground. The carnival music that rang in her head earlier, now drifted through the night. Her mouth watered at the sweet smells that filled the air. Animals and brightly dressed performers bustled around and waved at the Ringmaster. Her wide eyes struggled to take everything in as she ran to his position at the twinkling entrance.

He smiled back at her, "Do you like it, dearie?" he asked.

"I love it! I have never seen anything like it," she answered childishly.

His cheerful laughter boomed through the circus, "I knew you would!" He grabbed her hands and danced her through the crowd. Everyone made way for them and greeted them with a knowing smile. "Come! They've been waiting for you!" he said, leading her to the largest tent.

She had been caught up by the incredible scene, but

slowly came to her senses. Who were all these people that suddenly appeared in a circus? Why were they in the middle of a forest? Why was everything so maddeningly familiar to her? She stumbled behind him and was starting to pant while trying to keep up with him; he skipped effortlessly through the circus. This man must be crazy, she was sure of it. Maybe she was. As her mind raced for answers, the Ringmaster took her by her small hand and burst into the purple tent.

Inside there were around 10 performers chatting idly. They all turned to look at their guest and sadness washed over their faces. A small brunette boy exclaimed, "B-but Rosette…"

A gigantic, dark haired man nudged the boy harshly. The boy stopped speaking. The rest of the performers became silent.

Ringmaster frowned for only a moment, but quickly regained his fake grin. "Dearie, this is the family. They are your family if you so choose," he said, tipping his hat. "Guys, greet the beauty!" he demanded, with a hand on her shoulder. The family hesitantly gathered around her with solemn looks.

Ringmaster jumped over beside the very tall man with a grin and said, "Now this is Jumbo! He can lift more than 500 pounds!" He gestured to the weightlifting performer and the big man smiled back bashfully and scratched the back of his neck with a wave.

After an awkward moment, the big man managed to say, "Hey."

"Hello," she answered back.

Ringmaster then made his way over to a set of onyx-haired twins and a red headed woman. He bowed at the twins and smiled, "These two are our best acrobats, Gam and Kur."

They both had their faces painted like theatrical masks. The happy one cheered, "I'm Gam!" His sad twin brother raised a palm. "Kur," he mumbled.

She smiled back.

Ringmaster pulled her over to the red head. "This is our resident beast-tamer. Lash!" he said twirling around her.

The woman gulped and glanced at the small girl in the tent. The red head appeared hesitant to greet her, but finally raised a palm and managed a small smile, "Hello, Rosette..."

The Ringmaster introduced a few more performers to Rosette and then got to a small boy. The boy was ringing his wrists nervously and wouldn't look at her. When he finally managed to look up at her, Rosette gave the boy a warm smile. But he frowned.

Ringmaster broke the awkward silence by putting his arm around the small boy and announcing, "Love, this is our knife thrower..."

The boy interrupted Ringmaster's introduction and dashed toward the girl. He jumped into her arms and wrapped his small arms tightly around her. Bursting into hysterics, he wept, "W-why?"

"Knives!" yelled Jumbo. "Knives, stop," he said firmly while pulling the boy off her like one would remove lint. The boy continued to sob, burying his face into Jumbo's chest. Rosette thought she heard Knives whispering about how it was unfair.

The Ringmaster reassuring voice then rang threw the tent, "Well, that's everybody, love! Closing time!" he called out, putting an arm around her shoulders. "Let's go, dearie, you must be tired."

She only nodded and looked back at her new family. They looked back somber and quiet. The Ringmaster led her through some smaller tents, smiling and bidding "goodnight" to all who passed him. He seemed to be a very kind man, she thought.

He entered the last tent and led her gently inside. He smiled brightly at her and gestured to one of the two beds in the left corner of the room. "You had a big day. Get some shut eye. I have many papers to finish and shall be joining you in sleep soon."

She nodded sleepily and crawled into the bed.

***

Ringmaster chuckled warmly as she pulled up the covers. He hung up his bright coat and hat, sat down at a large wooden desk, and ran a hand through his wild, blond locks. She was confused as to who he really was and why she was there, but she soon felt sleep wash over her. As she drifted off, a vivid thought raced into her mind. All at once visions came pouring back to her. She was younger and was smiling as a young, blond haired man dashed up to her with the wide smile and wrapped his arms around her. He lifted her into the air and the two of them exploded in laughter. The next scene was of her laughing with the circus family, her hand grasping Ringmaster's hand.

Jumbo was laughing heartily and patted her back, making her stumble on account of his sheer strength. They all laughed and she ruffled up Knives' hair with her hand. She then had a vision of practicing the trapeze with Gam and Kur. She remembered having sleep-over parties with Lash. But the majority of her dreams consisted of loving moments with Ringmaster. They would have picnics and fun times with their family. He would grab her at random and dance with her. They would talk till the early morning hours. The most precious moment of all was when he proposed to her during a show.

She woke up breathing frantically. She realized: These were not dreams or delusions. These were memories! She darted her wide eyes to the ring on her finger and then to the desk in the corner. She found Ringmaster leaning his head on his arm as tears streamed down his face, ruining his paint. He had let down his guard and was sobbing heavily. He ran his shaking hand through his hair and rambled on about how sorry he was.

"R-Ringmaster?" she mumbled.

He threw his head up and quickly wiped away the tears. "Oh, oh, love. You're up!" he said, smiling weakly.

"I finally remember!" she blurted.

"Remember what, dearie?" he said frowning slightly.

"I remember you," she said in a determined voice.

He peeked at her through his bangs and gave an empty chuckle, "I was hoping you would remember. But, how much do you remember this time, love?" he asked walking over to her.

She looked up at him, confused. He smiled sadly at her and tried to comfort her, "Not everything this time round, then, huh? Love, we were very happy together, and were to be wed in a week actually. You were practicing on the trapeze with Gam. For fun of course," he spoke as if he had practiced the lines or as if he had said the same thing many times to her. His eyes began to water again.

"And you slipped. Your head was injured. You suffer from severe memory loss, love. It's all my fault, all of it! I shouldn't have let you on the trapeze!" said the once joyous man.

"It wasn't your fault," she reassured him.

He smiled half-heartedly and sighed, "That was two years ago."

Her eyes shot wide. "Two years?" she gasped.

"I didn't just lose you once. I keep losing you. For a few months I get you back, and... then you pass out and forget everything. Gone," he said staring at the floor, blond strands hanging in his face.

Tears began to stream down her face as it all sunk in.

He clenched his fists, "I'm going to get you back for good, one of these times. I will try until my last breath, I swear to you, Rosette."

IT'S US

Jamie Moubarak

"**N**o one has ever come out," I told my friend, Rose, trying to scare her.

"Don't you mean 'No one has ever come out alive?'"

"Well, no one, dead or alive, has ever walked back out of the doors of that house."

We were standing right in front of the house. She glared at me, obviously doubting everything I'd said. It's hard to make Rose believe in paranormal activity – she's never fearful.

"Hey, Emily, it would be cool if we stayed the night – tonight. You know, to prove me wrong and all," she snickered.

"You mean... in the house?" I smiled back at Rose.

Tonight we were going into the creepiest house ever, the same house that "Six people previously had disappeared in," according to a parapsychologist's report that had been on the news for the past two weeks.

"If you're scared, I can get Gale to stay with us," Rose mocked me.

I hate when she does that. Gale is my friend and I guess it would be a bit of an understatement to say that Gale and Rose hate each other – they despise each other. Sometimes I wish they would just get along. Rose is my best friend so I don't like it when Gale insults her. He believes in paranormal activity, and he says that it's a coincidence that Rose and I are friends. I never understood what he meant.

Heading in our direction was none other than Rose's enemy. When I mess with Rose, he always plays along.

"Gale! You know about ghosts and stuff, right?" I excitedly ask.

Rose rolled her eyes at me. "Give it up already," she muttered. Gale and I ignored her.

"There's no such thing as ghosts," he switched his attention from me and looked over at Rose, "but there is such a thing as the presence of an apparition. Exclusively found at that house." He pointed at the place where Rose and I were planning to spend the night. Rose just rolled her eyes again and crossed her arms. "I heard you guys saying you were going to stay there tonight. Rose, I think I'll miss you least of all," he joked.

I put my hand over my mouth to keep from laughing. He winked at me and continued down the block, probably back to his house.

A man who was clipping the bushes nearby overheard us talking and walked up to us. "How old are you kids?" he asked us.

"We're 16," Rose said, as we exchanged glances.

"You're going in that house to stay the night? Be careful," he warned.

"Do you know anything about it? Emily's been trying to scare me, but I'm not buying it."

"Oh, please, Rose. It was on the news!" I tried backing myself up. The man cocked his head in recognition.

"You're Emily and she's Rose, right? Emily and Rose. Emily Rose," the maintenance worker stuttered. A shocked expression crossed his face.

Rose and I exchanged glances again. I nodded, remembering a movie Rose and I saw a few months ago. It was called "The Exorcism of Emily Rose," a true story based on a girl named Anneliese Michel. Her demonic possession was recognized by the Roman Catholic Church.

The maintenance worker, looking quite tense, turned and just walked away.

***

"Well," Rose began, "that was strange." I looked down at my feet.

Soon enough, the sun went down and it was time for my best friend and I to spend the night in probably the most petrifying place we'd ever experience. Doing foolish things is what we're best at; we've been at it for 16 years.

We neared the shattered glass by the entrance of the

house. I remember, years ago, a family lived here. They had a sweet daughter. She always tried to help others in every way that she could. I never knew what happened to her because the family suddenly left one day. Honestly, out of fear, I didn't ever want to know what happened to them. The residence was very menacing, something even both Rose and Gale could agree on. Rose closed the door behind us, looking calm, but I knew that, on the inside, she was afraid.

We walked around the house, only to realize it wasn't as scary as people made it out to be. In fact, it was just a normal, old house. I could almost faintly hear the laughter of the happy, little girl running around the long halls. Sure, it could have used a little renovation, but that didn't make it "paranormal."

After we found a comfortable place to sit down, Rose and I noticed a cool breeze that returned every so often. I stayed on my guard even though Rose assured me there was nothing peculiar going on. To me, the recurring breeze was peculiar enough. I turned on my phone to tell my mom we were alright, but I lost the signal. I hoped that she didn't worry too much. Then, suddenly, from the corner of my eye I thought I saw the curtains move. I turned – but it was just my imagination – I hoped.

"Do you have signal?" I asked Rose.

She looked up from her nail filer and shook her head. "I don't see how you would get a signal. It's an abandoned house, it's not like someone's still paying for Wi Fi."

"Not just Wi Fi. I don't have any cellular connection! I did have some outside."

"Don't make a big deal of this. If you're chicken, you can leave now and prove yourself wrong. Or we can stay, no matter what, to see if there really are 'ghosts,'" Rose mocked me. I looked back down at my lifeless phone. Maybe my parents would understand why I didn't assure them I was alright when I tell them about the signal. Even better, maybe they'd think something was wrong and come to get me!

The floor was very uncomfortable and dirty, but the furniture was even more appalling. I rested my head on my arm. Memories of the scary movie we had seen a while back slowly, yet vividly, came back to me as the night went on. I remembered that a cold spot usually means there was a paranormal presence.

Rose glared over at me and snapped, "Would you stop chattering your teeth? It's driving me wild!"

I apologized. I didn't realize I was chattering my teeth. The air felt a little colder than the usual breeze that whipped past us, but I tried to ignore it.

Just as I was falling asleep, I felt a tug at my leg. "Rose, what do you want? I just wanna sleep," I complained.

But, when I looked over at Rose, I saw that she was fast asleep! "Rose," I spoke louder. She opened an eye and grumbled. I sat straight up and stared at her. How obnoxious of her to wake me up for no reason and then pretend to be asleep. Who did she think she was?

"What?" she asked half asleep.

"Stop pulling my leg. It's really annoying," I responded. "And stop pretending you are asleep.

"Very funny. I didn't pull your leg," she retorted. Almost simultaneously, we both shot right up from our sleeping positions. Something was wrong, and we both knew it.

***

I had brought an apple with me from home in case I needed a snack. I put it on the counter in the kitchen and turned to Rose. Another cool breeze whipped past me. I guess the heating bills had not been paid in quite some time. My stomach rumbled so I decided to reach out for my red apple. As I bit into it, blood ran from my mouth and down my arm. In fear, I threw the apple across the room and it hit the cupboard. Just as I was about to scream at the top of my lungs, Rose put her hand over my bloody mouth to stop me. "Shh! We don't know what could be here to hear us," her eyes almost teered up as she spoke.

I was sure that now she was afraid, too. I've been afraid ever since she brought up the stupid idea of staying here for the night. If it was daytime, we could just call for help. At night, no one was around to hear us. Everyone was asleep. My mouth stopped bleeding, but now my heart was racing uncontrollably fast. The fun was just about to begin.

Rose and I heard tapping against the cupboard where I

had thrown the apple. The tapping gradually got faster and faster, until the cupboard flew open. Nothing was inside, or at least nothing that we could see. Every time I tried to say something, I felt my throat tighten, so I limited my words. We slowly backed away from the kitchen, but we were still staring at the cupboard. I was sure something was going to pop out in front of us, like in scary movies.

I wiped my clammy hands against my jeans and was positive my heart sank into my stomach. Strangely enough, a bruise appeared on my left arm. It wasn't there earlier. I shifted my attention to the kitchen once again. I could almost see it, like a precognition of an apparition. Soon enough, in the cupboard, a faint specter began to shape itself. Rose and I stood, frozen in our footsteps, unsure of what to do.

The more I thought about it, the more I wished this was a dream. But I was positive this was no dream. A chill went down my spine as something quickly brushed against my shoulder, almost knocking me off balance. Vaguely, I could imagine what would happen next. Just like in scary movies, the exit door is most definitely locked. Rose verified that as she violently shook the door knob. I felt like a clairvoyant.

Now I was really questioning the idea of coming to the haunted house. Maybe I should have told Gale to stay with us. Although he probably would have made fun of us, because he didn't know there really was paranormal activity in the house. I didn't want to die; I was only 16! I was excited about driving and was getting my first car in a couple of days.

I had my whole life ahead of me, so this couldn't be the end! I took some comfort in the fact that at least I was with my friend – being alone would have been much worse. I would be balling hysterically if I was alone. I began to feel like we would have had better chances of winning the lottery than getting out of here in one piece. I should have talked Rose out of this when I had the chance.

"Why did I let you talk me into this? You should think twice about your genius ideas," I mumbled.

"I don't even think once. What makes you believe I would think twice? You shouldn't have listened to me, this is all your fault," Rose responded. She managed to make a joke out of our situation, which was typical of her.

We dragged our frightened legs down a dark hall and into a bedroom. Toys were scattered everywhere. This must have been the little girl's room. I smiled because it brought back memories of childhood. Her bed was big and the sheets had bright, eye-popping colors. The bed was not made, though. My smile faded away when I looked closer.

The wood frame had six thin scratch marks on it. They were long strokes from top to bottom. The sheets were torn in six places and were draped on the floor. Something very bad happened. On the other side of the room, a window had six deep cracks. Maybe we could smash it and get out, I thought! I pushed the cracks to see if they were loose, but as if by magic, the cracks sealed themselves. Someone – or something – wants us trapped. My mouth dried up as I realized the pattern going on. Six cracks, six rips, six scratches. I tried not to think about it anymore, but the idea lingered on my mind – 666. "Why sixes?" I thought aloud.

I turned and saw my reflection staring back at me. A tall mirror, about the width of a human body, was against a wall adjacent to me. In the reflection, I thought I saw something behind me, but it was just Rose. My overactive imagination had gotten the best of me once again. I squinted to see the initials "E.R." etched into the metal frame.

"Who do you think it has the initials, 'E.R.?'" I asked as my best friend steadied herself with the mirror's metal frame. Rose's once pink lips started to look duller, they looked almost blue. Her eyes were fixed into the mirror as if something was talking to her.

"Do you think the movie we saw could have been more than just a movie?" Rose questioned as she neared me. Her eyes followed the frame down and she finally said, "It's us..."

I didn't understand what she meant at first, but when I finally did, I wish I hadn't. She rested her palm face-down on the glass. I stood alone, wide-eyed, staring in shock at her as she sank into the mirror – it sucked her in.

***

A force flung me through the bedroom door and against the front entrance. I screamed uncontrollably for help.

Kicking and punching the door was all I could think of doing. Hot tears streamed down my cold face. The front door's handle began to shake, so I backed away. I kept my guard on. The door quickly flung open, and there stood Gale. I threw my arms around him and cried even harder. Once again, the door closed and locked itself.

"What's going on? Where's Rose?" he interrogated me. I shook my head, unable to speak. Once I was able to catch my breath, I looked up at him and told him everything that had happened tonight. He looked back at me, clearly believing everything.

"It's over here," I led him to the bedroom. We ducked through the hole in the wall made by my body when I was flung against it. Gale cautiously stepped inside before me, confirming the surroundings were safe. The mirror was still there, but it moved to the closet. "We can go inside like she did. We can save her, I know we can," I begged him.

"Are you crazy? What if we get hurt?" Gale objected.

"I know you don't like Rose, but she's my friend, and I will save her." I turned and placed my hand on the frame.

A gust of violent wind blew my hair behind my shoulders and a vivid vision came to me. I saw a baby in the hospital. Across from her room was another baby girl. The two were born on the same day and time. The doctors were arguing that the babies were six months early, they said it was something they had never seen before.

The first baby was to be named Sarah and the second baby

was to be Elizabeth. Every time the parents tried to name their daughters, the doctors would write down Emily for one, and Rose for the other. Those babies are my best friend and I – this vision is from the past! Could it be true? The vision went away and I returned to reality.

***

Gale decided to follow me, so we both stepped into the eerie mirror. The ambience of our new surroundings was formidable and the lighting gave off a maroon color. As we continued down the stone pathway looking for Rose, we noticed the strangest things going on around us. One man gripped a long rope connected to a machine. On the other side, another man with a petrified look in his eyes was laying down on a wooden bed, his head in the hole of a guillotine. Gale and I watched the rope release as the suffering man's head fell into the basket. I put my hand to my mouth and turned away instantaneously. Where were we? What was this place?

To my right, I saw a woman being pulled away from her child. A teenage boy held her child as a man forced the woman to sit in a chair and then strapped her in. She was burned alive in an electric chair. I was about to bolt for the child, but Gale grabbed my arm.

"Wait, don't get us in any trouble," Gale told me.

I turned to him and spoke in an angry tone, "And let those

monsters hurt that poor little girl? No thanks!" Running to the little girl, I heard Gale's footsteps chasing me. I reached out for her to save her, but my hands went right through her.

My heart almost skipped a beat. "What's going on?" I asked Gale.

"No one's even looking at us. It's like we're not even here."

"How? That's not even possible," I asked.

"Look," Gale pointed to a slim, blonde girl. I shift my attention to her. She looked dizzy. I quickly walked over to her. "Rose? Is that you?" I was so relieved I found her! She was going to be so happy to see us. But when she turned around, there were purple rings under her eyes, as if she hadn't slept for days.

I put my arm on her shoulder and smiled to reassure her. She didn't look too happy, but I was hoping that once we got out of there, she would start acting more like herself. It was then that I noticed a couple scratches on her collar bone.

"Don't worry we're here, let's g…," I began to say.

Rose's hands were around my neck. I could barely breathe. I counted three scratch marks. She violently shook my head back and forth until the veins in my eyes felt like they would pop. I counted another three scratch marks – six in total. I tried stopping her but I wasn't strong enough. I took one last breath before the world faded away.

I awoke to Gale's face. I was lying in a cave. "Where?" was all I could manage to say.

"We're still in the mirror, but I found a place to hide," Gale explained. "Was Rose mad at you before?"

"No," I coughed as I tried to regain my normal heartbeat. "But she's possessed. I know it."

Gale looked at the hand marks on my neck for a moment, then returned his attention to me. "You're right. We have to help her, she's our friend," Gale said. I was surprised to hear him call her his friend.

"Can't we do one of those things to make a ghost come out of her?" I asked.

"An exorcism? Do I look like a priest to you?"

"Well, we have to try! Do you have a better idea?" I questioned.

"Even if I knew how, which I don't, she would probably try to kill us before we could perform one?" Gale scoffed.

I turned away from him and began to tear up. My best friend tried to kill me. What if she stayed like this forever? What if Gale and I couldn't get out of here? How did she see us when no one else in the mirror world could? A million questions pounded in my brain as tears clouded my vision.

"Don't cry," Gale ordered. Still, I wouldn't look at him. I knew it wasn't his fault, we were both scared and tired. He put his hand on my shoulder. "We'll get out of here soon."

"What about Rose?" I queried.

"Look I know you want to save her, but let's face it, how can we? I don't want her to get hurt just as much as you do, trust me. But, honestly, we can't do this alone." I turned to him as he continued to speak. "We've been up all night. Let's get some sleep. Plus, nothing can find us in here."

Did he just call Rose a thing, I thought to myself? It was difficult, but I was exhausted and managed to drift off to sleep. I dreamed about Rose trying to kill me, so I woke up in terror.

Gale was still fast asleep. He slept with his mouth open. I smiled for the first time that night. "Gale, wake up. We've been asleep for a few hours." Truthfully, I woke him up because I was scared to be awake by myself and half expected that he would be gone when I awoke.

He opened one eye after another and had a paranoid look on his face. "I was hoping I'd wake up and all of this would be a dream," he muttered. I agreed with him.

"Do you feel better today? How's your neck?" He asked as he touched my sore skin.

I winced and brought my hand to his. "Still hurts," I said.

"Sorry," he apologized as he put his hand back down.

"How can we get out of here?" I asked.

"You know, you have really long eyelashes," he said, changing the subject.

I wasn't sure if he was trying to distract me from our situation or if he meant more. I let out a loud laugh. "Thanks for letting me know."

"So, anyway," he began as his cheeks flushed a little, "let's go out."

My eyes widened, and I was unsure of what to say. He quickly said, "I don't mean out! You know, I don't mean out on a date. I meant, like, outside of the cave! Not that you're ugly, you're not ugly, you're pretty… but I'm not asking you out! Well, I am asking if we should go out because we need to get out of here… and I should stop talking." He was blabbing on and on.

I burst into laughter after he finished stumbling over his own words. "Yeah, okay. Let's go outside," I giggled as he walked out of the cave before me. But the mirror's exit was nowhere to be seen, just as I had expected.

***

"Looking for a way out?" A tall man in clothing as white as snow asked us. He could actually see us!

"Yes, can you help us? Where are we?" I asked him. Gale positioned himself in between the man and me, as if protecting me.

"Where does it look like you are?" smirked the mysterious man. "A realm of evil and suffering. It's where all the possessed come to suffer for all eternity. The evil beings possess chosen humans, and… well, they come here through a mirror."

Gale and I exchanged worried glances, but Gale looked even more uneasy than me. "You're possessed?" Gale questioned him.

"Does it look like I am?" he shook his head slowly. "I almost was, but the evil being spared my life as long as I agreed to work here, cleaning up after the 'job' is done. Cleaning ashes and stuff is what I do."

"Free my friend from possession! We won't tell anyone! Please, let us all go!" I pleaded. The man tapped the stubble on his chin. "Maybe we can arrange something with the one who took control over her. What're your names?"

"He's Gale, I'm Emily, and the possessed one is Rose."

He straightened his back and chuckled with a creepy smile before he spoke. "Well, I'll be! Emily and Rose! We've been expecting you two to show up for years now. You two have been possessed even before you were born! Let me tell you everything."

Gale looked at me in a suspicious way as the mysterious man explained what was happening.

"Some evil spirit got a hold of your mothers, so it could create two super evil minion children. The early delivery was its doing, of course, but it ended up losing control over you two. Something happened. We never knew what, but somehow you two were partly freed of the curse. The chosen names 'Emily' and 'Rose' stayed, but your bodies were free of possession. Now that Rose has been captured, the evil spirit will let her go under one condition. The both of you must agree to sacrifice one of your own children in the future."

Gale scratched the back of his neck and fixed his eyes on me. "What're you going to do?" he asked me. I tried to take it all in, but it was just too overwhelming. How could I sacrifice one of my own future children to a devil? Would sacrificing myself be a better choice?

"Maybe if I have more than one child when I'm older, I

could give one up," I tried to justify the decision. "Rose can do the same; I'm sure it'll be alright."

A dark fog suddenly filled our surroundings. A deep voice came from the fog, "If you keep your promise, all three can go. But mark my words, if you back down from your vow, all of your lives will be destroyed." Suddenly, the fog cleared up and Rose appeared. The rings were gone from under her eyes. She came running toward us and gave us a huge hug.

"I was so scared! I'll never doubt you again, Emily. Gale, I still hate you," she said in between sobs. It made us smile, despite the predicament we were in.

"Hey! Without Gale we wouldn't have gotten out of this mess. You owe him an apology," I scolded her. She rolled her eyes at him.

The man in white snapped his fingers and, as if by magic, we appeared in the haunted house's closet. Within seconds, we all bolted out of it and ran to my house. Police cars were parked in my driveway, their lights flashing.

"We can't tell anyone about this," I said. My friends nodded in unison.

"I'm glad you're alright, Rose," Gale smiled at her. I couldn't believe that he was being nice to her for the first time. He could be such a gentleman when he wasn't acting like a five year old. The scene was broken up when my parents came rushing out of the house.

"Where were you? We were worried sick!" My mom shouted.

"If you ever do that again, I'll… I don't know what I'll do! But you can guarantee yourself grounded until you get married," my dad scolded me.

If only they knew what happened, then they wouldn't be yelling at me, I thought.

"Actually, sir, she was volunteering at a nursery home for the night, and her phone lost the signal," Gale pulled a brilliant excuse from thin air. It worked; my parents believed every word of it and even ungrounded me. Technically, it's safer if they don't know the truth.

My mom let Rose sleep over that night. Rose was still scared out of her mind. Gale stood on my driveway for another moment, then said bye to Rose. He turned to me and smiled. I admitted to him, "Rose and I wouldn't be alive right now if it wasn't for you. Thanks!"

"Anytime," he replied. I felt safe again now that I was at home and my friends were safe too.

But then Gale reminded us of the deal we had made. "What if you forget about the promise?" he warned.

I took a deep breath. Let's just hope I don't.

FINDING KAYA

Kaitlyn Osmond

saw a Vigorion apartment, and we started to run toward that building in hope for shelter. We entered the apartment and ran up the stairs as fast as our legs would take us. The thought of keeping her alive was what kept me going, so stopping was not an option. But when I looked back, I saw her at a halt. I whispered to her, "Kaya, you can't stop. For me please, one more stride!"

Kaya wiped her tears from her soaked face and ran as fast as a speeding bullet. When we make it to the top floor, we reached a bedroom that had a shrine of Vigor. We hid under the bed and were as silent as a mouse. As the older sister, I felt that I had to keep Kaya alive, even if that meant risking my life.

We stayed under that bed for what seemed like a year. I finally heard creaks of the floor board and tried to make myself invisible to all surroundings, but nothing seemed to work. The only thing I could do was pray to Acumen. Being born from a family who followed the Acumenism religion, we all believed in the power of intellect and cleverness. But as I started to pray, the door swung open and there stood a soldier pointing his submachine gun at me. I could see he had on an Opulence necklace. I wanted to run, but my limbs did not move; besides, there was nowhere to go. All I could do was wait to see my fate had in store for me. But the soldier just looked at me with a daze. I did not know if it was a look of confusion or a deep threat. He finally took my arm and dragged me to the floor where my mother was supposed to meet us. With no sight of her anywhere, I knew something tragic had to have happened.

The soldier took me outside, where other soldiers were threatening people who did not believe in Opulencism. When we were outside, he pushed me to my knees and pointed the gun at my head. The other soldiers just watched as if it was some kind of show. The solider that had me hostage told the other men to leave without him; that he would take care of me. I watched the other soldiers get inside the truck full of people with necklaces of Vigor, Agroterra, Affinity, and Acumen. The truck was overflowing with many people I knew and a few I didn't know. It then drove off to a building only 10 miles away from the apartment. I suddenly saw my mother. She was on the truck. I could not help but tear up. She had been found and was being taken to the camp. I was so devastated that I forgot the problem at hand.

I fixed my teary eyes back on the soldier who had my life in his hands. His fierce face seemed to fade into a gentle one. He looked around as if he was making sure no one was still there, and then he told me his name was John. He looked into my eyes and I said nothing.

He spoke to me, "I don't wish to kill you, but this is my duty." His face was still gentle, but my face now depicted the terror I felt. I started to squirm and get nervous.

"But I would rather lose my job than kill you," he finally said. I knew this to be untrue; not the part about killing me, but the part about losing his job. If he would fail to carry out this task, he would be executed at the camp as if he was a Dissenter himself. A Dissenter was a rebel group that tried to overthrow Opulence. The group of Dissenters included Vigorions, Aggroterrians, Affinists, and Acumentists.

***

The soldier took my arm and lifted me from my knees. I was still pondering what was going on. He told me, "Do not be afraid, why don't you go back inside." I did as I was told, still not knowing if there were any tricks up his sleeve. John told me to sit and asked why I was in the Vigorion's apartment.

I was still frazzled by the thought of my mother gone, so I said nothing.

"There is nothing to be afraid of. If I wanted to hurt you I would have done so outside in front of all the troops," said John.

This made sense, so I told him my name was Rosa. I asked John why he saved me and he replied, "You are not saved until the war is over."

I was confused as to whether or not he was on the Opulencism or the Dissenter side. Not until that moment, did I realize that John was a blond, masculine boy with a stunning smile.

Without thinking, I ran upstairs to find Kaya. I felt a pit in my stomach – Kaya was nowhere to be found! I looked under the bed, out the window, and anywhere you could think of. I was sickened by the thought of her running away or being taken. Although I never saw that happen, it very well could have occurred during all the commotion. If we were not at war, then I would have shouted her name. But the fact that I could put Kaya, John, and I in danger was heart-wrenching. Instead, I ran back downstairs to tell John what happened. He had no idea what had become of her and I started to panic, wondering what to do next. With no lead on exactly where she was, it would be almost impossible to find her. John tried to tell me it was okay, but it only made it worse.

"My mother is gone, my sister is gone, and my father is gone! So don't you dare tell me it's okay, because, in reality, everything is falling apart!" I said.

He just listened and nodded. I apologized for the rage, but I was not sure I really was sorry.

John then said, "As an Opulencist, I should have killed

you. But I do not believe that one religion is more important than another. I am sure the Gods are looking down on us in disappointment."

I was amazed at his words of wisdom and could not help but to break down into tears. He soothed me, but I just pushed him away. I felt that if I let someone get close to me again, I would be heartbroken if I lost them. I had to put everything in the past, but one thing: I will never forget Kaya, and would not stop until I found her.

***

"So are you an Opulencist or a Dissenter?" I asked John.

He replied, "I am an undercover Dissenter, although I am a believer in the God of riches. If I have to, I will fight Opulencism to get the world back to where it used to be. The five gods should have equal power." He was referring to the gods of our world: Vigor was the god of healing, Agroterra the goddess of nature, Affinity the god of relationships, Acumen the goddess of intellect, and Opulence the god of riches.

I knew that Oppulenism wanted control over all other religions but the only way to do that was to eliminate them. I asked John if he would ever actually turn to Dissention instead of being undercover. He told me only if I joined the Dissenters would he join it himself. I never thought of being a rebel, but then again, I never thought Oppulencism would become in command.

The war had been going on for 13 years, so it was a faint memory of what life was like before the war. As a two year old, my only priorities were eating and sleeping. I decided to take John's offer and join the rebel side for my mother and my sister. As for my father, he had left my family members to join Oppulenism. He did not give us any forewarning, he just left. My mother had to keep my sister and me alive by herself. So being a strong woman ran in the family. I have no idea where the Dissenter headquarters was, but I had a feeling that John did.

Without any words, John took me to a small building that had the Opulence logo on it. I thought it was a great idea; no one would ever think that Dissenters would be in there. We stepped into the poorly lit apartment and I saw him – the leader of Dissenters was a very muscular man with dark, brown hair. He must have been at least 30 years old. He gave John a hand shake and asked who I was.

"I am Rosa, and I am an Acumentist," I said. John filled him in with everything that happened to Kaya, Mother, and me.

"I have a plan, but I need your help. We have about 150 people here who are willing to fight, but I need you," Paul told me.

All of a sudden, there was a noise – it sounded like a woman crying. And then all of a sudden, I heard gun shots and started to panic. I froze in my footsteps, but got picked up and dragged out the backdoor. I heard more shouts, and then silence. I realized that Paul, John ,and I were the only ones that came out of the back door. If John had not picked me up and ran, I would have been dead. The Oppulenists had found the Headquarters and planned to demolish it. We stayed behind the building for the night, not knowing how safe it was at the front.

***

At daylight, we decided to leave the back of the building to see what damage had been done. We entered the building to see almost everyone shot to death. One boy was huddled in the corner shaking. Although he was not hurt, he was obviously scared. I decided to talk to him, but there was only silence from him. I helped him to his feet and he finally said something: "My mother has been shot!"

I did not dare tell him everything was okay because I know those words were a lie. Instead, I told him that we had a plan and if he wanted to survive he should follow us. The boy agreed with our proposal. Before we departed the building, we checked on the boy's mother. By the time we found her, it was too late. We headed out the front of the building with not much of a plan. Our only chance was John. If we used John to get us into the Oppulnist Headquarters, we might be able to find my sister and my mother.

We had no mode of transportation, so we walked. We walked past the old Vigorion building that we hid in. We walked about half way to the camp, when I found her on the side of the road, helpless, bundled, and bloody. It was my mother! I tried to feel for a pulse, but my hands were shaking. John carefully took my hand and tried to stabilize it. I finally felt the pulse and was excited. John decided to carry her to the nearest Vigorion building to try to find some medicine and some other medical equipment. He set her down on a table and examined the wound on her calve. Although it was not very deep, he could tell it had been infected for at least two days. He disinfected the wound and bandaged it up. Because of the injury, my mother could not walk and we had to wait for it to heal before we continued our expedition.

On the last day before we departed the building, I decided to wake her up from her sleep. "Hey, it's me, Rosa," I smiled. She has a confused look on her face but she finally smiled.

"Darling, I thought I would never see you again." My mother started to cry so I saved the questions for when we hit the road tomorrow. I told my mother to go back to sleep and she did not oppose. There were two more days of walking, so I decided to ask her the question that had been in my mind.

"Mother, why did you not meet us back at the Vigorion building?"

It did not take long before she answered my question.

"I was out getting food, as you know. I heard gun shots, so I decided to start running. When I saw the troops roll onto the street I panicked. I decided to hide in an old alley, but the troops already had spotted my presence."

I decided to say nothing the rest of the trip and let her concentrate on healing and keeping up with us. We finally made it to the headquarters, so John acted the part of a loyal soldier. He put Paul, Mother, Billy, and I into wrist restraints, then went inside the building, pulling us behind him and telling the guard that he found us on the street. The guard told him to put us in a cell and to see the headmaster. John was fearful of what would happen to us, so he decided instead to put us inside of his dormitory and lock his door. We all slept in there for the night.

In the morning, we discussed our next plan of attack. We decided that John would invite the headmaster to his room to have brunch. It worked. He called the headmaster and he agreed to eat brunch with John. John put us inside his closet, with each of us holding a gun for protection.

When the door opened, the headmaster walked in, followed by a young, female guard holding a gun.

"Welcome, Sir Omar," said John as he bowed. All of a sudden, I noticed the name. I was shocked when I heard his voice.

"Hello, Johnathan. It's a pleasure to be in your company."

I became light-headed and almost fell out of the closet. The voice was sharp and fierce; it was so unique, that it was impossible to forget. I came to conclusion that the man was my father. I glared at my mother and she fought back the tears. I did not have to say a word; I knew she recognized his voice too. I heard John's throat clear and I knew it was time.

***

We stormed out of the closet and pointed the guns at Omar. His security guard did not have time to react. The boy took the rope from the closet and tied my father's hands. He did not even try to fight back, because our guns were pointed at him. The boy was very good at tying the knots and almost cut off the circulation to Omar's wrists. We propped him up against the wall and began the interrogation, with John asking the first question.

"How did all of this start?"

My father replied, "Well, it all started when the Oppulnists wanted more say in who gets how much money. They thought that they should be in charge of that spectrum because they believe in the god of fortune. When they were granted that power, the whole dynamic of equality shifted. Oppulnism gained too much control. They needed a leader, so I stepped up."

I then followed up with a second question, "How did you become the leader when you were not even an Oppulnist?"

My father then replied, "I am indeed a member of Oppulnism. Your mother was the one who was an Acumentist. We could have chosen between the two, but I let your mother have the say. I became leader because the people believed that whoever had the highest paying job would be best with their money and should be in charge."

"Why did you not tell us you were leaving?" asked mother with a whimper.

"I could not tell anyone about why I was leaving, because it could put you all in danger. If the rebel group knew that I would become a leader, they would kill you first and then me," he replied.

"Why did everything go downhill from there?" asked John.

"Well… I had to kill my own brother, because they needed me to prove my loyalty. After that, everyone thought that killing was okay. So, they started to go and kill innocent people who were not members of the Oppulnism faith. I tried to stop them, but it was impossible."

Paul stepped forward violently. "Omar, it was silly for you to think that I was dead!" He shouted and then pointed his gun at Omar and pulled the trigger. The bullet found its target.

"Why did you do that?" I shouted.

"Because he tried to kill me, and he thought I was dead."

Now everything is was coming back to me. Mother always told me about how much my father always hated his brother. Now I know that Paul is my uncle, and other things became clear. The little girl at the door was so quiet, I almost forgot that she was there. I looked at her and noticed that Kaya had changed. She looked brainwashed and now had a tattoo on her wrist. It was the symbol of Oppulensim and she stared at me with a blank look on her face.

I summoned John to come over to me. "John, when you were here, what happened to the minors when they were brought to the camp?"

He told me that they were brought to a training station that allowed them to be brainwashed into becoming heartless soldiers. I looked back at Kaya and saw that the raised a gun and pointed it at my head. With lightning reflexes, John dove and tackled her, knowcking the gun free from Kaya's hands. She struggled, but then finally stopped fighting. John picked her up and said, "Cover her tattoo with a handkerchief. It will help calm her, but the tattoo will resurface in an hour so we must hurry before she tries to attack us again."

He ran out the door and beckoned for us to follow him. We ran down five flights of the metal stairs to finally reach a laboratory. There, John injected Kaya her with a blue liquid and told me the antidote would wipe away her memory of the last 48 hours. He then grabbed a tattoo gun and added a salve to numb her skin. He marked over the tattoo.

Once it was gone, John propped up Kaya and asked, "Hello. Who are you, and what is your religion?"

She replied in a lifeless voice, "My name is Kaya and I am an Acumentist."

I ran to Kaya and hugged her hard. Slowly, her familiar expression returned and she began to cry when she recognized me. The easy part was behind us; now for the hard part: Trying to escape this place.

As we were making our plans, the whole building descended into chaos. Dissenters in large squad trucks began to storm into the building and threatened to shoot everyone unless they surrendered. John looked at me and I looked back unless they surrendered. John looked at me and I looked back at him. What should we do? How had the Dissenters survived the purge? As we were staring at one another, Paul put his hand on my shoulder and smiled a disgusting grin. Every single Oppulenist dropped their gun and knelt down.

Paul stepped up and said, "Listen! You must follow me or else you will be executed on the spot!" He forced everyone in the trucks. John, Mother, Billy, Kaya, and I ran. We hoped to find an escape route. Behind us, a group of Dissenter guards snatched John and dragged him away to one of the trucks. We managed to reach a room filled with all sorts of vehicles. We quickly hopped on motorcycles, Billy and I on one, and Kaya on the back of Mother's.

We raced out of that garage and followed the trucks. No one needed to speak. We were all in agreement that, instead of saving ourselves, we needed to rescue John and stop the evil leaders from taking complete control of everything. We had no idea where those trucks were headed, but we took off after them. Now, instead of finding Kaya, I was finding John.

ALONE

Tommy Reid

Journal Entry 1; December 19, 2015

Why can't anyone see me? Every day of my life is spent thinking about that night. And every time I cringe at the thought of it. I just wish that it could just go away, that I would forget about it... it seems almost impossible. I go to school every day and no one sees me; so I sit down at lunch and sulk. I mean, I have "friends," but I don't think they are actually friends. If I want to do something with them, I have to suggest it to make sure I'm invited. I have to say "hi" in the hallways, even though they don't say it back. I am the one who starts the conversations. They never do anything for me.

And on top of all that, I don't think my family even knows I exist. They always wonder why the cereal's gone or the milk carton is empty. They can never figure out why. My family went to IKEA today; of course, it was without me. I found out because of the note they left for my little brother.

He wasn't home from school, his last day before break. The note said "We are going to buy a new table at IKEA. I'm sorry, we couldn't wait for you. If we would've waited, we would never get the table. I hope you had a great day at school! :) We didn't want to leave you alone, but we just had to go. See you when you get home!"

Can you believe that they completely forgot me? And the worst part is that when they got home, the table only had four chairs, when there was five of us. Guess who's the one who had to find a seat somewhere else? You guessed it…me. But, hey, at least the couch is comfortable.

We even have a dog, but I don't exist, so it doesn't matter anyways. I just wish someday someone will find me and see me. Notice me. Feel what I'm feeling. Know what I know. And then maybe, just maybe, I will finally be understood.

Journal Entry 2; December 20, 2014

Today's my birthday; but it's not like anyone cares anyway. I'm turning 17; yup, 17 years of me cooped up in my little "shell," as my mother would say. She was the only one that ever understood me. Today's not just my birthday, today is the anniversary of what happened that night. Last year was when it happened, supposedly the most important birthday ever. The big 1-6, the sweet 16. Except for me, it was anything but sweet. It was the most retched, horrible, saddest day of my life.

Why did he have to come? Of all of the nights he could've come, why that night? He is the most ungrateful son of a... Don't think like this on your birthday, I thought to myself; you're better than this. C'mon, if you were there, you would understand. If you only knew... Now that I think about it, I don't even understand. But I know and I... NO ONE CAN EVER KNOW.

Journal Entry 3; December 21, 2014

Only four days until Christmas. Yea! I just can't wait until I am the only person without a gift under the tree. I get to watch my dad, my two older sisters, and younger brother opening gifts – a new IPhone, a new gaming system, clothes, and even more clothes. Then they get my gifts. When they open them, their reaction is always the same. "Oh yes! I wanted his!" or "I needed this!" And when they go to look for whom to thank for the gift, they say, "Who's Jared, Dad" or "I don't know who this is from." They just act like it never happened and just go about their lives... But to see them happy and to see another year of successful presents makes me happy... but that's also when it hurts the most.

Journal Entry 4; December 25, 2014

Yea, it's Christmas. I really hope my family likes the gifts I got them this year. I got my dad a new set of tools to fix things like the leaking sink that only I know about, because no one listens to me. He looked a little disappointed when he opened them, but I know that he will eventually use them for the sink. I bought a brand new bow staff to match the nun chucks that I got my little brother Nick last year. I got my older sister Ziva the newest and best laptop I could find, so she can use it to become the computer designer she has always wanted to be. When she opened it she was so happy. Now, for me oldest sister Abby I got a college sponsor to come to one of her lacrosse games. The sponsor was from the college that she wanted to go to.

I don't know how he actually noticed me, but I didn't worry about. And he kind of looked familiar, but like I said, I didn't worry about. When the college sponsor got back to me, he said that he could get a full scholarship for Abby. I was so excited, but not as excited as Abby was when she opened the envelope that contained the letter that saying that she was accepted and with a full scholarship. The thing was this: as soon as I got happy, something happened... and it hurt.

Journal Entry 5; January 1, 2015

Happy New Year! Yea, I don't know if I will be happy at all this year. I'm sorry that I haven't said anything in a while. I was... well, let's just say that I was doing something. My dad threw a party for New Year's Eve. I think he is trying to get a girlfriend or something. He was hitting on this one girl the whole night. YUCK! I don't see how he could ever think about replacing mom. I don't get how he could just throw away what he had with my mother and go for another girl so soon. I mean, yea it has been a year, but compared to the 12 years they spent together, that is nothing. It makes me think that he never even loved my mother at all. He just loved her for her looks or just started to fake it after a year or so. I am just so angry with him right now!

Journal Entry 6; January 17, 2015

Sorry about the 16 days of you waiting for me to write. I was just too angry at my dad and I couldn't write. I felt so emotional that I had to go do something. I ended up going to this abandoned house. It was really creepy there. I felt like the house was going to fall on me, but I also felt that if it did I would be able to stop it. I have no idea why; such a feeling makes absolutely no sense at all. I wish I could understand.

I apparently made a lot of noise, because someone complained about the commotion. Only one police officer came. I wasn't too worried about it though, because no one can see me. When the police officer came, I just relaxed and kept doing what I was doing because nothing was going to happen. But... THE POLICE OFFICER SAW ME! HOW DID HE SEE ME?

When he saw me, I had to run or I was going to jail. I ran as fast as I could and somehow, someway, I outran the police officer. I ran like I had never run before. I was as fast as a cheetah! How? I don't know. I am not a fast runner; any other day, I would have been caught and taken to jail. But what happened today? What was different today? I have absolutely no clue, but I will find out…

Journal Entry 7; February 13, 2014

Okay, I can't hold it in anymore. I need to tell someone. You have to promise that you will not tell anyone, ever. I need to know that I can trust you. C'mon, say something! Fine! But I should also mention that if you read the next sentence you will be in danger. Not minor danger, but I'm talking about serious danger. This could get you killed.

Okay, here it goes: I have some type of power, this unmistakable power, and I don't know what it is. You see, what this "magic power" does is that it makes me invisible to the ones that don't have it or don't suffer from the same losses, anger, or pain. It was never me; I wasn't another person to ignore – I am special. Wait a second, if the college scout saw me, does that mean he has the "magic" or is he just in pain? I THINK I KNOW WHY HE LOOKED FAMILIAR!

Journal Entry 8; June 5, 2015

Sorry it took so long to write again. I lost my journal and couldn't find it. It was in a school locker and we just cleaned it out today. Ah, cleaning out lockers, the symbol of the last day of school. I can finally go and find that college scout. I can find out what happened to my mother; even what this "magic power" is, how to control it, and why I have it. I have so many questions to ask him. I need to find him. Well, if he is who I think he is, I need to find him..

Journal Entry 9; June 23, 2015

So, the reason I haven't been contacting you in a while is because I found out. I got my answers. It all started like this: I was walking down the vacant street right after the previous journal entry when I saw him. As soon as I saw him, I had this sudden urge in my stomach not to chase him, but what else could I have done? There I was standing like a deer in headlights, as he was fumbling with his keys to open his 2002 off-white convertible BMW. That's when he saw me; and as soon as he did, he started to move fast, as if he could see into my soul and see my anger or sense that I could see into his.

As he tried to quickly put the key in the keyhole, I was able to catch him before he opened the door. He tried to open the door, but the door was not budging for some strange reason. Then suddenly, he stepped back from his car and stared like a maniac at his car door. And within an instant, the car door flew open and down I went. Some robust force sent me flying across the street. I hit my head firmly against the ground and I can't remember anything else after that...

Journal Entry 10; June 24, 2015

Now that you know what happened those past couple of da... Oh yea, I almost forgot to tell you: I was in the hospital with a coma for 17 days. Crazy right? I can't believe it myself. But I have to believe, because when I was in a coma I saw someone. Someone very important... my mother.

The memory I saw was the one when I was eight. It was Christmas, one where I actually got presents. When I opened my present, it was my first journal – the journal that started it all. I have gone through about 100 by now. The journals are probably the only thing keeping me alive today. But... Oh, I also completely forgot that I was about to tell you about what happened...

Okay, so after I got out of the hospital, I saw it. I saw the 2002 BMW, the same 2002 BMW! I was astonished and I was in pursuit of the car – more covertly this time, of course. But I didn't need to be careful because he just let me in his car. So why did he put up such a fight when I saw him the first time?

Journal Entry 11; June 25, 2015

So we're in the car, right? And he keeps trying to convince me he didn't mean to send me to the hospital. Yea, like I'm gonna believe him. How inconsiderate can you be? I'm going to throw this kid across the street by "accident" and expect him to forgive me. Wow, such a great plan. But, anyway, so apparently his name is Kai and has the "magic power" like me. He said that he was trying to escape to power the "magic" in me because it's fueled by anger or pain or something like that. He was testing how powerful I was in order to get a basic understanding of how he should train me.

I didn't even know that I was the reason why he couldn't open the door. And I guess that when he was staring at the door, he was using his "magic" to open it. Clearly he is stronger than me; but he is almost twice my age. We are driving to god knows where. He won't tell me where we are going. The only thing he'll tell me is that it is "something for... training." He said it just like that, cause that's not suspicious or anything, not at all. Anyway, I'm gonna sleep until we get there, wherever there is.

Journal Entry 12; June 26, 2015

We just got there and Kai woke me up. We are at some medieval-looking place. I guess it looks medieval because of the fact that it's one colossal castle with miniature castles linked to the main one. Kai went inside and told me to wait outside. A couple of minutes later, he came out with and elderly lady. Her name was Renee. Kai said that Renee was his trainer and he wants her to train me.

But I said, "I don't know if I want to be trained by such a fragile lady." Renee responded by turning around and looking at the castle and, without even moving, she lifted the whole entire castle off the ground. Not just the main castle, but all of the miniature castles, too. How did she do that without a single body motion? She simply looked at it, lifted it off the ground, and put it back down like nothing happened. She turned around and gave me a smirk.

"Okay, let's get this thing started," I replied.

Journal Entry 13; June 27, 2015

"Okay, to 'get this thing started' we will first see how much supremacy you actually have," Renee smirked.

"What do I have to do?" I responded.

We sit in silence for a couple of seconds; then she looks at me as if she can see my soul, just as Kai did. But she doesn't run or try to fight – she just stares at me. After an uncomfortable five minutes of staring, she says one word – the most excruciating and heart-wrenching word she could say. She looks deeper into my soul and says it again. I can't take it anymore; I have to break the gaze, but I can't. She holds tight and says it once more. I'm trying to escape when I realize that she was never talking. She wasn't the one saying the word... I was.

Why would I say that word? Does it have to do with the gaze that she is giving me? I say it again once more. Over and over, again and again, I say the word until I can't say it anymore. I can feel it gurgling in my chest and out it goes, louder than a herd of elephants: MOTHER!

I scream it again and again, until I feel the ground start shaking, which doesn't make sense because we are at the top of the castle on the watchtower. Then the ground stops shaking and I look up. We are 60 feet into the air. I did that. I lifted all the castles. Through the rage, I realize that I able to lift the castles; the loss of my mom allowed me to unlock my potential. My mom, even though she is long gone, is still here with me and is still helping me get through life.

Journal Entry 14; June 28, 2015

"That was a very good start, yesterday," Renee said.

"Well, well! I did amazing! I lifted all the castles just like you did," I boasted. "I'm probably the best student you've had, right?"

"Well, let's not get to arrogant," she replied. "And yes, you did lift the castles, but not like me. I did it without even moving, or screaming for that matter."

"But I am the best student you've had though, right?" I asked.

"Well... no, but the best that I have had in a while," she answered. "And don't get a big head from this!" she added.

I laughed and we got on with today's training. So this time she didn't stare into my soul, but instead we talked. That's all we did. But what was important about it was what we were talking about. Obviously, she heard me say "mother" yesterday, so she knew who I lost. That's what I found out: Anyone who has this "magic" has had a tragic loss of a parent. I'm not alone. And get this, the "parent that the person lost had the 'magic' too," announced Renee.

"Had the magic?" I ask.

"Yes, once the child reaches 18, he or she has the choice to have a child. Before they choose, we tell them the consequences."

"Consequences?" I ask.

"Yes, consequences like knowing that once they have the child their magic with flow from them to their baby. Also, that once their child turns 16, the parent will end up dying unless they can escape, but that has only happened once," she answered.

"Who? Who escaped?' I swiftly asked.

"Alright, that's enough for today," she replied.

"Wait!" I demanded.

But she didn't wait. She got up like nothing happened and briskly walked away. I wonder who it was...

Journal Entry 15; July 4, 2015

Happy 4th of July! I haven't written in a while, because I have been training. I got a break today because it's a holiday – even though I wanted to train, because Renee is amazing. I am learning how to control my sadness from my mother and harness it into this "magic power." Also, Renee told me that what this "magic power" is, is actually more scientific than supernatural. She said that the "magic" is actually telekinesis in a way. See, there is a supernatural factor to it, because of the way it is transferred from parent to child. What the people with the "magic" have is a semi-functional brain. What she meant was that regular humans have about 10 percent of their brain unlocked, while "special" humans have roughly double that.

But what I was really surprised about, was that Renee got back to the topic of the person who escaped. No matter what I did, I could not get a name out of her. She did say, however, that this person was someone who happened to unlock 100 percent of their brain. Renee tried to stop her, but couldn't. Now, that's when I realized I got a clue out of her. Later I realized that I didn't get it out of her, she purposely gave me the hint. I could see it in her eyes. Anyway, she said that the person could be anyone because, for every 10 percent of your brain power you unlock, you get a new "superpower." At 10 percent, we get life and comprehension, at 20 we get telekinesis, at 30 we get shapeshifting, at 40 we get flying, at 50 we get invisibility, at 60 we get mind-reading, at 70 we get super speed, at 80 we get super strength, at 90 we get healing, and at 100 percent we get complete control over all of the abilities. Wow!

She also said that those who have it and have gotten to 100 percent, need no training at all. But if they got to 99, for example, they would just learn very quickly and do not need to train as frequently as those who have only 20. Due to the ability of shapeshifting, she said that the person that escaped could be anyone. Also, with the power of healing, they could live forever unless they are physically killed by a special staff that's been missing for 200 years. After she explained this to me, she did what she did last time: She simply got up and walked away like nothing happened. I need to find out more information.

Journal Entry 15; June 20, 2015

I kept nagging her and nagging her about the person, and she didn't budge. But I feel that she is on the breaking point of telling me. Since she hasn't told me who it is, there isn't much to talk abo... Right! I almost forgot to tell you that my training has been going really well. You know how Renee lifted the castles when I first met her? Well, I can do that now with ease. All that is different is that I only use minimal movement instead of no movement at all. I feel so proud of myself.

"You have been coming along quite nicely," Renee said.

"Thank you," I replied. "But there is just one thing that I have to ask you. It's about my mother, Robin Waterwo..."

"Wait, your mother was Robin Waterworks?" Renee quickly asked.

"Yes, of course, I'm Jared Waterworks. That would make sense, we do have the same last name," I answered.

"Your mother was my student 200 years ago!" Renee stated.

"What? How is that even poss... Doesn't that make my mother the person that unlocked all of her brain?"

"Yes, yes it does," Renee quickly responded.

"Does that mean that I have all of my brain unlocked?" I asked.

"No, not necessarily. A person only unlocks all of their brain; it doesn't mean they pass along all of the abilities. Only about 20 percent of the brain can be passed on. However, to get 100 percent of one's brain, both parents would have to have the 'magic'."

"Oh that makes sense...sorta," I stated uneasily. "Forgive me if I don't believe you. But if I did unlock all of my brain, how come my father wasn't killed?" I asked.

"Well, it's different for the father. When the father turns 18, he has a choice if he wants children. He is told about the consequences, but they are different. The father's consequences are that he loses his 'magic' right then and there. Then the father will forget all about the 'magic'."

"So, my father ignoring me was him trying to give me my best shot. What?" I was shocked.

Journal Entry 16; June 21, 2015

I decided to test out whether or not I have all of my brain unlocked. Renee said I shouldn't test it, because I could get seriously hurt or die. I don't believe that. I believe that I have all of my brain unlocked, because I can feel it. I told Renee that I was going outside to get some fresh air after our little "disagreement." But what I was really doing was going to the top of the castle... To the watchtower. As soon I got to the watchtower, I knew what I had to do... I had to jump. I debated it myself, but I have to believe that my father was a better person than I thought he was. I can do this. I have to!

With the cool wind gently blowing against my frigid face, I do it. I jumped...

Journal Entry 17; June 22, 2015

See, I told you I could do it. All I had to do was believe in myself, which I did. I HAVE 100 PERCENT OF MY BRAIN UNLOCKED!

As soon as I hit the hard ground, I blacked out. When I woke, only minutes passed and I felt like I could have run a marathon. I healed myself – a sign that I unlocked 90 percent of my brain. I did it. When I opened my eyes, I was a little dreary at first, but then I saw Renee standing there. But she looked different. She looked younger... but how?

"When you hit the ground, I came rushing over," she explained. "After about three minutes, I got worried. Just as I was losing hope, you started to glow. Then all of a sudden you were back to normal. I started crying, and then without warning, a purple cloud emanated from your body and when you were awoke, I was young again. You made me young again. Now I can train the "special" for a couple of more years. How can I ever repay you?"

"You already have."

Journal Entry 18; December 20, 2016

Sorry I haven't been writing in a while. I left my journal at the medieval castles. But I summoned it back today, since I'm 18 now.

"You have a choice," Renee said. "You can either keep your 'magic' or not have children, or you can give up your 'magic' and pass it on to your children."

"I can't choose," I answer her. "I have to run away."

"You can't run away from this, Jared. They will find you," Renee warned me.

"I can't. I have to run. I can use my invisibility power to stay hidden," I explained.

"That didn't work for your mother, now did it? What makes you think it will work for you?" she cautioned.

"I don't know. But I am leaving now, whether you like it or not!" I roared.

"No, you have to wait. You can't run away for the rest of your life. Just stop and face it."

Journal Entry 19; Augustus 14, 2036

15024 Lila Street. California, Alaska 65246. No time for explaining. I can hear them coming. They are trying to get in. You need to get here fast. Oh No! They got in. Come save m…

MARKS

Cadence Rochlen

Maeve clutched the small necklace that had just been placed in her hand. Below her lay the body of a young woman, stone cold. Nothing left of the smiling, caring person she knew as her mother. She opened her hand slowly, a tear rolling down her cheek as she peered upon her mother's last gift. The necklace shined – three loops moved slightly, encircling a small hourglass filled with pure white sand. She turned and the old floorboards creaked under her bare feet as she walked through the hallway, which now contained only wisps of memory. She shuffled through the small door at the end of the hall, as if in a trance.

Maeve looked around the unfamiliar room, and her heart sank. She realized that it was actually the same; that she had lost this part of her. She would never again see this place as home. The death of one person caused the birth of a new person. She did not like the new person she would become; the new tore itself apart, picking at its own weakness until there was nothing left but a scared girl clutching to a small lifeline. The old Maeve loved. The old Maeve felt infinity and clung to it, stayed fixed there always. She saw now that the old way of life was not returning. She could not go back. Time didn't favor her.

After

It was becoming quite clear that Maeve was not going to get to school on time. She yanked on her hairbrush, which was currently stuck in her bright, red tangled mess of hair. He father poked his head in the room, asking the necessary question: "your ETA?" She thought about this, factoring in a little leeway – better to be earlier with the ETA than later. "About 7:55" she replied. He nodded and left to enter this into the ledger. She sighed as she remembered that this would cause her to lose marks. Oh well, there was nothing she could do about that now.

Quickly, Maeve braided her hair, and put it up into a bun. Hopefully, it would stay in place today. Yesterday she had received a mark down because of a few hairs that had wandered out of the bun. She then put away her brush, turned off her light, and walked to the train stop.

The train was much quieter than usual. This was to be expected, considering that the young students where all away at school now. The train car was currently occupied by several young adults, obviously college students on their way to their morning lectures. They stared at her. Maeve was so obviously out of place it was almost comedic: instead of their clean button-down shirts and ironed jeans, she was wearing her mother's necklace, and the typical middle learning outfit of a polo shirt and skirt.

They knew Maeve was late, and she could almost feel their judgmental eyes scanning her. As if she didn't know it; as if the mark she would lose wasn't punishment enough. She leaned back and closed her eyes, still tired from staying up late the night before. She had been studying, as she should. But she still hadn't learned a key skill: time management.

Just then, Maeve's bracelet dinged, alerting her to the fact that she was officially late. This meant that she had already lost two of her 100 marks for the day. The display listed this in all caps: MARK: 98. The train slowed carefully to a stop and Maeve got off. She walked as quickly as possible toward the platform counter. The counter beeped as she passed, and the display on her wrist flashed once again: MARK 93. She frowned, realizing that she would be walking on eggshells today, trying to keep what little she had left of her points. She didn't want to be sent to Finis. She had already been transferred once.

Maeve didn't remember much of that experience. She was very young at the time. Her mother had just died and her father was doing nothing, just staring blankly for hours on end. The doctors said it was shock. She remembered being cold and watching her frozen breath decorate the air as she shivered in her coat. The part of town she was in was not meant for the eyes of the many, and didn't hold the same sterile feeling that everything else did in Purgare (her old district). Maeve was being transferred to a new district, one she did not yet know the name of. She and her father were the only ones their, which was surprising, considering the number of people she had seen getting transferred. Then the train whistle blared, and her memory faded away.

When she arrived at the school, the class was already in progress. Again, she scanned her bracelet (and watched it remove two more marks) and then walked into the building. She walked to her first class, arriving just as Ms. Benignus was beginning her lecture for the day. Maeve smiled, and to her relief, the teacher let her sit in her seat without saying anything; Maeve was already embarrassed enough.

Maeve reached into her gray shoulder bag and pulled out her tablet: the machine assigned to her at birth that held a record of all her achievements – from her first baby scribbles to her honor roll certificates. The screen flashed open to today's note guide, and she began typing. But she only half listened; Maeve's mind was still on the marks she had lost that morning. If she got transferred again, her father would not go with her – you only get one full family transfer.

The ringing of the bell startled her out of her thoughts, and she quickly got up to go to her next class.

"Hey" said a voice behind her. Maeve turned, startled, but smiled when she realized who it was. "Hey Em," Maeve smiled to the tall, curly-haired blonde.

Emily frowned, obviously concerned about her friend's tardiness. "What happened?" she asked.

"Just slept through my alarm."

Emily nodded understandingly and the two girls walked out of the classroom and down the hall to their next lesson: anatomy.

Anatomy happened to be Maeve's favorite class. Since she planned to pursue a career in medicine, she found the class very useful. Emily had always envied Maeve for already knowing what it was she wanted to do with her life – teachers always praised students that already had good goals set. Emily was still torn between two options: childcare and government. These two options were as completely different sides of the spectrum, and many adults viewed Emily's indecision as laziness a lack of direction.

Maeve, however, recognized it for what it was: nervousness. The thought of deciding on one career for the rest of her life was very daunting to Emily, as it should be. Maeve had always believed that the other kids her age were somehow too comfortable with such lasting decisions.

The class was nothing out of the ordinary. Today was a normal day, and the teacher spoke with the same cadence he always did, until a piercing scream broke the regular rhythm. The whole class jumped, and Maeve, the teacher, and a few others ran out into the hallway to see what had happened, and if they could help in some way.

Hannah

As the sun rose, Hannah Benignus thought about what she had learned. The information had been given to her by a friend who was a government worker. She thought about Finis: Finis was the end; Finis was death. Now that she knew the truth, she could not keep the information secret. This was wrong. Her basic human instinct told her this. But if they found out about her knowledge there was no doubt in her mind where she would be sent. It was almost ironic, really.

They would suspect something was wrong if she didn't go to her job; she knew this. She doubted she could act normal around everyone. But she had no choice. Slowly, she got out of bed and got dressed. Her heart raced and her palms sweated, wondering if anyone at the school would notice this change. She walked to the bus stop and sat down on a bench, looking at the people around her. Most of them she saw every morning – a combination of teachers and young students.

But it wasn't them she was paying attention to. It was the man in the suit, looking at his watch nervously, that she was observing. He was clearly late. There was a pang in her chest as she thought about the marks he would lose for it. If he got to zero… well… she wouldn't be seeing him again.

The transfers to Finis were not rare. Everyone knew how to manage their minutes. But problems and transfers still happened. Being a teacher, she had even caused a few. A few marks here, another there; it was a cruel fact that she was slowly killing them? She thought the strict system was put in place to better the society, to create a world where everyone had a place. But she was wrong.

The train pulled into the stop, and Hannah walked, trance-like, onto the platform. Her thoughts wandered to all the people she knew who had been transferred: Her father, her cousin, and a few of her students. A tear streaked down her cheek as she thought of them. Her father hadn't committed any crime. He simply had an off day. He overspent his marks and was sent away, with the rest of the transfers. She never thought twice about it, she forced herself to think he was just in another district, that he would be happy there, that he would fit into that society better.

As the train's whistle sounded, alerting passengers to disembark at the stop, Hannah dried her eyes. She couldn't let anyone she knew see her like this. She tried to act normal, which is not as easy as it sounds. Her classroom was almost at the back of the school. She had chosen the location, and she now regretted the decision: she had to walk by all the other classrooms on the way to hers and there was clearly no way to avoid "hello's" from fellow teachers. The first one came from the anatomy teacher, Mr. Gaudium.

"Good morning, Hannah."

She smiled back like usual and waved good naturedly, hurrying down the brightly lit hallway.

Her first class went almost without a hitch. One of her female students – a girl named Maeve – came in late, which concerned her, but she managed to act naturally. She lectured about Greek architecture, the subject her class was currently studying, and then reminded them to read the pages that they were supposed to finish by Friday. When the bell rang, the class shuffled out slowly, like a herd of cattle, and she breathed a sigh of relief. She had a prep period next, and she needed the time to clear her head. The final bell rang, signaling to the students that they needed to be in their next class. A boy she recognized, Thomas, ran past her room and she frowned: He would lose marks for being late.

Hannah got up and went to use the bathroom. As she was walking toward it, she saw a man she did not recognize walking toward her. He stopped directly in front of her and spoke:

"Hannah Benignus, you are being transferred to Finis." And in response, she let out a terrified cry for help.

Maeve

Maeve she ran out into the hallway and saw that it had only two occupants: Ms. Benignus and a man she did not recognize. "Ms. Benignus, what is happening?" she asked her teacher.

Ms. Benignus looked as if she had seen a ghost, and simply replied, "I am being transferred."

Maeve pondered this reality. She had seen many other people transferred but none had acted in such a strange way.

But everyone who now poured out into the hallway, except for the strange man, stood in shock. The man carefully led Ms. Benignus out of the school by her arm, and nothing more was said.

This was life. And no one seemed to question it.

DREAMCHASER

Devereaux Stephens and Etienne Stephens

I awoke in a dark and damp cave, the silence of the blackness before me shook me to my core. I groped around to find my way, my hands tracing what I hoped was the wall of the cave. I searched the unending darkness for something, anything that would tell me where I was and how I could leave. Then, I spotted a single, almost unnoticeable gold dot. I slowly made my way to it, not knowing if I was slowly walking to my salvation or my demise. The dot seemed to grow larger and larger, until the light began piercing the blackness that sought to consume me.

My path dimly illuminated. My confidence grew and so did the pace of my steps. I stumbled on my way out, but it did not matter. I could see the mouth of the cave. I began to run faster and faster, until I was sprinting toward the vast field that lay before the cave. Before I could register what was going on, the ground beneath my feet began shaking. I looked all around me and could not find what was causing *this terrible shaking. Terrified, I stood at the exit, trying to gather my courage. After about three more minutes, I saw it.*

THUD! A foot the size of a house crashed into the grass before me. The shockwave sent me stumbling back in surprise and in awe. I rushed back to the cave's mouth to get a better look at what I had just witnessed. It was a giant beast of some sort, one of those beasts that you hear about in fairy tales and myths. Without realizing, I had walked to where its foot was, and before I could process what was going on, its huge shadow loomed over me, and its other foot was yards away from my head and getting closer, fast.

A few hours earlier...

"Jiro! Jiro! It's time to wake up! You're going to be late for school!" wailed an annoying voice.

I groaned and got up from my nice, nine-hour sleep. If that wakeup call didn't point it out, I'm Jiro, Jiro Brooks. Actually, since my dad left, I've taken my mother's maiden name – Fukui. It's supposed to mean "lucky" or something, what a laugh. If I'm so lucky, why is my sister yelling at me to wake up?

I'm 16 and live with my mother and sister; I'm outnumbered and very annoyed right now. After slowly getting ready, I made my way downstairs for breakfast. But I could barely get my foot to hit the first step before getting shoved into the wall by a troll, otherwise known as Stephanie – or the person I regrettably relate to as my sister.

"Move out of the way, idiot! Some of us actually want to leave for school" she said condescendingly.

Most people would have a quick retort or would otherwise react to something like this, but why bother? Stuff like this happens all the time and I have gotten used to her behavior. I know that if I actually decide to respond, I'll have a 20-minute long shouting match with someone who's IQ is that of a snail. So, I brushed it off and finally made it downstairs for breakfast.

I grabbed something quick and tried to sneak out before I was spotted; but, like every morning, I was seen by "The all seeing eye," also known as Mom.

"Good morning, sweetheart! I didn't hear you get up! Normally that crazed siren you call your alarm clock would be blaring and I wouldn't have to send your sister to wake you up," she said lovingly.

"Well, considering I only need to be in school in person twice a week, I figured that I'd go in tomorrow. But 'the witch' didn't think to ask me anything," I replied.

"Oh, she's just looking out for you! She knows that you've had a tough time making friends and just wants you to get out there and enjoy your time at school."

Just then, my sister appeared, with her black hair done in a long braid and her bright blue streak screaming down the middle of her head like a racing stripe painted on the hood of a car. Her small, wiry frame held her confidently as she said, "Why would I look out for someone as dumb as you? Ha! I don't have enough time to deal with a charity case like him, but as student body president, I have a duty to help out the less fortunate. So I'm forced to waste my precious breath to say 'Get your butt in gear we need to leave'... now!" She added extra malice and aggression to the last word.

"Okay, settle down you two," said my mom "Steph, please be nice to your brother."

"I'll consider it," pouted Stephanie

"Maybe I'll consider not nagging about how you refuse to show... I mean, you have the same beautiful brown hair as your father! And it suits you better than..."

"Fine! I'll be nice! But I'm going to leave now before I change my mind," yelled Stephanie as she was running off.

I chuckled as my mom beamed at me. "Beep-beep, beep-beep." My eyes bulged, remembering that I left my personal project unattended in my room. I walked to my desk and grabbed a blue box no longer than six inches. I sat in my computer chair and quickly fumbled for the mouse. When my screen saver dissipated, I hurriedly opened a program that I have been working on I call "Pileus," which is Latin for freedom. Considering what it can do, I think it's appropriate.

Pileus is a program that will give anyone the ability to dream lucidly. In the day-to-day bland reality that I call my life, I realized that if I'm not able to control my surroundings during the day, then why should I let my brain run on autopilot at night? So for the last few months, I've been using an external stimulus to help me induce a super lucid state in my dreams in the form of my alarm.

Reprogramming my clock was child's play, but the difficult part has been trying to keep the dream state. The electronic waves that my alarm has been silently producing have not been powerful enough. So I used my school's 3D printer and created a physical medium. I have named the interface "Icarus" and to mimic the name Icarus, I designed the nodes to look like a pair of wings. They are simply electronic stickers that amplify my brain's alpha waves and then send whatever I have programmed in Pileus straight into my dream. Last night was the final beta test. I just have to remember to put in the termination trigger.

"Jiro. Sweetheart, you have to get to school!" yelled my mother from the kitchen.

"Okay! I'll be right down!" I replied.

I took the blue box which housed the Icarus nodes or Icarus' "wings," opened it, and gently placed each wing on my temples. I have to make sure that they calibrate properly the software in relation to my brain activity, so I'm going to keep them on all day. I need to record my biorhythms, so my first real dream submersion will be more real.

After setting the program to run on my computer, I rushed downstairs and, as I was on my way out, I saw my mom looking at a picture as she sat on the couch. She was in the living room, which was squashed next to the kitchen. Sitting sideways on the red armchair like she always did, her back was turned to me and I didn't have to see what she was holding to know that it was my dad's picture. I know because it's the only frame whose wood finish is worn and slightly warped by her tears. Rather than announce that I was leaving, I slipped out without a sound. My head felt a little heavy as I walked to school.

My mind started to wonder why my mom can still cry after he left while Steph was so angry. Actually it was easy to figure it out; she can be so transparent sometimes. You can see that my sister doesn't really like me, it's because our father left when she was young and I am a spitting image of him. With the wrath that she directs toward me, you'd think that I was his carbon copy. But according to her, I'm just an idiot and, if this idiot can connect the dots that easily, why should I have to suffer and go to school too? It's tortuous enough knowing that I'm smarter than the entire student body, but I have to deal with them in person!

I chose a school that would allow me to stay home as much as possible; the only drawback is that my annoying older sister goes there too. But I go for my mom, who says I need to "socialize." But I mean, how could I have an equal amongst those obnoxious, driving, brainless chimps. Luckily, I could take my wings on a small "test flight" today, which made my day go by quickly enough. It was just another day at school. I took my notes, did my work, and aced whatever test I had to, as I usually do.

Lunch time came around and I was so bored with school that I just grabbed my stuff and ducked out early. As I walked home from school, I thought of how amazing it would be if I could just go to my own little place where no one could bother me and where no one would ever worry about me. I better just keep dreaming, huh? Exhausted from life in general, I completely forgot that I was wearing my wings and my program was probably finished coding. I went straight home and made sure I was not followed or seen.

As I walk in, I was greeted by the sight of my sister standing in the doorway with her arms crossed and tapping her foot. "Oh no..." I thought to myself as I was about to consider running away.

"Well? What are you doing here?" she asked.

"Is there anything wrong with walking home to get lunch?" I retorted. I quickly ran upstairs to my room before she could say anything else. On my way upstairs, I looked in the living room to see my mother passed out on the carpet, with a half empty glass bottle in her hand and a few cans scattered around her. Ignoring the scene, I went into my room and locked the door. I peeled off the wings and put them in their blue box and closed the lid. I shook my mouse and, after a second, the screen displayed a finished program and the last command blinking on the bottom. It read "Termination code: ???"

Without much thought, I typed in something quickly and hit enter. I plugged the box into the computer's USB port and typed in a final command and let the program sync with the wings and their biorhythm readings. As the program was running, I made some minor adjustments to my room. I closed the shades and took a sleeping pill, and made my bed as comfortable as possible. I waited for what felt like forever and my eyelids began to increase in weight and I started to drift off when I heard, "ding ding."

My computer chimed to notify me that the wings were ready to fly. I opened the box lid and placed each wing on the side of my head. My arms felt like lead and I slowly walked to my clock and fumbled with a few buttons, then I flopped onto my bed. Without much warning, I slipped into a deep sleep. I woke up and I looked around to see only darkness. I stood up, slightly annoyed that my program didn't work. I fumbled my way to my desk, only find that I was groping a wall. I spun around quickly to find my bed again, only to trip on a rock and land face first on the floor. I could only see darkness, feel darkness; and I was slowly being consumed by the darkness.

Present time...

Before I could process what was going on, its huge shadow loomed over me, and its other foot was yards away from my head and getting closer, fast. I had to get out of its path. I dashed to the left and rolled, literally inches from being crushed. I stared at the giant creature in awe. What was that? Where am I? As I took a look around me, my heart nearly skipped a beat.

The landscape was... a rainbow. The grass was colored red, orange, yellow, green, blue, and violet. There were 1,000-foot trees sprouting out of the ground. The sun was shining extra-bright, making everything around look beautiful. The birds seemed to be the only normal things in this mysterious place. As I looked around, I saw a forest to my left and a village to my right. At that moment, I realized that my program worked! But I didn't have much time to rejoice in my success; I needed to see how well Pileus worked.

I looked in awe as the beast continued to stroll toward the forest. I remembered that I created a simple shell program which would give me general guidelines, but my subconscious and conscious mind helped shape my experiences. Luckily for the masses, I made it with their simple decision in mind.

Anyone who didn't choose the village was just adventure-thirsty. As I made my way toward to the village, I smelled smoke and a little warm feeling in the palm of my hand. When I looked, it was a tiny flame emerging from my hand. I instantly screamed and tried to pat it down, but the fire wouldn't go out. I began to flail like a mad man, screaming my head off. I tried all sorts of ways to put out the fire. I rolled on the ground. I tried to use the dirt to smother it and, after a few minutes and complete exhaustion, I looked at my hand and the fire.

"Wait," I said to myself. "Why isn't the fire burning me?" As soon as I started to stare at the fire in amazement, it just went out like that. Poof! What was that? I quickly recovered from the odd situation and head toward the village.

Suddenly, smelling the sweet smell of what I thought was a barbeque, my mouth began to water. I broke into a run toward the smell, when I heard a loud BOOM! Suddenly, I went flying into the air, then with the help of gravity my body made a "comforting" THUD!

"Ow! That did not need to happen," I complained as I sat up.

Wondering what that was, I felt my feet burning up. For some reason, my shoes were smoking, just like my hands. Now I was beginning to seriously question what was happening to my body. I wiped the dirt off my clothes and started again to head toward the village. Surprisingly, it looked as if the villagers knew I was coming and they greeted me.

"Welcome, Jiro, to our world!" exclaimed one of the villagers.

Before I could say anything I was interrupted.

"We have expected your arrival for quite some time now," said some old man that looked like the elder of the village. "Come inside and have some tea while I explain everything to you."

Rather than question him I just let the program run and kept my mouth shut. I followed him into a small hut.

As he poured me some tea, he said, "If you hadn't noticed already, this is not Earth. This is a place called Taria. 'Where exactly is this place?' you may be wondering, and to be complete honest, this is deep inside your psyche. This place is only images, thoughts, sensations, and feelings. In other words, this is a dream.

Widening my eyes, I said sarcastically, "A dream? How is that possible? I mean, I'm fully aware of all my actions! Usually dreams are fuzzy and distorted."

The elder just took a sip of his tea and smiled.

"Jiro, not many make it into this world. You have been chosen out of few. This world is yours. Have you ever heard of lucid dreaming? This is basically the same, except you are fully aware and you will not forget what happens."

"Are you serious? Okay this is getting tedious. Command: Program; Skip intro.exe" I said, becoming annoyed.

"Um, okay. Well, as I was going to say, do you have any questions before you explore Taria?" said the elder with an air of confusion.

I explained the whole fire situation to the elder and he simply responded, "You must figure that out yourself."

It took me a little while to process all the new thoughts. "What do you mean? I programmed you to explain it to me... weird. But, no mind, I'll just iron out that bug later."

The elder paused. "Before you leave, I am obligated to

tell you because you are fully aware of your actions, your brain is, too. If you died in this world, your brain would 'think' it is actually dead and will stop working completely."

My blood froze. "What was this AI saying?" I thought to myself. "How did it seem so intelligent about how the world around him works, but he can't explain how I control the fire I produced." This was no different than life itself. I still needed to be careful. I thanked the elder for explaining my status and headed off in the direction of a field, which actually had normal-colored grass. If there were going to be these fantastic creatures roaming around freely in this world, I needed a way to control this weird ability to create fire that I seemed to possess.

This is my world and I can do what I want. I walked back to the field where the cave was. There, I faced the enormous rock face that dwarfed the cave's mouth. I closed my eyes and focused on my feet. I concentrated on the warm feeling on the bottom of my feet, but it just wasn't enough. When I focused intensely, huge burning flames burst from under my feet and sent me rocketing into the sky uncontrollably. I screamed, "WHY DOES THIS KEEP HAPPENING TO ME?"

The fire began to dissipate and sputtered under my feet, while I tried to gain some control. I looked at the world which I was high above now. I saw vast fields, endless forests that disappeared into a colossal mountain range, and a blinding light that shined directly into my eyes. I blocked what light

I could with my hands in order to look at the source of this light, only to see that I was staring at a crystal clear lake.

But before I could admire the water, a loud noise seemed to surround me. The screaming wind tore at my cloths as a green wall barreled its way toward me. "That's odd. Why is this happening?" I thought. "I was in the air looking at the landscape and then..." My stomach dropped. I felt myself falling! I tried concentrating on the fire again, but this time it engulfed my entire body.

The ground was closing in fast and I was running out of time. BOOM! The fire burst from my feet again, and I was saved. The fire exploded with such force that I sped in a horizontal direction. I was away from danger, for the most part. I was exhilarated! I was flying! On fire yes, but I was flying!

I flew into the forest excitedly. In the dense forest, I sped between the large trees in amazement at the detail my program had produced. Flying toward the sky again, I raced toward an open field. I spotted a cluster of rocks and went to investigate them. I landed right next to them. I picked up one of the rocks and it felt warm. And with no warning, it squeaked.

Confused, I looked at it and said to myself, "It squeaked? How does a rock squeak?" I put it to my ear and again it squeaked and jumped out of my hand. The other rocks that were in a pile started squeaking too. They began to jump around and squeal louder and more frequently.

Before I could process what was happening, the earth began to shake. Expecting to see the beast looming over me, I looked up. But there was no shadow and no foot that I had to avoid. A cold sweat accumulated at the base of my spine. A violent vibration shook the earth and rattled my bones. I could barely stand and could not gather my focus. The squeaking was at a shrill pitch now and I could barely make out a dozen or so fin-shaped rocks making their way toward me.

Then, as suddenly as it began, the vibration came to a sudden halt. And before I could register what was happening, a large blur lunged at me and knocked me over. I rolled a few yards away from the rocks. I stood as quickly as my legs would allow. My eyes darted around to see what hit me; then I saw the fin-shaped rocks converging on me. And for an instant, I saw the body of what looked like a shark emerging from the ground. My eyes grew wide. But before I could vocalize my thoughts, one of the beasts flanked me and breached the ground to attack me. I concentrated: BOOM! The air beneath my feet exploded and I rose just high enough to avoid the gaping maw of what looked like a shark.

Without thinking twice, I sped away from the pack. Unfortunately, it seemed as though the pack was waiting for me to flee, because they rocketed after me. I had not recovered from the shock wave enough to fly any higher than a few dozen yards off the ground. I flew as fast as I could, all while dodging the beasts as they launched themselves from under the ground. I had to dart into the forest in an attempt to lose them, but they pursued more intensely.

They shot from beneath the ground with ease and they launched themselves at trees and knocked them down with ease. Using their fins like sails, they seemed to be flying all around me, like flying daggers trying to slice into my body. Leaving a trail of destruction in their wake, I slowly recovered and began to pick up speed. The beasts pursued me with an insatiable blood lust, when from the corner of my eye I spotted a cloaked figure riding a horse that seemed to be flying on the forest floor.

Looking to my left, I saw three more horses with riders. Looking behind me, I saw two more riders behind the pack. I heard a sharp whistle pierce the air as the riders surrounded me and the riders at my side drew small sticks from under their cloaks. Then, as suddenly as they drew them, the sticks extended and revealed themselves to be spears with a blue spark on their tips. I sighed, thinking that this could not be happening.

Until a spear whizzed past my head. "Hey! Watch it! That nearly hit me!" I yelled to no avail. I had a few seconds to dodge the three other spears that were clearly aimed at me. As I rolled out of the way, a chain wrapped around my ankles and a stream of electricity coursed through my body.

I nearly lost consciousness. I did lost control and started to fall toward the ground. I recovered quickly and tried to raise my speed and increase altitude, when a shadow bounced between the trees and was above me in an instant and threw a net at me. BOOM! I changed directions explosively and shot toward the ground. BOOM! I shot in a different horizontal direction when I felt a sting and a shooting pain invade my train of thought. A spear made its entrance into my field of vision and, without thinking, I thrust out my hand and grabbed it and screamed in pain.

As I screamed, my hand burned with an uncontrollable white heat. And I shot into the air uncontrollably again. This time, I broke through the canopy and I looked at the chain that was wrapped around my feet to see a hooded figure clinging to the chain and slowly climbing. I reached out for the chain and inadvertently shot a burst of flame at the cloaked figure. The hood was being consumed by the flame and, in one swift motion, the figure removed the hood, revealing long, flowing red and pink hair, green eyes, and a face adorned with a few blue tattoos. The girl at the bottom of the chain glared at me. With a surprising amount of strength, she pulled the chain and caused me to spin uncontrollably.

As my consciousness began to fade, I saw her slender figure dance in the air. She twisted in the air and threw a second chain that coiled itself around my left arm. She pulled and twisted the chain; as we fell, she swung the chain into a spiral, which coiled around my body. With an effortless pull, the chain then wrapped around my body as if it were a full-body straight-jacket. Pulling me close, her feet were on my back. As we plummeted toward the ground, I released whatever fire I had left to control our fall, but I was fading fast.

But the tattooed warrior on my back was sharp and alert and she used the last burst I gave to slow us just enough to throw another chain around a tree branch. It worked. We swung around the area of the tree in a spiral descent and, when we were close enough to the ground, she kicked my back and, WHAM, I slammed into a tree. Spots filled my vision and the sky became overcast and slowly all became black.

The last voice I heard was, "What the heck was that and why was it flying?"